SUPERMAN

SHADOWS LINGER

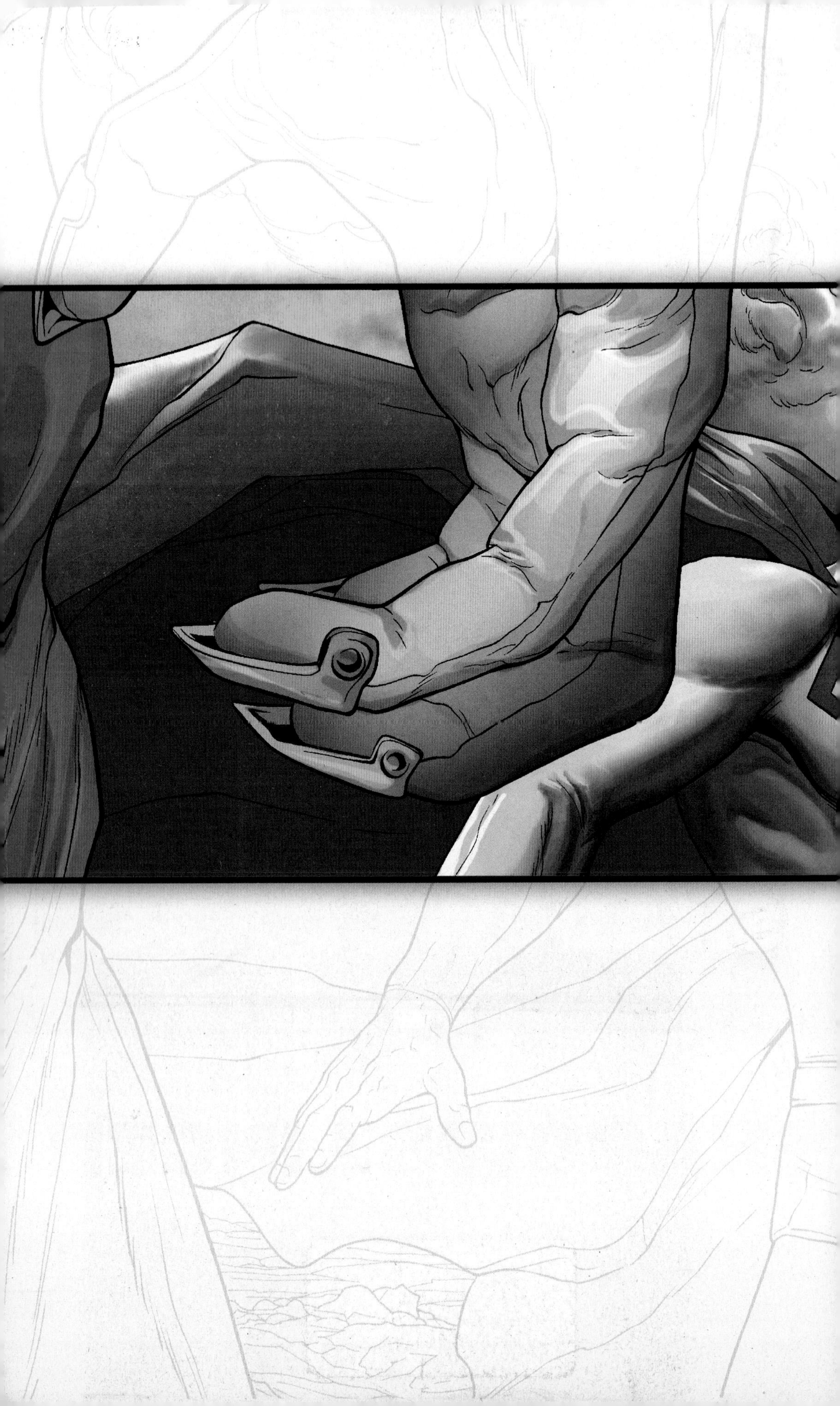

SUPERMAN

SHADOWS LINGER

KURT BUSIEK writer

PETER VALE	**JESÚS MERINO**
JESÚS MERINO	**WELLINGTON DIAS**
RENATO GUEDES	**JOSÉ WILSON MAGALHÁES**
JORGÉ CORREA JR.	**JORGÉ CORREA JR.**
pencillers	inkers

COMICRAFT	**KANILA TRIPP**
PAT BROSSEAU	**DAVID CURIEL**
letterers	colorists

Superman created by Jerry Siegel and Joe Shuster

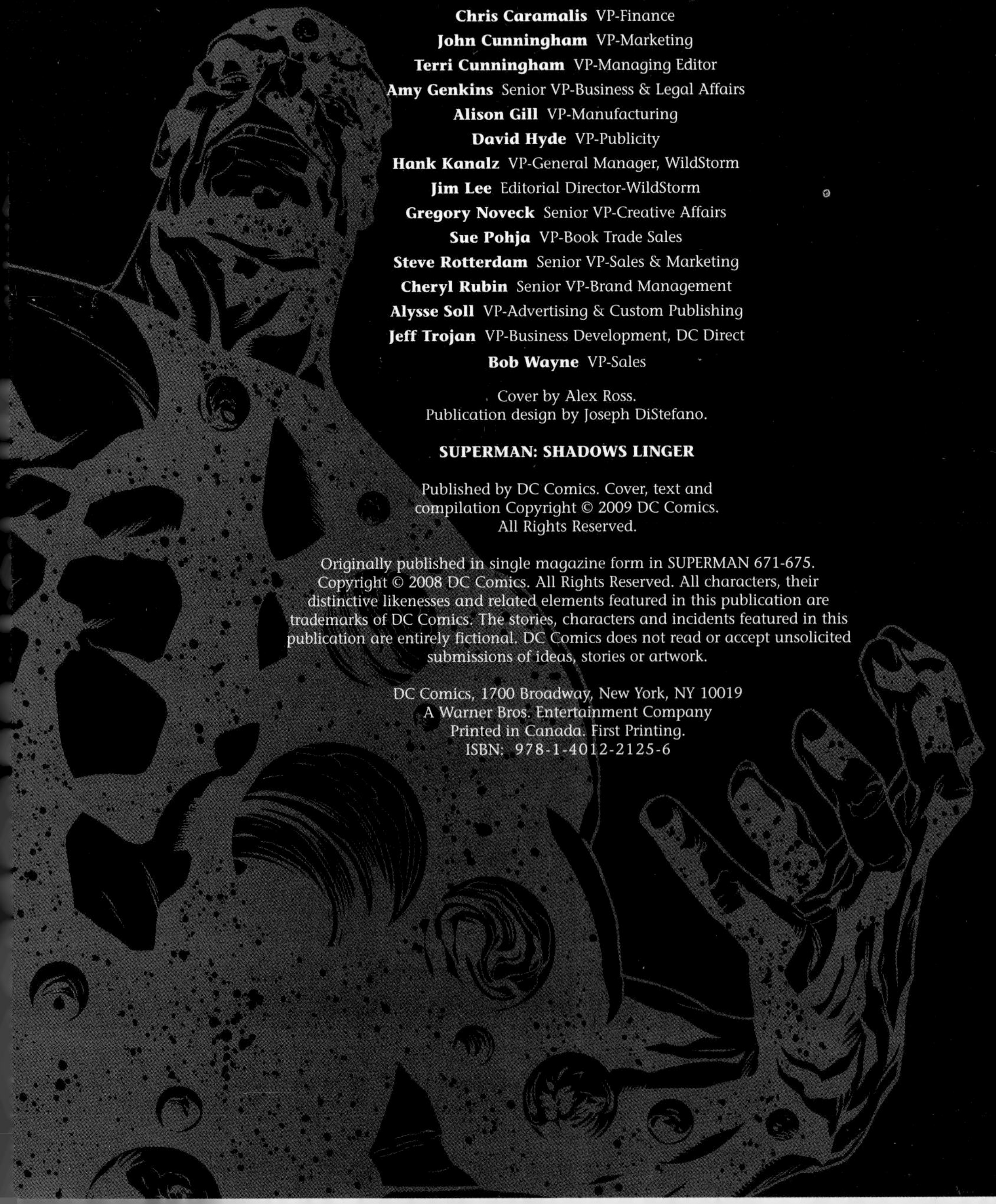

Dan DiDio Senior VP-Executive Editor
Matt Idelson Editor-original series
Tom Palmer Jr. Associate Editor-original series
Sean Mackiewicz Editor-collected edition
Robbin Brosterman Senior Art Director
Paul Levitz President & Publisher
Georg Brewer VP-Design & DC Direct Creative
Richard Bruning Senior VP-Creative Director
Patrick Caldon Executive VP-Finance & Operations
Chris Caramalis VP-Finance
John Cunningham VP-Marketing
Terri Cunningham VP-Managing Editor
Amy Genkins Senior VP-Business & Legal Affairs
Alison Gill VP-Manufacturing
David Hyde VP-Publicity
Hank Kanalz VP-General Manager, WildStorm
Jim Lee Editorial Director-WildStorm
Gregory Noveck Senior VP-Creative Affairs
Sue Pohja VP-Book Trade Sales
Steve Rotterdam Senior VP-Sales & Marketing
Cheryl Rubin Senior VP-Brand Management
Alysse Soll VP-Advertising & Custom Publishing
Jeff Trojan VP-Business Development, DC Direct
Bob Wayne VP-Sales

Cover by Alex Ross.
Publication design by Joseph DiStefano.

SUPERMAN: SHADOWS LINGER

COVER ART BY PETER VALE & WELLINGTON DIAS

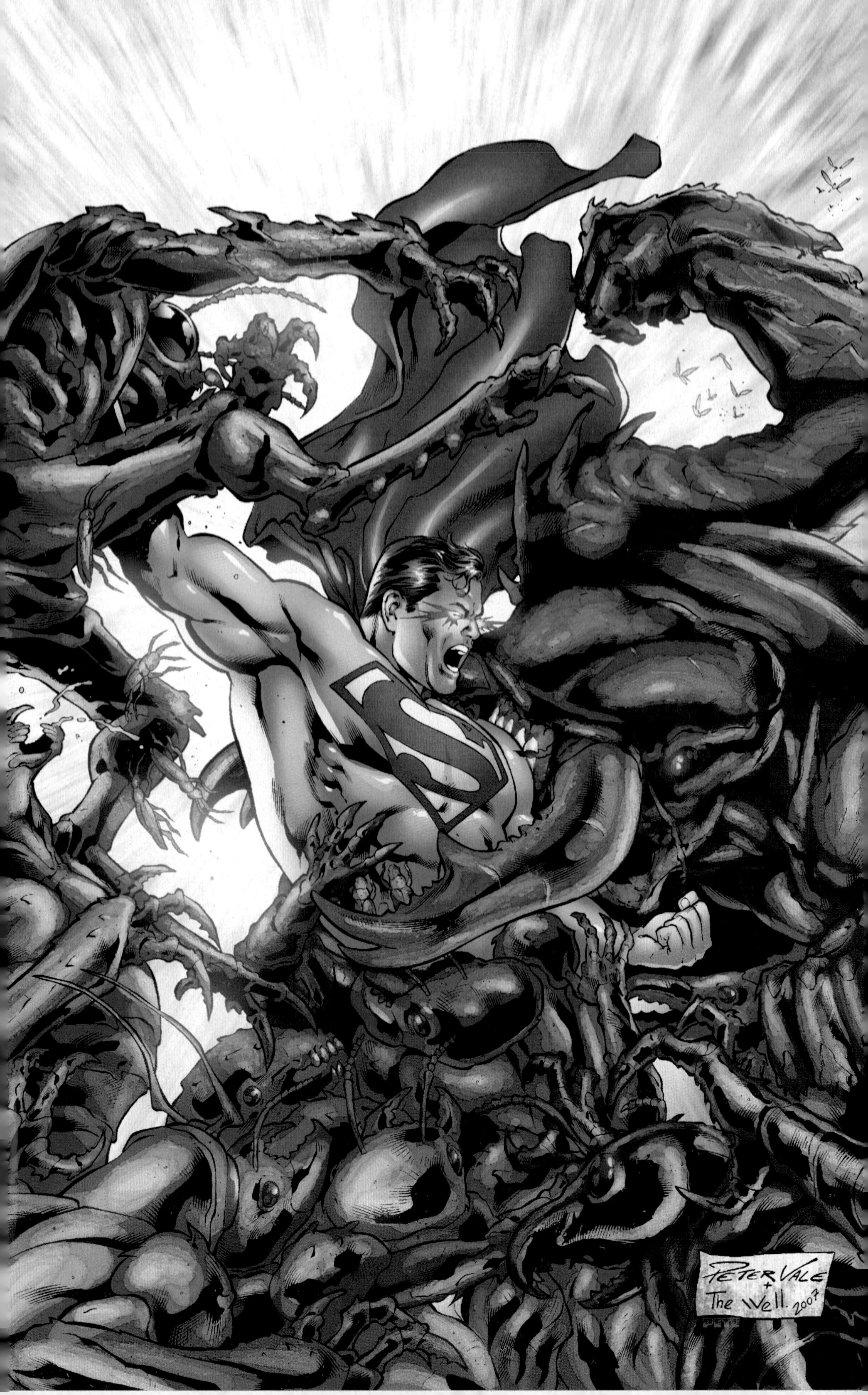
PETER VALE
+
The Well. 2007

INSECT QUEEN
PART ONE:

A FALL OF MOONDUST

ART BY **PETER VALE** & **JESÚS MERINO**
COLORS BY **KANILA TRIPP**

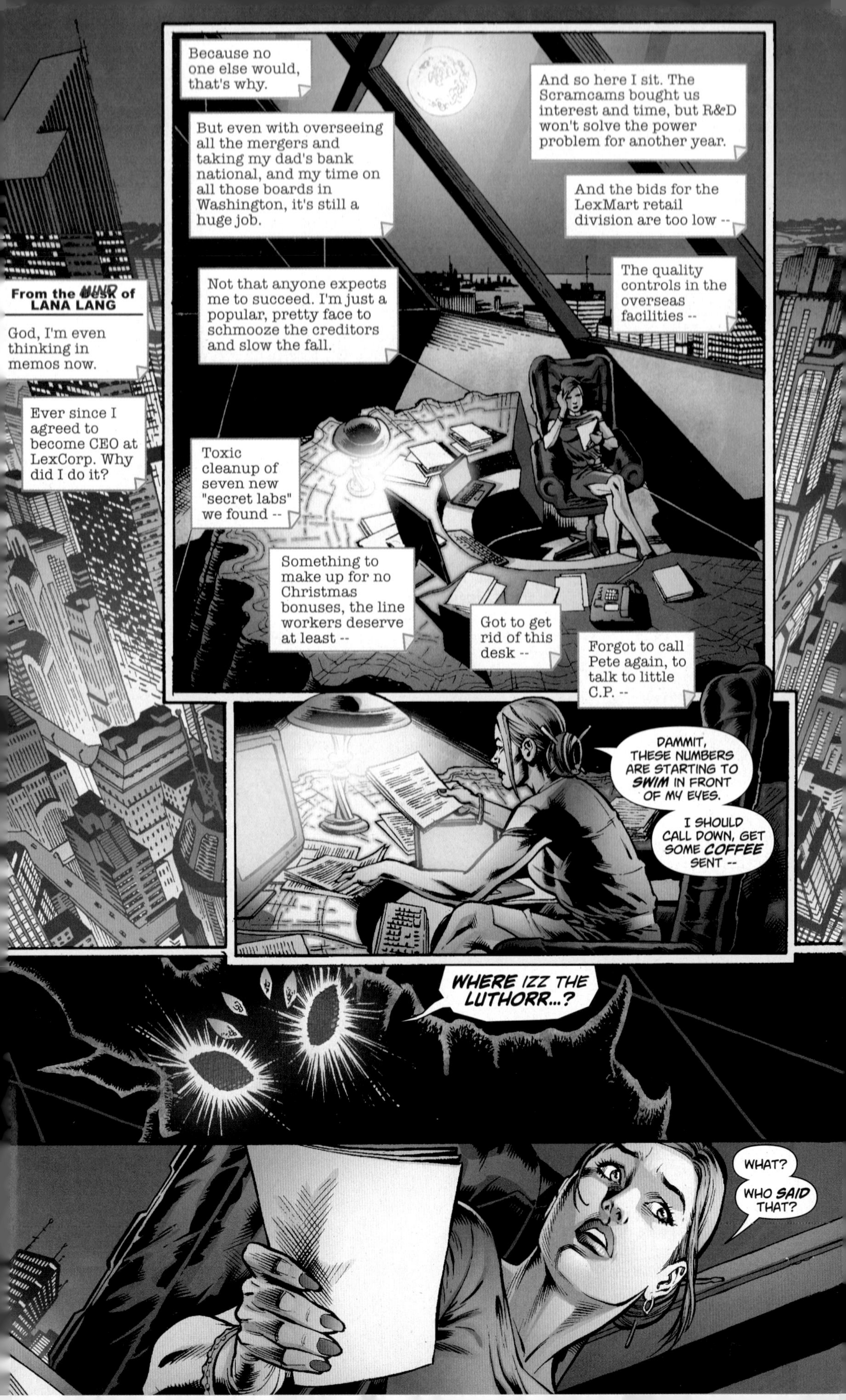
From the ~~Desk~~ MIND of LANA LANG
God, I'm even thinking in memos now.
Ever since I agreed to become CEO at LexCorp. Why did I do it?
Because no one else would, that's why.
But even with overseeing all the mergers and taking my dad's bank national, and my time on all those boards in Washington, it's still a huge job.
Not that anyone expects me to succeed. I'm just a popular, pretty face to schmooze the creditors and slow the fall.
And so here I sit. The Scramcams bought us interest and time, but R&D won't solve the power problem for another year.
And the bids for the LexMart retail division are too low --
The quality controls in the overseas facilities --
Toxic cleanup of seven new "secret labs" we found --
Something to make up for no Christmas bonuses, the line workers deserve at least --
Got to get rid of this desk --
Forgot to call Pete again, to talk to little C.P. --
DAMMIT, THESE NUMBERS ARE STARTING TO SWIM IN FRONT OF MY EYES.
I SHOULD CALL DOWN, GET SOME COFFEE SENT --
WHERE IZZ THE LUTHORR...?
WHAT?
WHO SAID THAT?

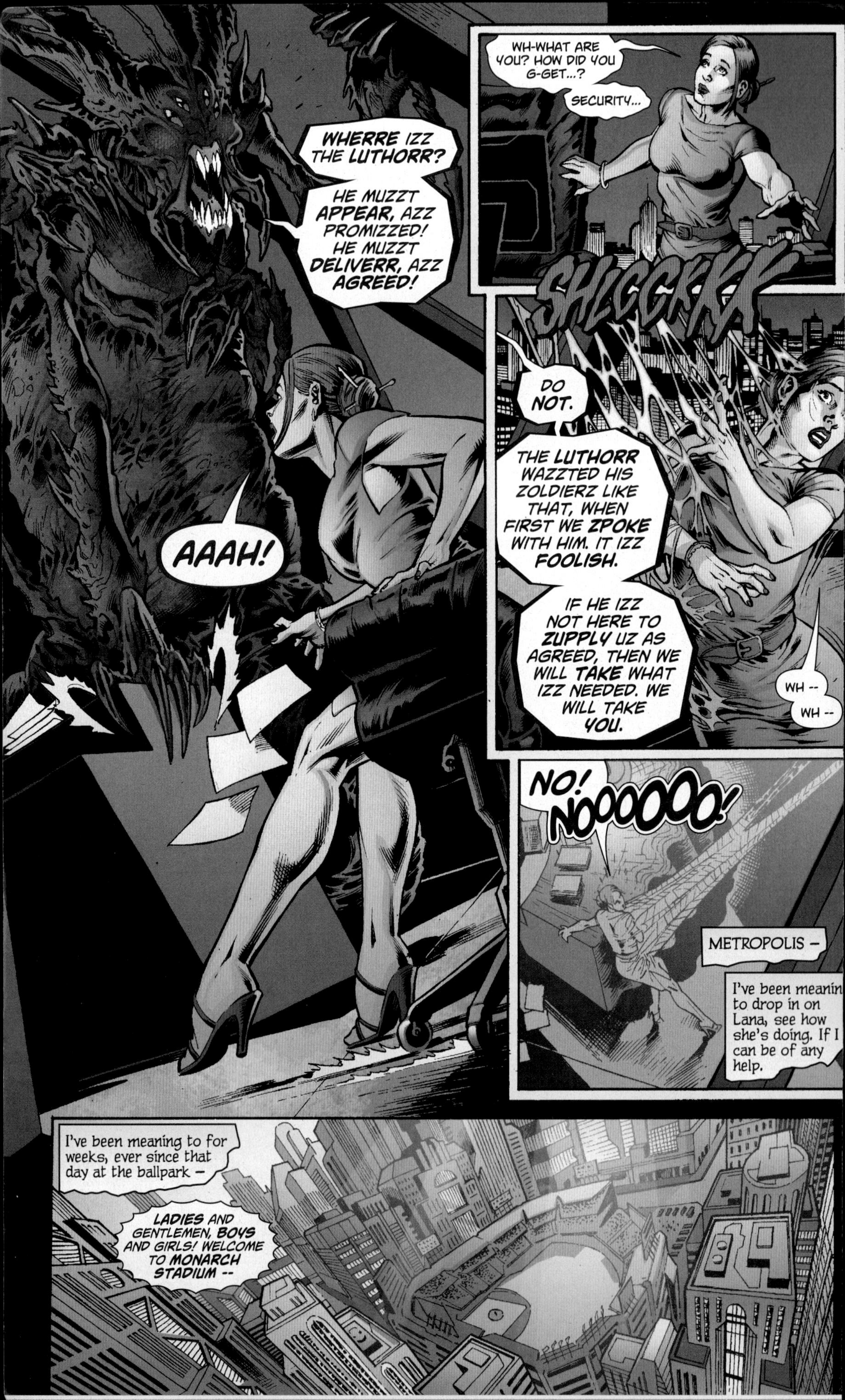

WHERRE IZZ THE LUTHORR?
HE MUZZT APPEAR, AZZ PROMIZZED! HE MUZZT DELIVERR, AZZ AGREED!
AAAH!
WH-WHAT ARE YOU? HOW DID YOU G-GET...?
SECURITY...
SHLCCKKK
DO NOT.
THE LUTHORR WAZZTED HIS ZOLDIERZ LIKE THAT, WHEN FIRST WE ZPOKE WITH HIM. IT IZZ FOOLISH.
IF HE IZZ NOT HERE TO ZUPPLY UZ AS AGREED, THEN WE WILL TAKE WHAT IZZ NEEDED. WE WILL TAKE YOU.
WH --
WH --
NO! NOOOOOO!
METROPOLIS –
I've been meanin to drop in on Lana, see how she's doing. If I can be of any help.
I've been meaning to for weeks, ever since that day at the ballpark –
LADIES AND GENTLEMEN, BOYS AND GIRLS! WELCOME TO MONARCH STADIUM --

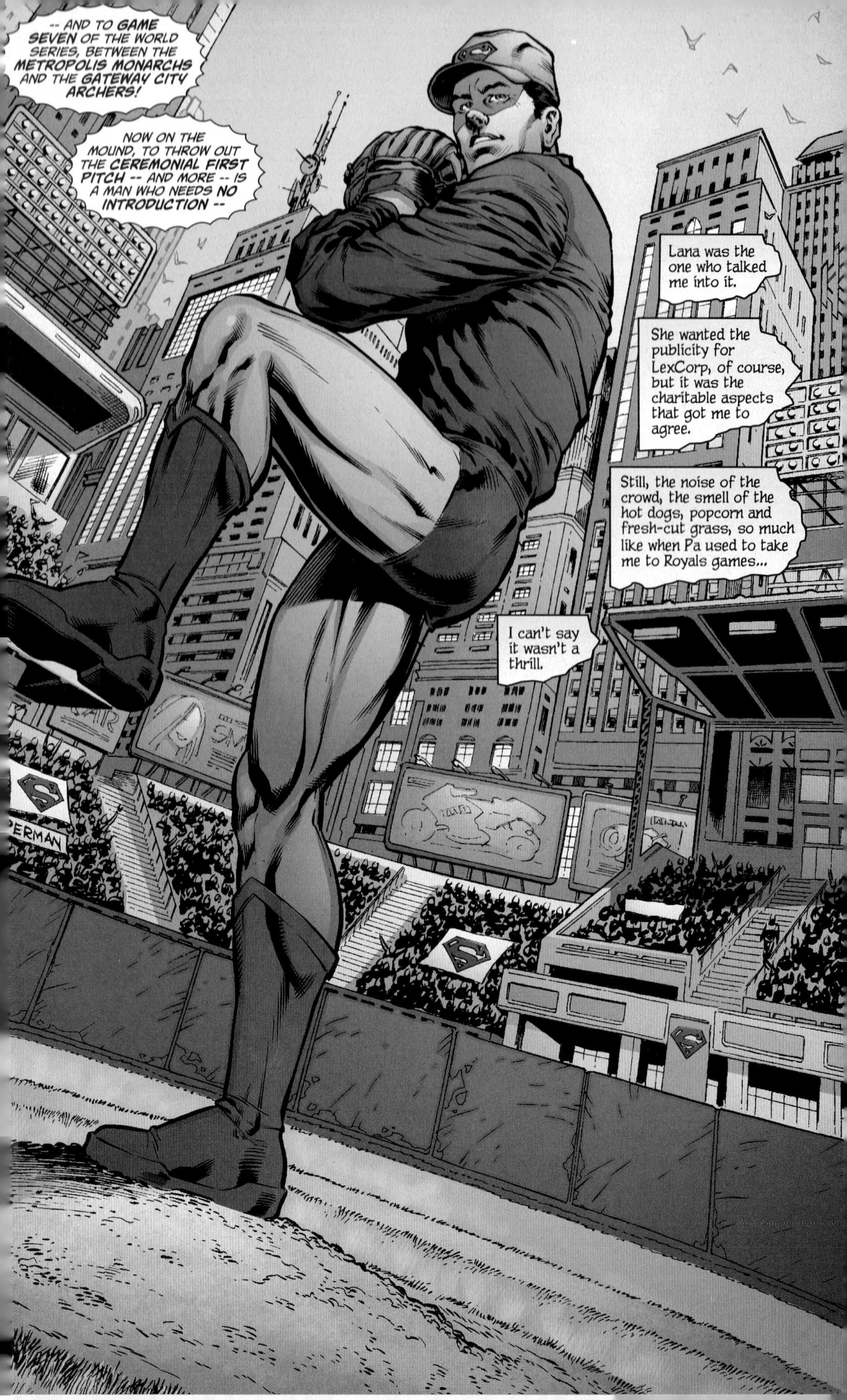
-- AND TO GAME SEVEN OF THE WORLD SERIES, BETWEEN THE METROPOLIS MONARCHS AND THE GATEWAY CITY ARCHERS!
NOW ON THE MOUND, TO THROW OUT THE CEREMONIAL FIRST PITCH -- AND MORE -- IS A MAN WHO NEEDS NO INTRODUCTION --
Lana was the one who talked me into it.
She wanted the publicity for LexCorp, of course, but it was the charitable aspects that got me to agree.
Still, the noise of the crowd, the smell of the hot dogs, popcorn and fresh-cut grass, so much like when Pa used to take me to Royals games...
I can't say it wasn't a thrill.
PERMAN

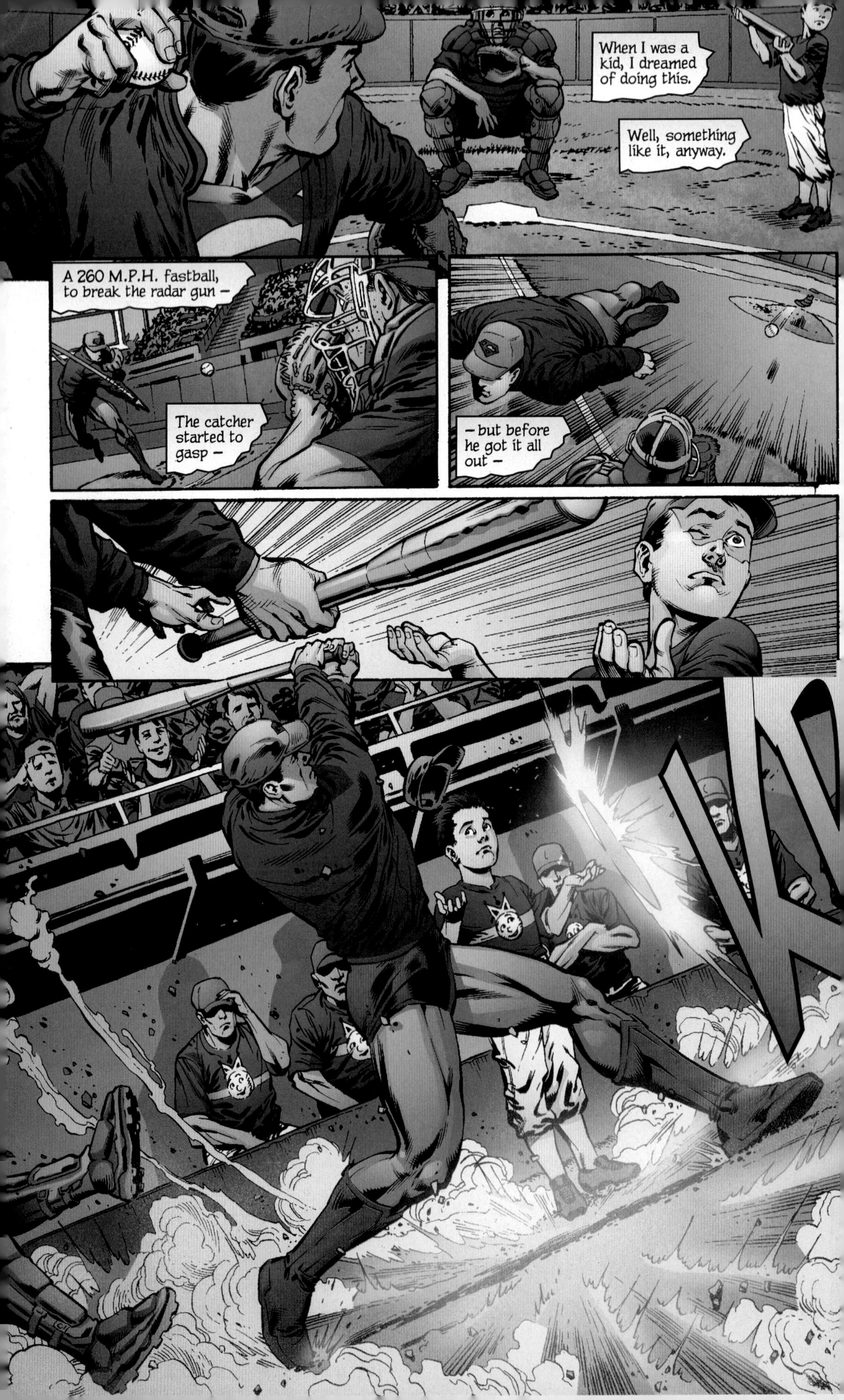
When I was a kid, I dreamed of doing this.
Well, something like it, anyway.
A 260 M.P.H. fastball, to break the radar gun —
The catcher started to gasp —
— but before he got it all out —

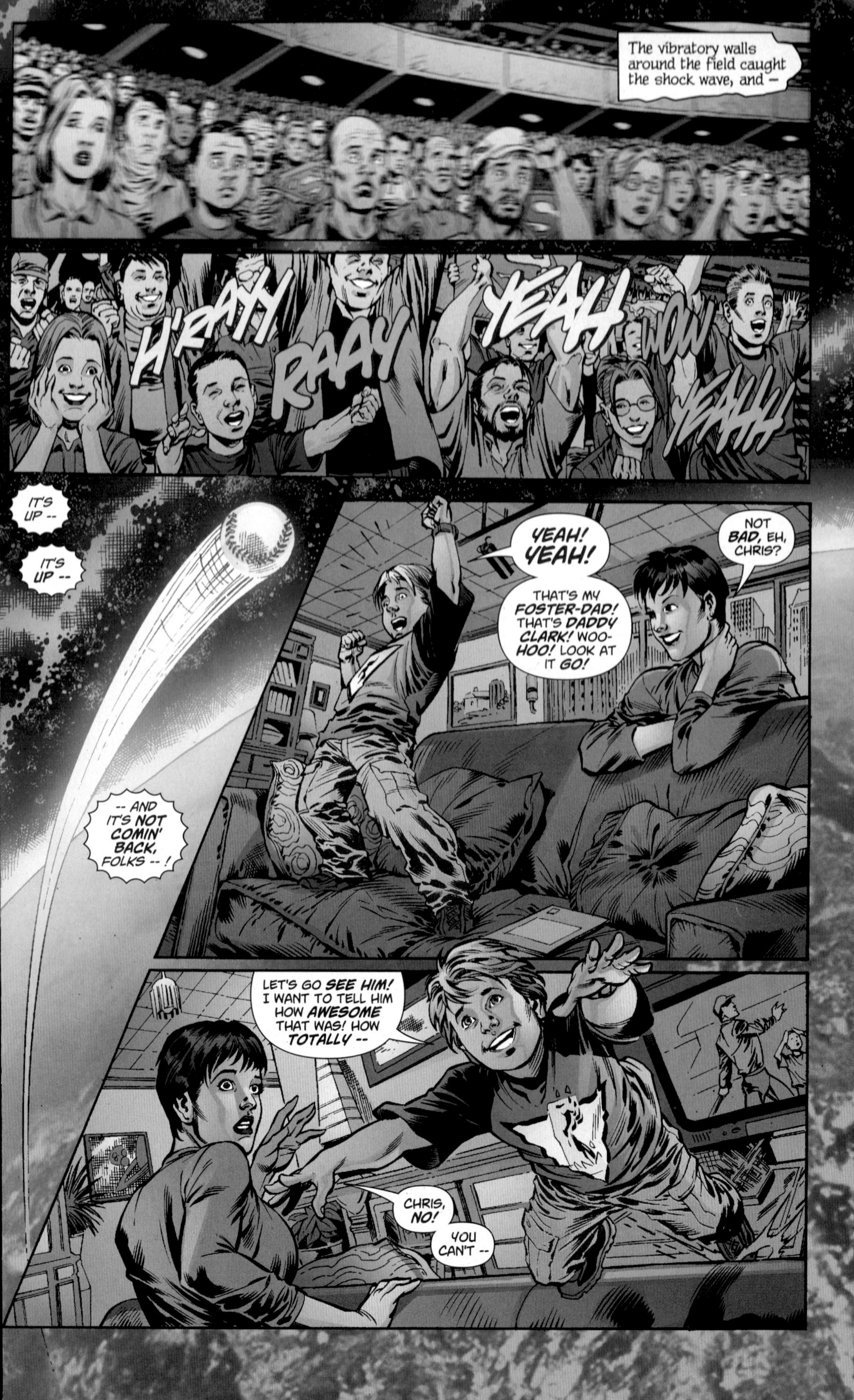
The vibratory walls around the field caught the shock wave, and —
H'RAYY
RAAY
YEAH
WOW
YEAHH
IT'S UP --
IT'S UP --
-- AND IT'S NOT COMIN' BACK, FOLKS -- !
YEAH! YEAH!
THAT'S MY FOSTER-DAD! THAT'S DADDY CLARK! WOO-HOO! LOOK AT IT GO!
NOT BAD, EH, CHRIS?
LET'S GO SEE HIM! I WANT TO TELL HIM HOW AWESOME THAT WAS! HOW TOTALLY --
CHRIS, NO!
YOU CAN'T --

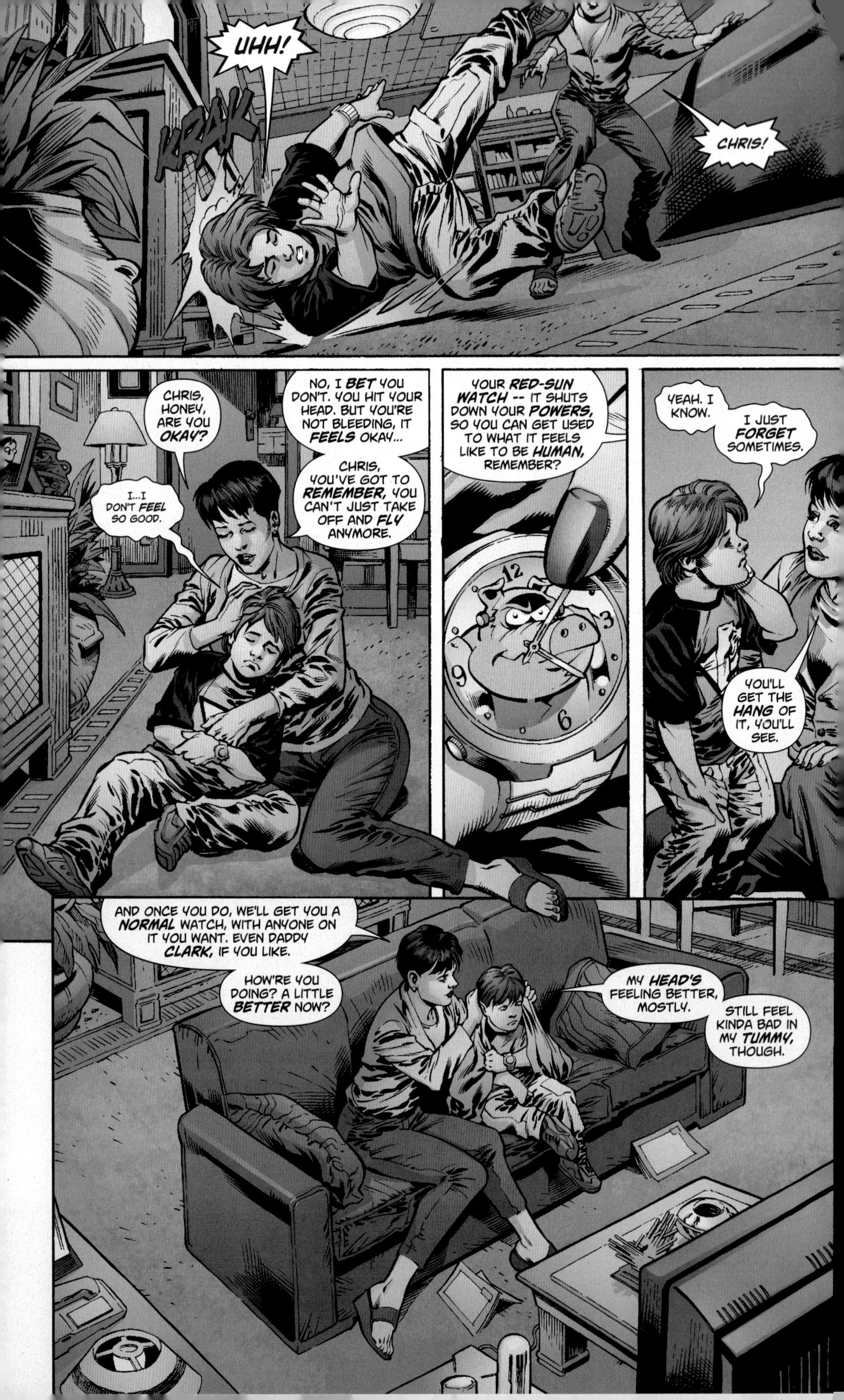
UHH!
KRAK
CHRIS!
CHRIS, HONEY, ARE YOU OKAY?
I...I DON'T FEEL SO GOOD.
NO, I BET YOU DON'T. YOU HIT YOUR HEAD. BUT YOU'RE NOT BLEEDING, IT FEELS OKAY...
CHRIS, YOU'VE GOT TO REMEMBER, YOU CAN'T JUST TAKE OFF AND FLY ANYMORE.
YOUR RED-SUN WATCH -- IT SHUTS DOWN YOUR POWERS, SO YOU CAN GET USED TO WHAT IT FEELS LIKE TO BE HUMAN, REMEMBER?
YEAH. I KNOW.
I JUST FORGET SOMETIMES.
YOU'LL GET THE HANG OF IT, YOU'LL SEE.
AND ONCE YOU DO, WE'LL GET YOU A NORMAL WATCH, WITH ANYONE ON IT YOU WANT. EVEN DADDY CLARK, IF YOU LIKE.
HOW'RE YOU DOING? A LITTLE BETTER NOW?
MY HEAD'S FEELING BETTER, MOSTLY.
STILL FEEL KINDA BAD IN MY TUMMY, THOUGH.

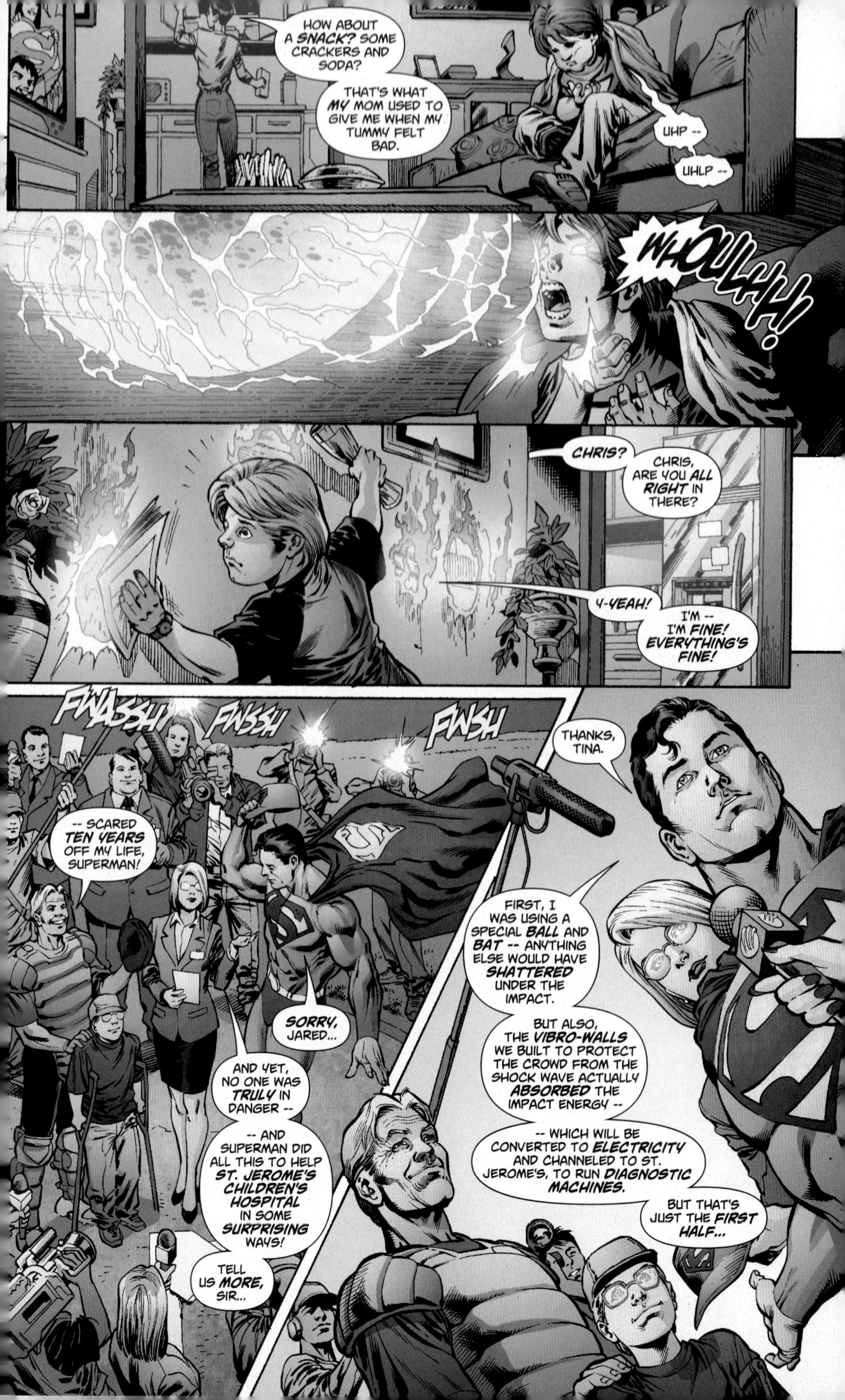
HOW ABOUT A SNACK? SOME CRACKERS AND SODA?
THAT'S WHAT MY MOM USED TO GIVE ME WHEN MY TUMMY FELT BAD.
UHP --
UHLP --
WHOULHH!
CHRIS?
CHRIS, ARE YOU ALL RIGHT IN THERE?
Y-YEAH!
I'M -- I'M FINE! EVERYTHING'S FINE!
FWASSH
FWSSH
FWSH
-- SCARED TEN YEARS OFF MY LIFE, SUPERMAN!
SORRY, JARED...
AND YET, NO ONE WAS TRULY IN DANGER --
-- AND SUPERMAN DID ALL THIS TO HELP ST. JEROME'S CHILDREN'S HOSPITAL IN SOME SURPRISING WAYS!
TELL US MORE, SIR...
THANKS, TINA.
FIRST, I WAS USING A SPECIAL BALL AND BAT -- ANYTHING ELSE WOULD HAVE SHATTERED UNDER THE IMPACT.
BUT ALSO, THE VIBRO-WALLS WE BUILT TO PROTECT THE CROWD FROM THE SHOCK WAVE ACTUALLY ABSORBED THE IMPACT ENERGY --
-- WHICH WILL BE CONVERTED TO ELECTRICITY AND CHANNELED TO ST. JEROME'S, TO RUN DIAGNOSTIC MACHINES.
BUT THAT'S JUST THE FIRST HALF...

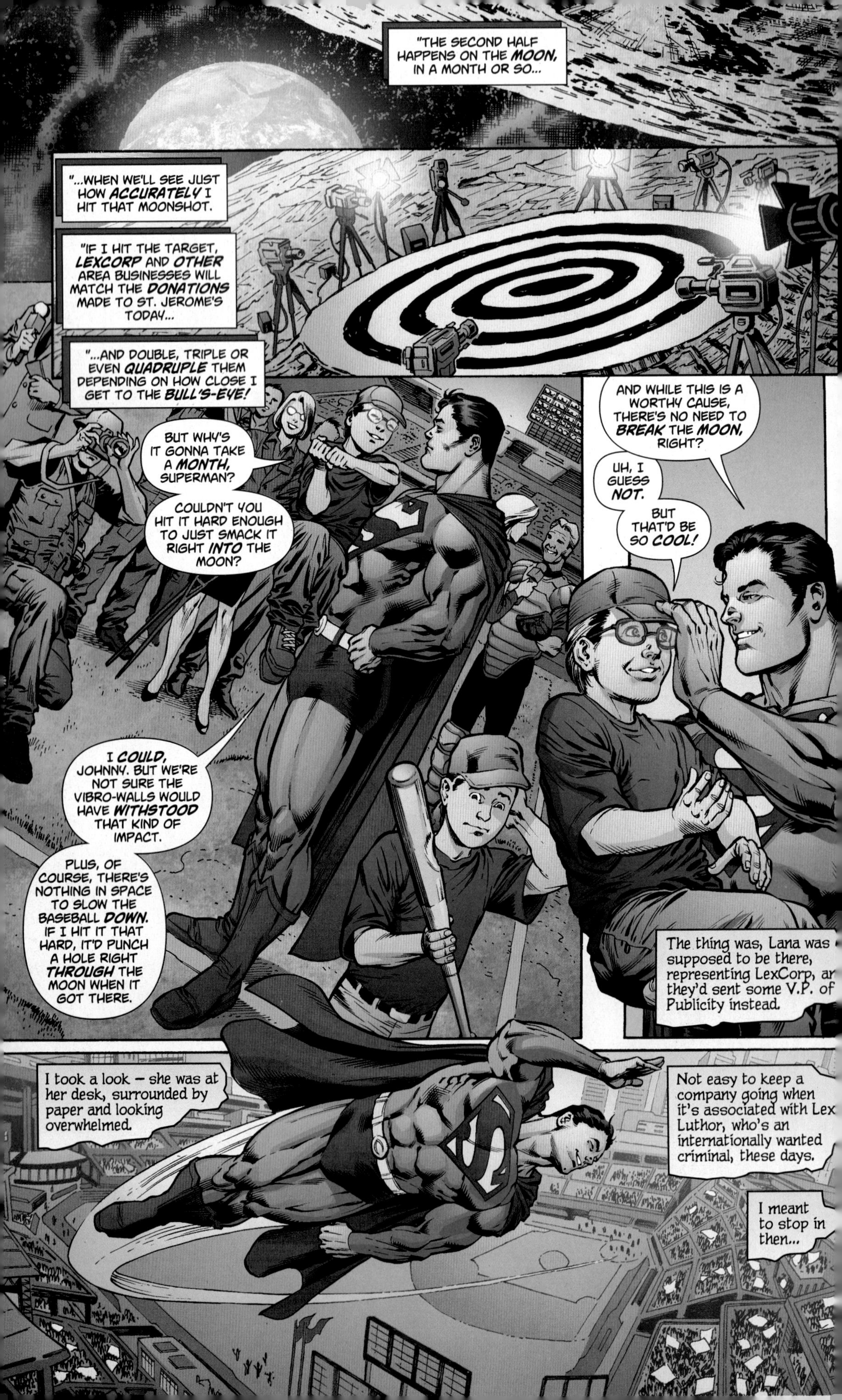
"THE SECOND HALF HAPPENS ON THE MOON, IN A MONTH OR SO...
"...WHEN WE'LL SEE JUST HOW ACCURATELY I HIT THAT MOONSHOT.
"IF I HIT THE TARGET, LEXCORP AND OTHER AREA BUSINESSES WILL MATCH THE DONATIONS MADE TO ST. JEROME'S TODAY...
"...AND DOUBLE, TRIPLE OR EVEN QUADRUPLE THEM DEPENDING ON HOW CLOSE I GET TO THE BULL'S-EYE!
BUT WHY'S IT GONNA TAKE A MONTH, SUPERMAN?
COULDN'T YOU HIT IT HARD ENOUGH TO JUST SMACK IT RIGHT INTO THE MOON?
I COULD, JOHNNY. BUT WE'RE NOT SURE THE VIBRO-WALLS WOULD HAVE WITHSTOOD THAT KIND OF IMPACT.
PLUS, OF COURSE, THERE'S NOTHING IN SPACE TO SLOW THE BASEBALL DOWN. IF I HIT IT THAT HARD, IT'D PUNCH A HOLE RIGHT THROUGH THE MOON WHEN IT GOT THERE.
AND WHILE THIS IS A WORTHY CAUSE, THERE'S NO NEED TO BREAK THE MOON, RIGHT?
UH, I GUESS NOT.
BUT THAT'D BE SO COOL!
The thing was, Lana was supposed to be there, representing LexCorp, ar they'd sent some V.P. of Publicity instead.
I took a look — she was at her desk, surrounded by paper and looking overwhelmed.
Not easy to keep a company going when it's associated with Lex Luthor, who's an internationally wanted criminal, these days.
I meant to stop in then...

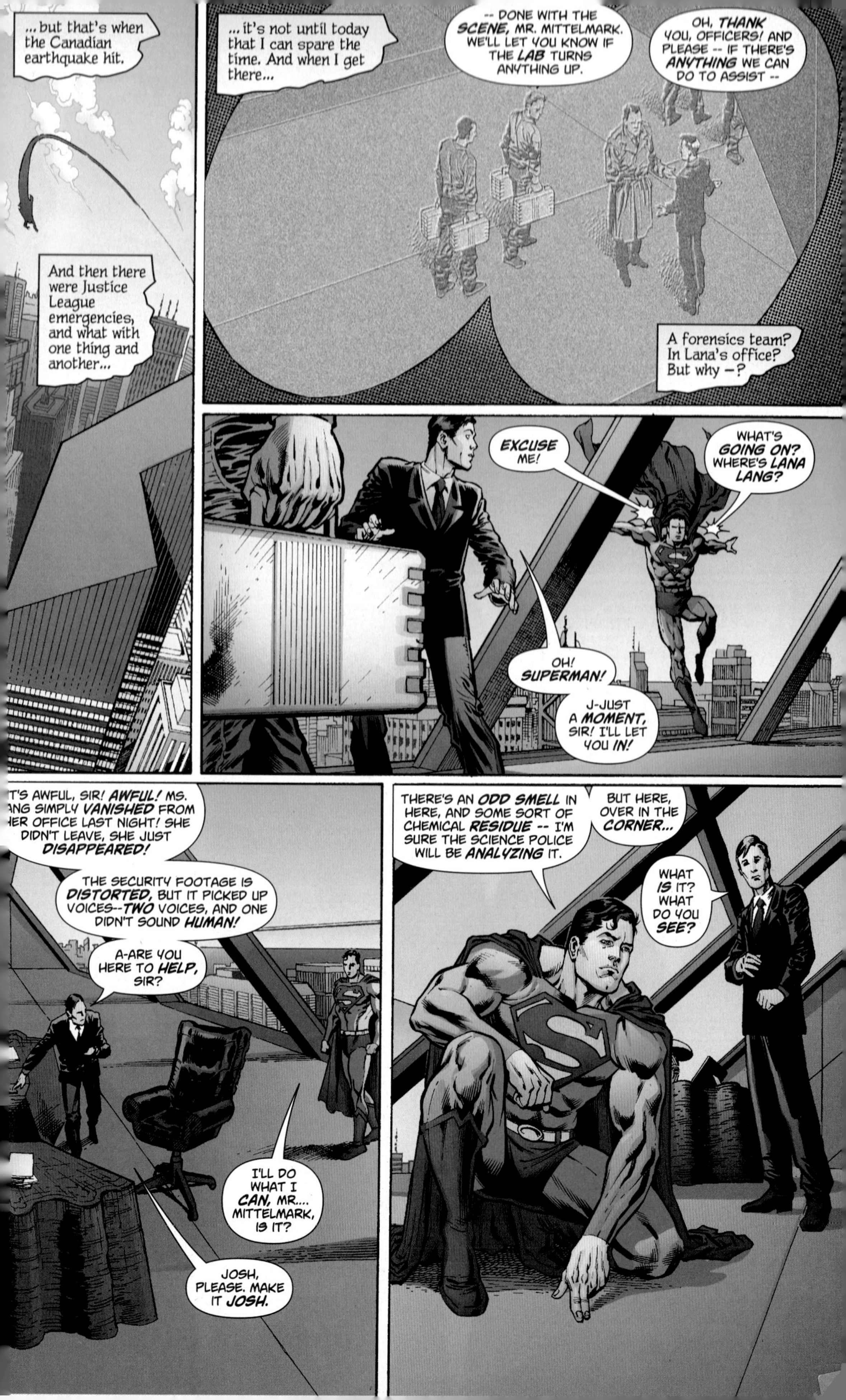
...but that's when the Canadian earthquake hit.
And then there were Justice League emergencies, and what with one thing and another...
...it's not until today that I can spare the time. And when I get there...
-- DONE WITH THE SCENE, MR. MITTELMARK. WE'LL LET YOU KNOW IF THE LAB TURNS ANYTHING UP.
OH, THANK YOU, OFFICERS! AND PLEASE -- IF THERE'S ANYTHING WE CAN DO TO ASSIST --
A forensics team? In Lana's office? But why --?
EXCUSE ME!
WHAT'S GOING ON? WHERE'S LANA LANG?
OH! SUPERMAN!
J-JUST A MOMENT, SIR! I'LL LET YOU IN!
IT'S AWFUL, SIR! AWFUL! MS. LANG SIMPLY VANISHED FROM HER OFFICE LAST NIGHT! SHE DIDN'T LEAVE, SHE JUST DISAPPEARED!
THE SECURITY FOOTAGE IS DISTORTED, BUT IT PICKED UP VOICES--TWO VOICES, AND ONE DIDN'T SOUND HUMAN!
A-ARE YOU HERE TO HELP, SIR?
I'LL DO WHAT I CAN, MR.... MITTELMARK, IS IT?
JOSH, PLEASE. MAKE IT JOSH.
THERE'S AN ODD SMELL IN HERE, AND SOME SORT OF CHEMICAL RESIDUE -- I'M SURE THE SCIENCE POLICE WILL BE ANALYZING IT.
BUT HERE, OVER IN THE CORNER...
WHAT IS IT? WHAT DO YOU SEE?

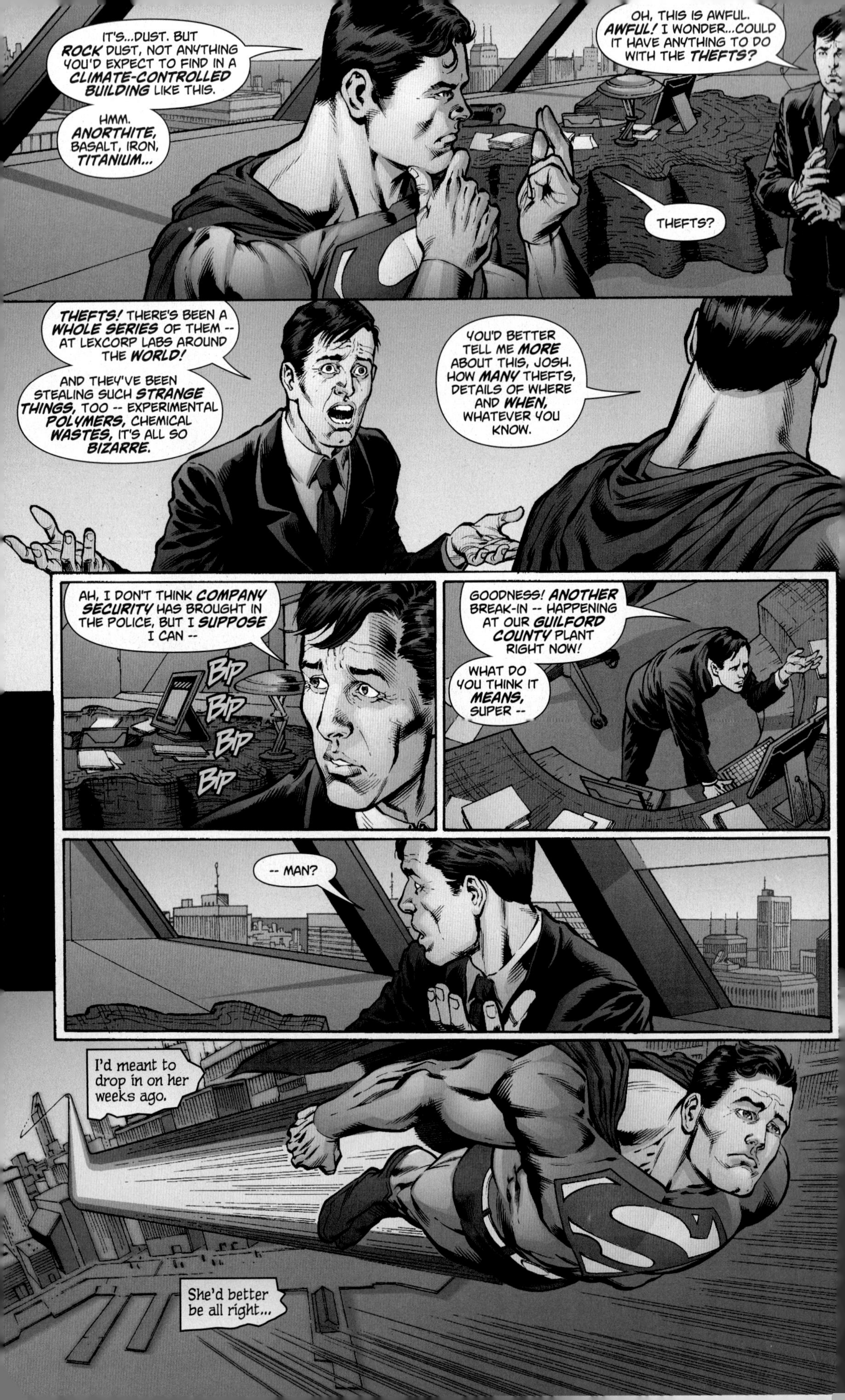

IT'S...DUST. BUT ROCK DUST, NOT ANYTHING YOU'D EXPECT TO FIND IN A CLIMATE-CONTROLLED BUILDING LIKE THIS.
HMM. ANORTHITE, BASALT, IRON, TITANIUM...
OH, THIS IS AWFUL. AWFUL! I WONDER...COULD IT HAVE ANYTHING TO DO WITH THE THEFTS?
THEFTS?
THEFTS! THERE'S BEEN A WHOLE SERIES OF THEM -- AT LEXCORP LABS AROUND THE WORLD!
AND THEY'VE BEEN STEALING SUCH STRANGE THINGS, TOO -- EXPERIMENTAL POLYMERS, CHEMICAL WASTES, IT'S ALL SO BIZARRE.
YOU'D BETTER TELL ME MORE ABOUT THIS, JOSH. HOW MANY THEFTS, DETAILS OF WHERE AND WHEN, WHATEVER YOU KNOW.
AH, I DON'T THINK COMPANY SECURITY HAS BROUGHT IN THE POLICE, BUT I SUPPOSE I CAN --
BIP
BIP
BIP
BIP
GOODNESS! ANOTHER BREAK-IN -- HAPPENING AT OUR GUILFORD COUNTY PLANT RIGHT NOW!
WHAT DO YOU THINK IT MEANS, SUPER --
-- MAN?
I'd meant to drop in on her weeks ago.
She'd better be all right...

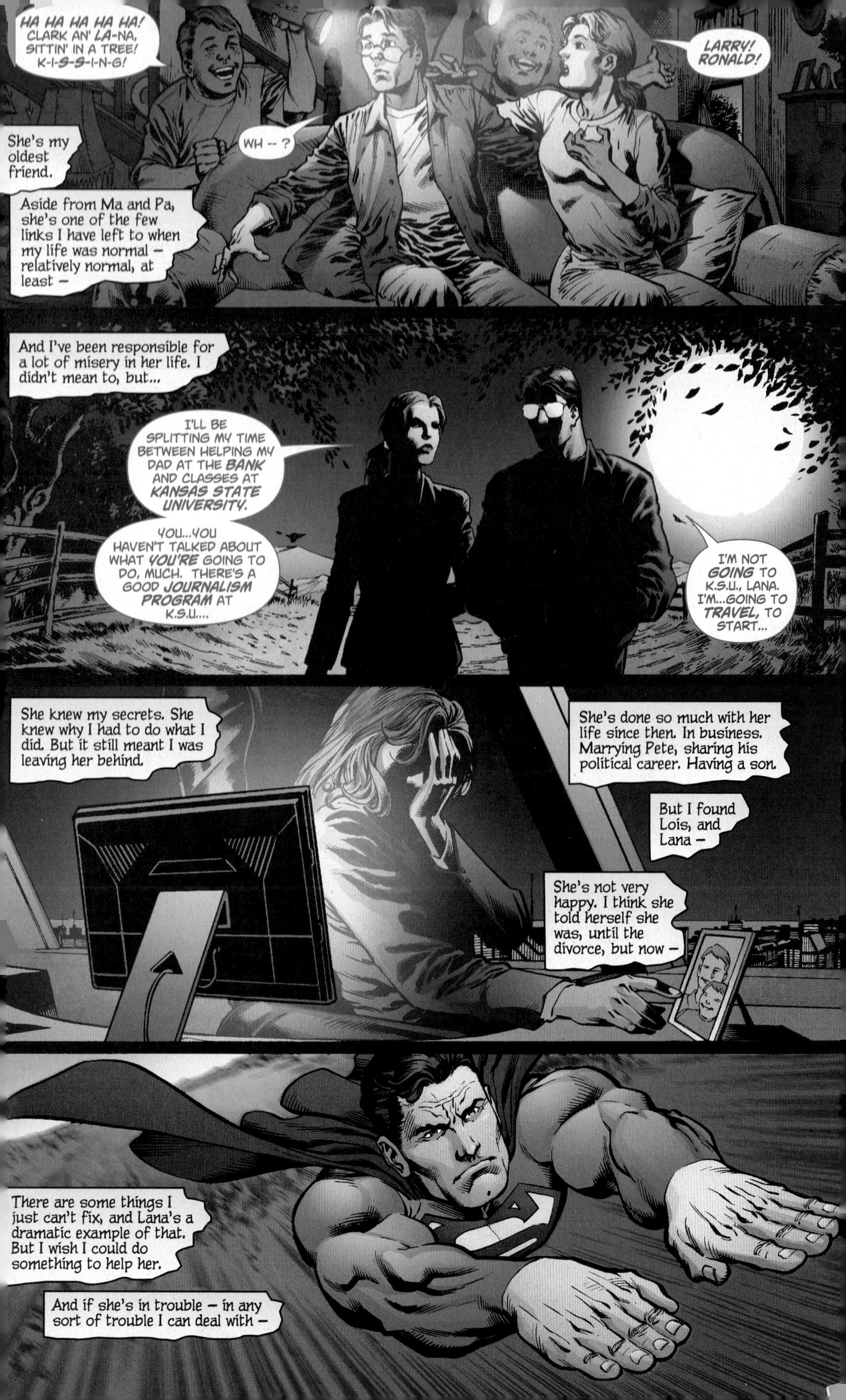
HA HA HA HA HA! CLARK AN' LA-NA, SITTIN' IN A TREE! K-I-S-S-I-N-G!
LARRY! RONALD!
She's my oldest friend.
WH -- ?
Aside from Ma and Pa, she's one of the few links I have left to when my life was normal – relatively normal, at least –
And I've been responsible for a lot of misery in her life. I didn't mean to, but...
I'LL BE SPLITTING MY TIME BETWEEN HELPING MY DAD AT THE BANK AND CLASSES AT KANSAS STATE UNIVERSITY.
YOU...YOU HAVEN'T TALKED ABOUT WHAT YOU'RE GOING TO DO, MUCH. THERE'S A GOOD JOURNALISM PROGRAM AT K.S.U....
I'M NOT GOING TO K.S.U., LANA. I'M...GOING TO TRAVEL, TO START...
She knew my secrets. She knew why I had to do what I did. But it still meant I was leaving her behind.
She's done so much with her life since then. In business. Marrying Pete, sharing his political career. Having a son.
But I found Lois, and Lana –
She's not very happy. I think she told herself she was, until the divorce, but now –
There are some things I just can't fix, and Lana's a dramatic example of that. But I wish I could do something to help her.
And if she's in trouble – in any sort of trouble I can deal with –

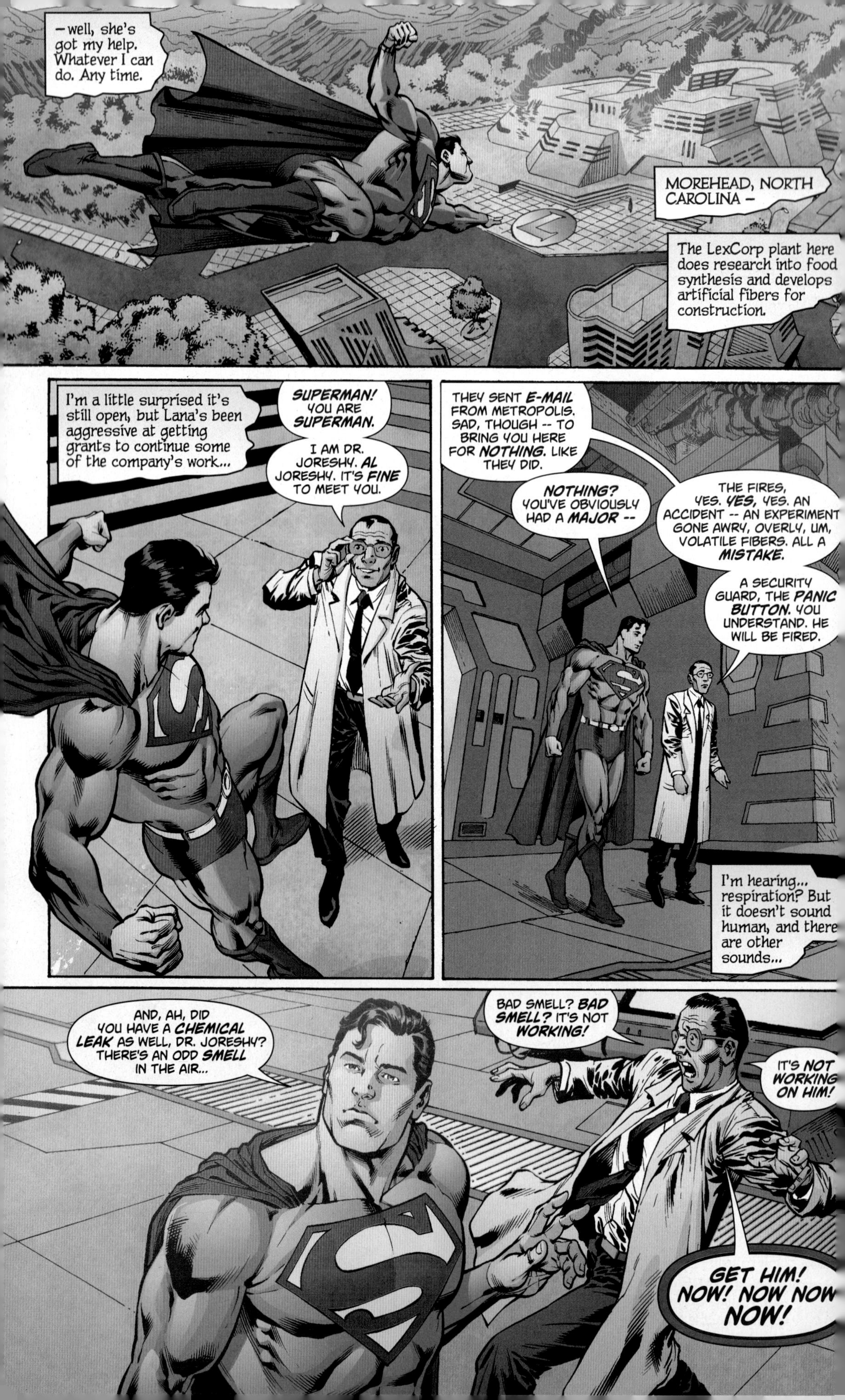
—well, she's got my help. Whatever I can do. Any time.
MOREHEAD, NORTH CAROLINA —
The LexCorp plant here does research into food synthesis and develops artificial fibers for construction.
I'm a little surprised it's still open, but Lana's been aggressive at getting grants to continue some of the company's work...
SUPERMAN! YOU ARE SUPERMAN.
I AM DR. JORESHY. AL JORESHY. IT'S FINE TO MEET YOU.
THEY SENT E-MAIL FROM METROPOLIS. SAD, THOUGH -- TO BRING YOU HERE FOR NOTHING. LIKE THEY DID.
NOTHING? YOU'VE OBVIOUSLY HAD A MAJOR --
THE FIRES, YES. YES, YES. AN ACCIDENT -- AN EXPERIMENT GONE AWRY, OVERLY, UM, VOLATILE FIBERS. ALL A MISTAKE.
A SECURITY GUARD, THE PANIC BUTTON. YOU UNDERSTAND. HE WILL BE FIRED.
I'm hearing... respiration? But it doesn't sound human, and there are other sounds...
AND, AH, DID YOU HAVE A CHEMICAL LEAK AS WELL, DR. JORESHY? THERE'S AN ODD SMELL IN THE AIR...
BAD SMELL? BAD SMELL? IT'S NOT WORKING!
IT'S NOT WORKING ON HIM!
GET HIM! NOW! NOW NOW NOW!

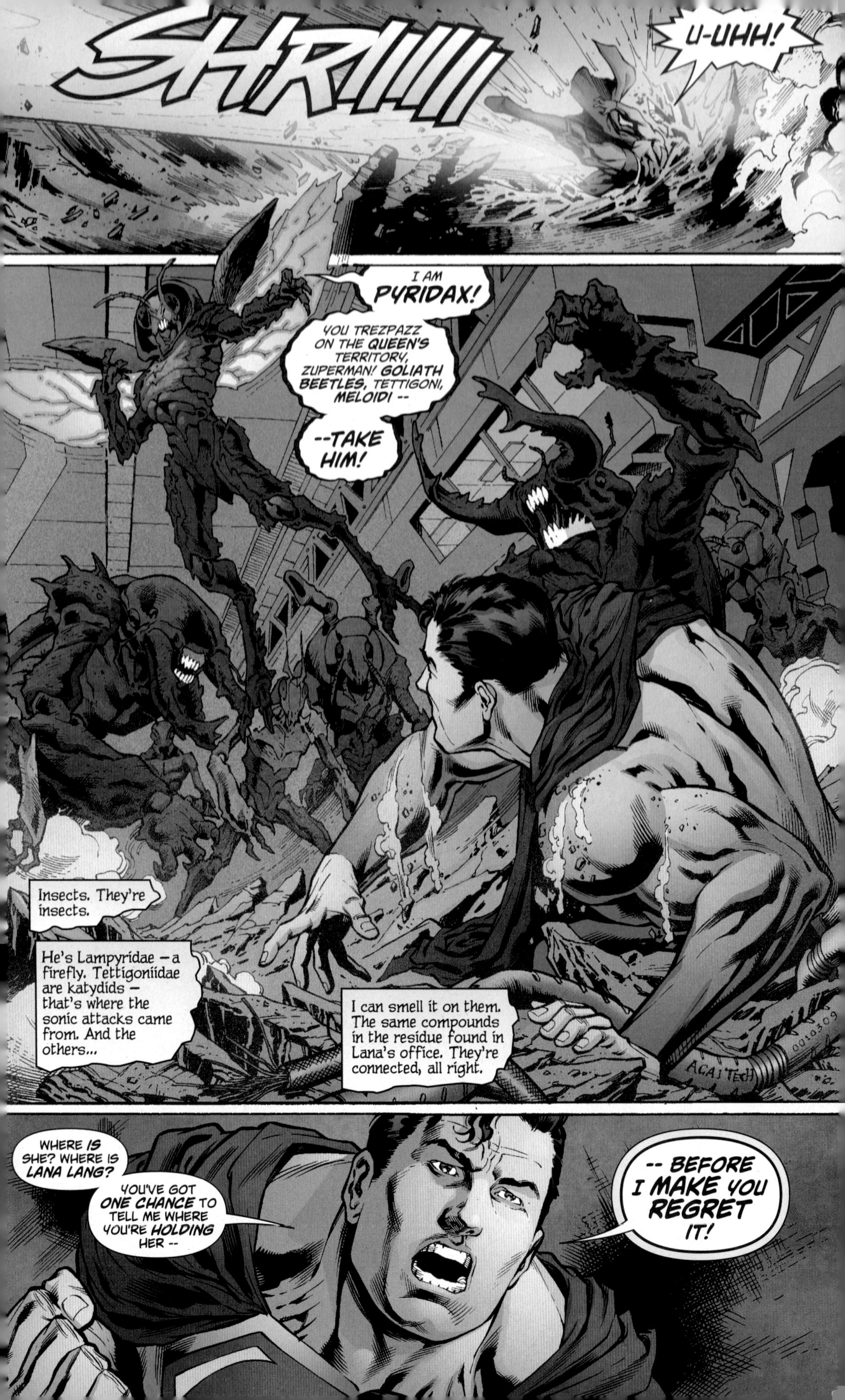

SHRIIIII
U-UHH!
I AM PYRIDAX!
YOU TREZPAZZ ON THE QUEEN'S TERRITORY, ZUPERMAN! GOLIATH BEETLES, TETTIGONI, MELOIDI --
--TAKE HIM!
Insects. They're insects.
He's Lampyridae – a firefly. Tettigoniidae are katydids – that's where the sonic attacks came from. And the others...
I can smell it on them. The same compounds in the residue found in Lana's office. They're connected, all right.
WHERE IS SHE? WHERE IS LANA LANG?
YOU'VE GOT ONE CHANCE TO TELL ME WHERE YOU'RE HOLDING HER --
-- BEFORE I MAKE YOU REGRET IT!

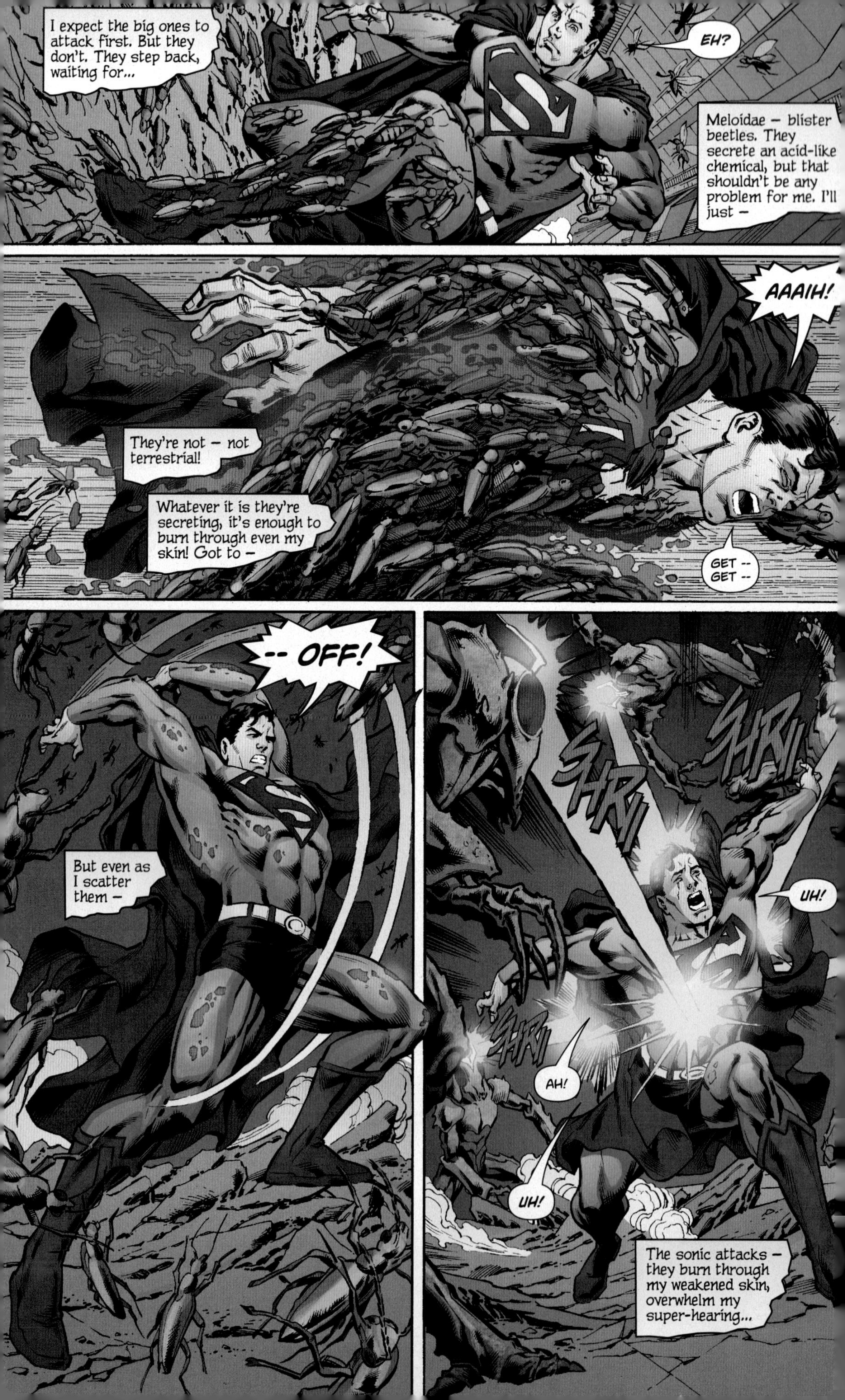
I expect the big ones to attack first. But they don't. They step back, waiting for...
EH?
Meloidae – blister beetles. They secrete an acid-like chemical, but that shouldn't be any problem for me. I'll just –
AAAIH!
They're not – not terrestrial!
Whatever it is they're secreting, it's enough to burn through even my skin! Got to –
GET -- GET --
-- OFF!
But even as I scatter them –
SHRI
SHRI
UH!
SHRI
AH!
UH!
The sonic attacks – they burn through my weakened skin, overwhelm my super-hearing...

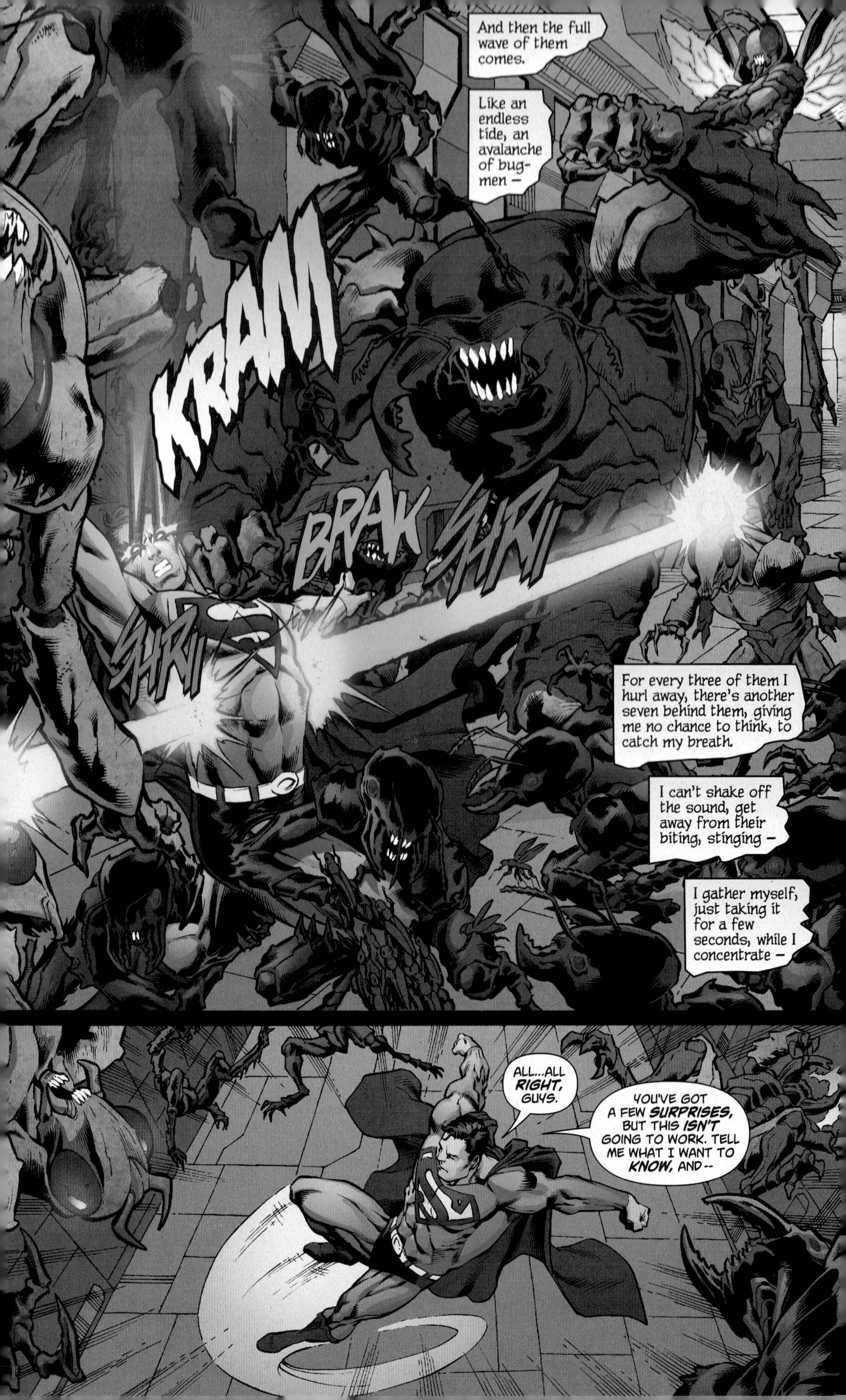

And then the full wave of them comes.
Like an endless tide, an avalanche of bug-men –
KRAM
BRAK
SKRI
SKRI
For every three of them I hurl away, there's another seven behind them, giving me no chance to think, to catch my breath.
I can't shake off the sound, get away from their biting, stinging –
I gather myself, just taking it for a few seconds, while I concentrate –
ALL...ALL RIGHT, GUYS.
YOU'VE GOT A FEW SURPRISES, BUT THIS ISN'T GOING TO WORK. TELL ME WHAT I WANT TO KNOW, AND --

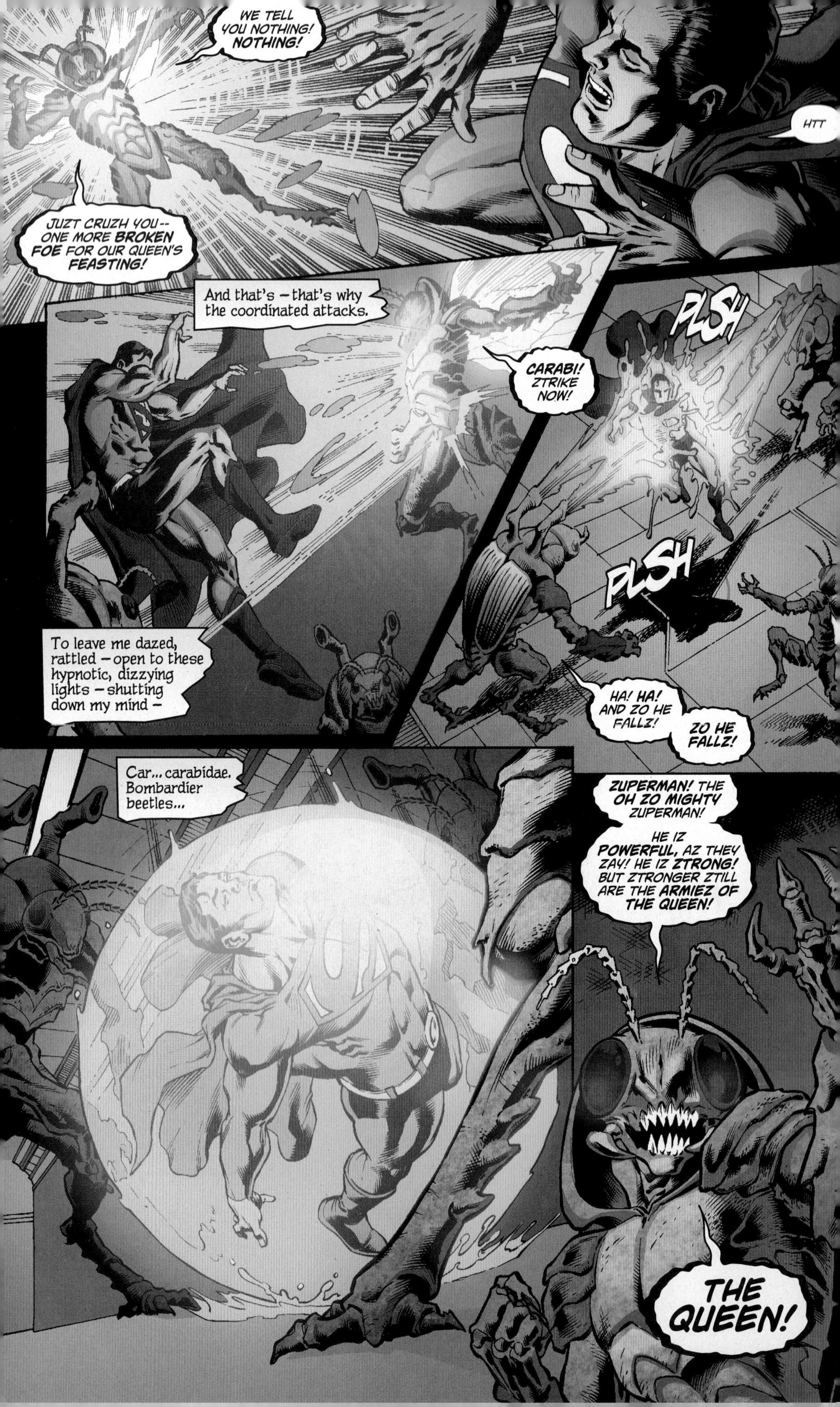
WE TELL YOU NOTHING! NOTHING!
HTT
JUZT CRUZH YOU-- ONE MORE BROKEN FOE FOR OUR QUEEN'S FEASTING!
And that's —that's why the coordinated attacks.
CARABI! ZTRIKE NOW!
To leave me dazed, rattled — open to these hypnotic, dizzying lights — shutting down my mind —
PLSH
PLSH
HA! HA! AND ZO HE FALLZ!
ZO HE FALLZ!
Car... carabidae. Bombardier beetles...
ZUPERMAN! THE OH ZO MIGHTY ZUPERMAN!
HE IZ POWERFUL, AZ THEY ZAY! HE IZ ZTRONG! BUT ZTRONGER ZTILL ARE THE ARMIEZ OF THE QUEEN!
THE QUEEN!

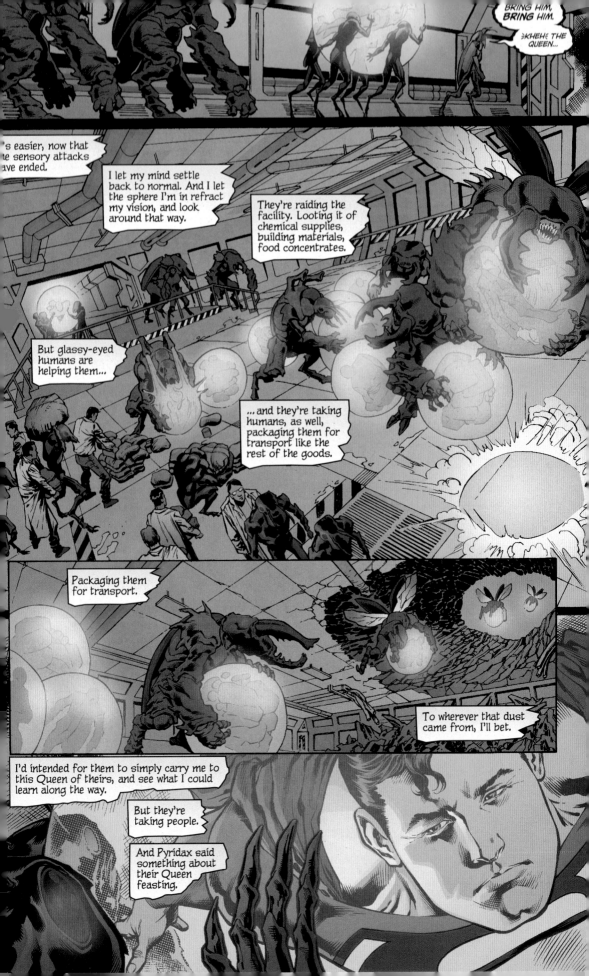

BRING HIM, BRING HIM.

ƎKHEHƷ THE QUEEN...

...'s easier, now that ne sensory attacks ave ended.

I let my mind settle back to normal. And I let the sphere I'm in refract my vision, and look around that way.

They're raiding the facility. Looting it of chemical supplies, building materials, food concentrates.

But glassy-eyed humans are helping them...

...and they're taking humans, as well, packaging them for transport like the rest of the goods.

Packaging them for transport.

To wherever that dust came from, I'll bet.

I'd intended for them to simply carry me to this Queen of theirs, and see what I could learn along the way.

But they're taking people.

And Pyridax said something about their Queen feasting.

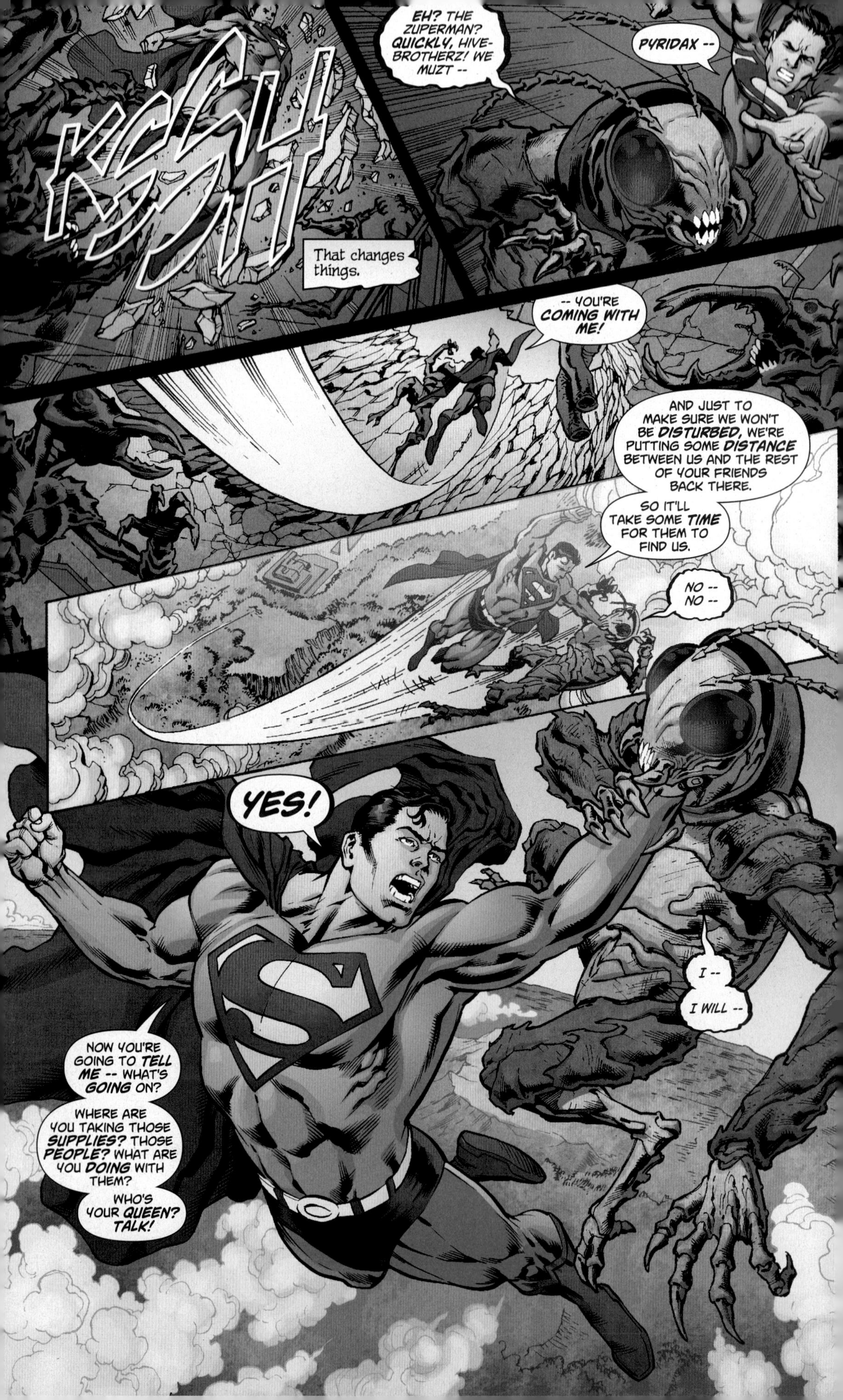
KCCHHH
That changes things.
EH? THE ZUPERMAN? QUICKLY, HIVE-BROTHERZ! WE MUZT --
PYRIDAX --
-- YOU'RE COMING WITH ME!
AND JUST TO MAKE SURE WE WON'T BE DISTURBED, WE'RE PUTTING SOME DISTANCE BETWEEN US AND THE REST OF YOUR FRIENDS BACK THERE.
SO IT'LL TAKE SOME TIME FOR THEM TO FIND US.
NO -- NO --
YES!
NOW YOU'RE GOING TO TELL ME -- WHAT'S GOING ON?
WHERE ARE YOU TAKING THOSE SUPPLIES? THOSE PEOPLE? WHAT ARE YOU DOING WITH THEM?
WHO'S YOUR QUEEN? TALK!
I --
I WILL --

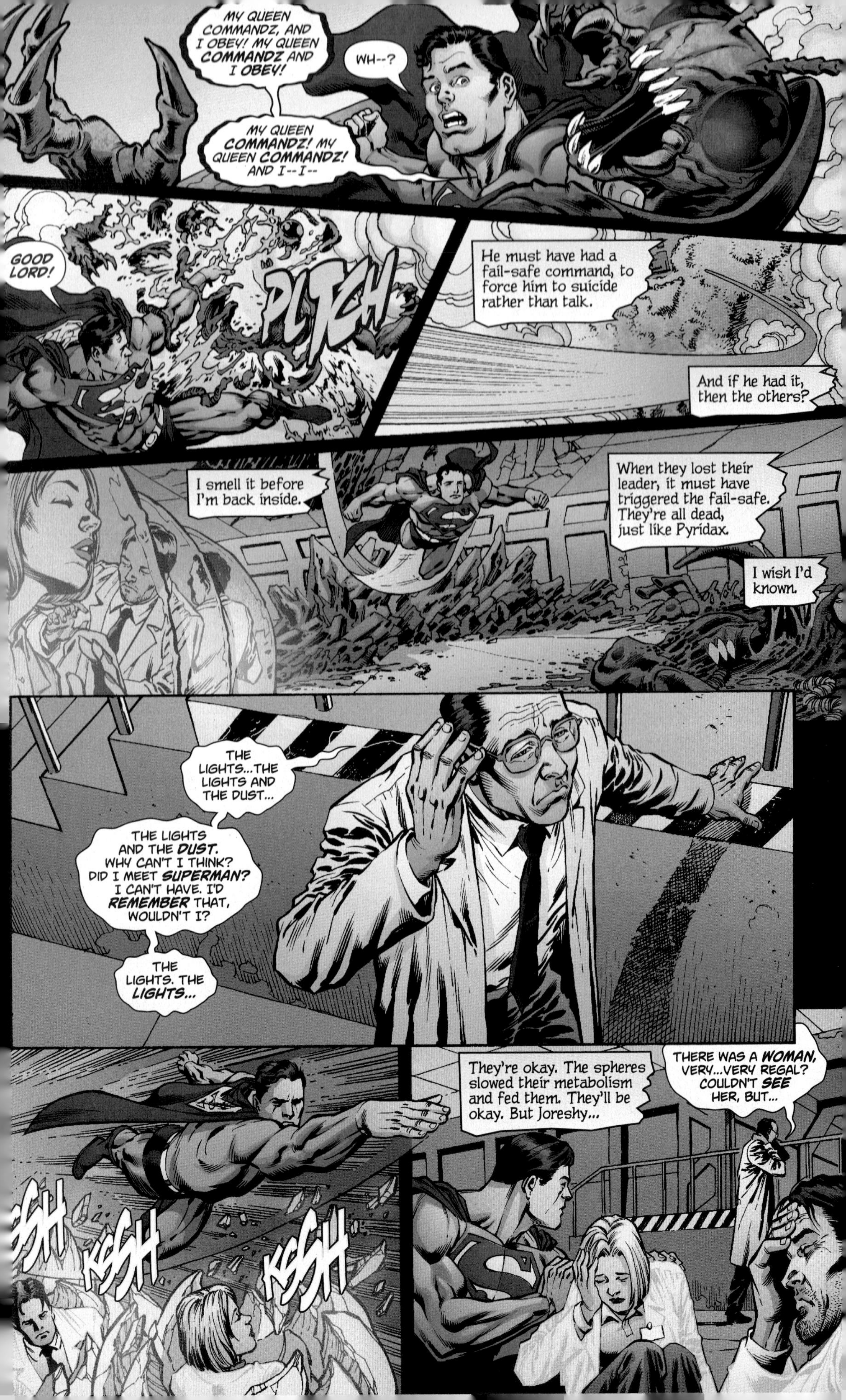
MY QUEEN COMMANDZ, AND I OBEY! MY QUEEN COMMANDZ AND I OBEY!
WH--?
MY QUEEN COMMANDZ! MY QUEEN COMMANDZ! AND I--I--
GOOD LORD!
PLTCH
He must have had a fail-safe command, to force him to suicide rather than talk.
And if he had it, then the others?
I smell it before I'm back inside.
When they lost their leader, it must have triggered the fail-safe. They're all dead, just like Pyridax.
I wish I'd known.
THE LIGHTS...THE LIGHTS AND THE DUST...
THE LIGHTS AND THE DUST. WHY CAN'T I THINK? DID I MEET SUPERMAN? I CAN'T HAVE. I'D REMEMBER THAT, WOULDN'T I?
THE LIGHTS. THE LIGHTS...
KSH
KSSH
They're okay. The spheres slowed their metabolism and fed them. They'll be okay. But Joreshy...
THERE WAS A WOMAN, VERY...VERY REGAL? COULDN'T SEE HER, BUT...

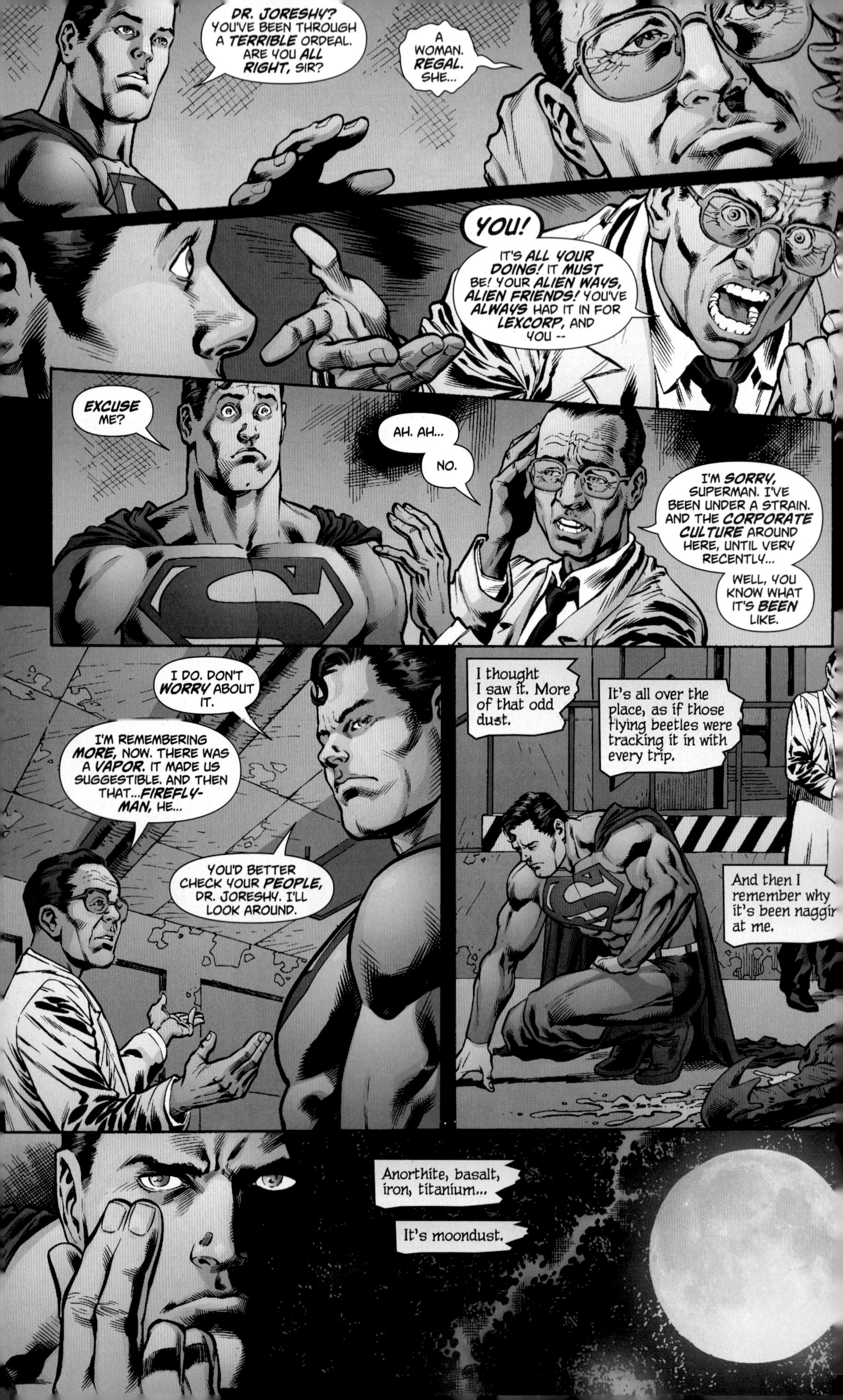
DR. JORESHY? YOU'VE BEEN THROUGH A TERRIBLE ORDEAL. ARE YOU ALL RIGHT, SIR?
A WOMAN. REGAL. SHE...
YOU!
IT'S ALL YOUR DOING! IT MUST BE! YOUR ALIEN WAYS, ALIEN FRIENDS! YOU'VE ALWAYS HAD IT IN FOR LEXCORP, AND YOU --
EXCUSE ME?
AH. AH...
NO.
I'M SORRY, SUPERMAN. I'VE BEEN UNDER A STRAIN. AND THE CORPORATE CULTURE AROUND HERE, UNTIL VERY RECENTLY...
WELL, YOU KNOW WHAT IT'S BEEN LIKE.
I DO. DON'T WORRY ABOUT IT.
I'M REMEMBERING MORE, NOW. THERE WAS A VAPOR. IT MADE US SUGGESTIBLE. AND THEN THAT...FIREFLY-MAN, HE...
YOU'D BETTER CHECK YOUR PEOPLE, DR. JORESHY. I'LL LOOK AROUND.
I thought I saw it. More of that odd dust.
It's all over the place, as if those flying beetles were tracking it in with every trip.
And then I remember why it's been naggir at me.
Anorthite, basalt, iron, titanium...
It's moondust.

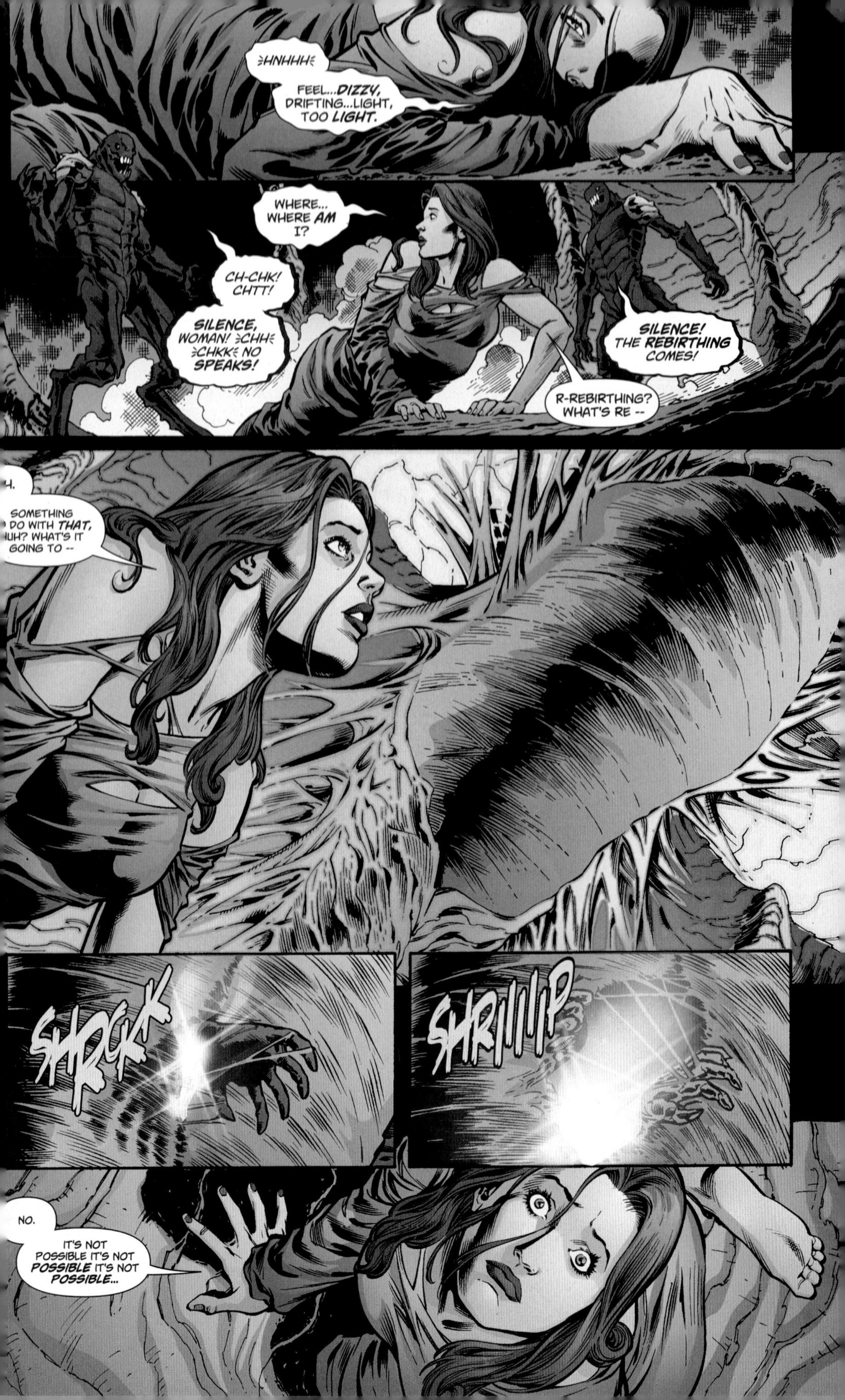

≥HNHHH≤
FEEL...DIZZY, DRIFTING...LIGHT, TOO LIGHT.
WHERE... WHERE AM I?
CH-CHK! CHTT!
SILENCE, WOMAN! ≥CHH≤ ≥CHKK≤ NO SPEAKS!
SILENCE! THE REBIRTHING COMES!
R-REBIRTHING? WHAT'S RE --
SOMETHING DO WITH THAT, HUH? WHAT'S IT GOING TO --
SHRCKK
SHRIIIIP
NO.
IT'S NOT POSSIBLE IT'S NOT POSSIBLE IT'S NOT POSSIBLE...

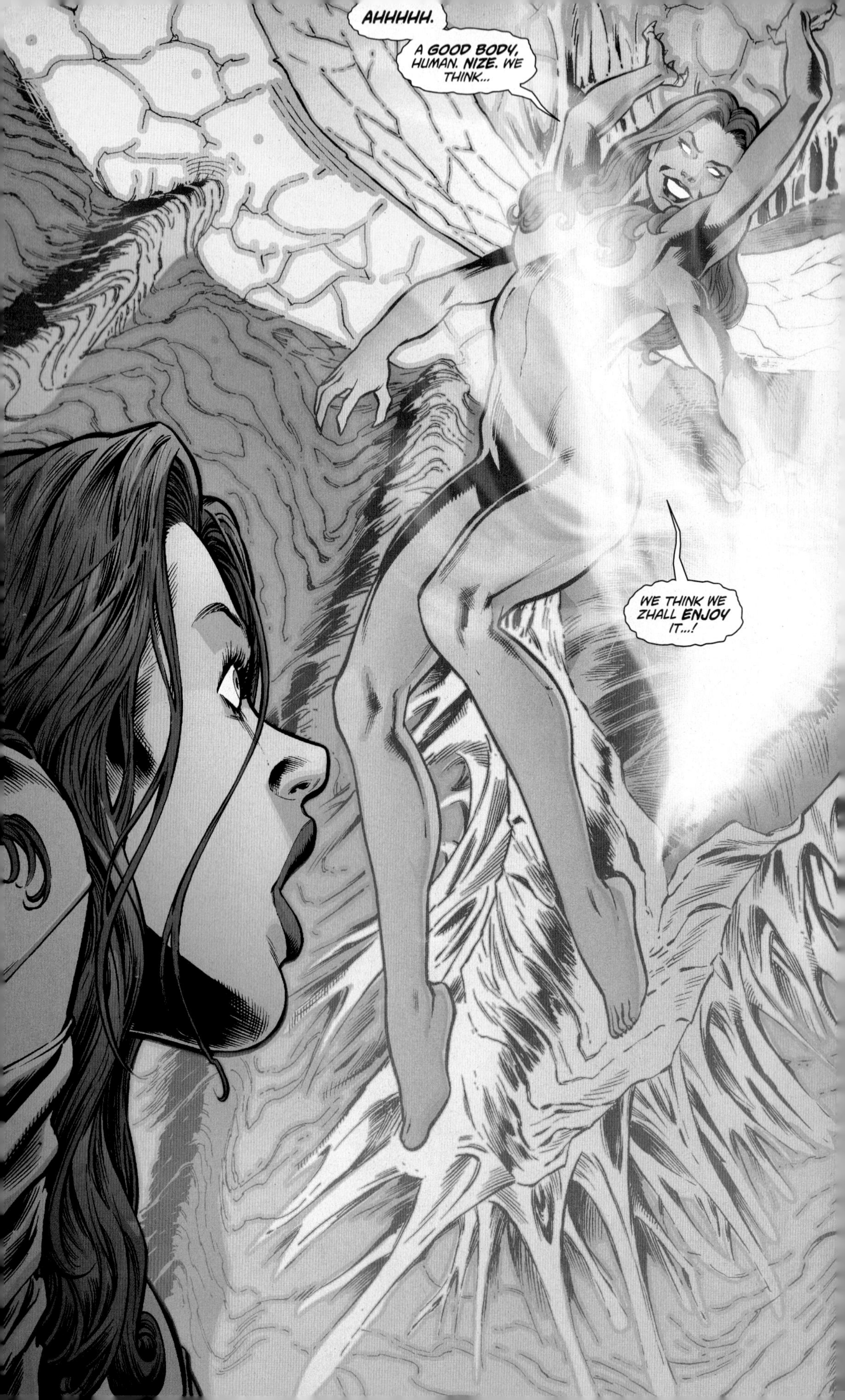
AHHHHH.
A GOOD BODY, HUMAN. NIZE. WE THINK...
WE THINK WE ZHALL ENJOY IT...!

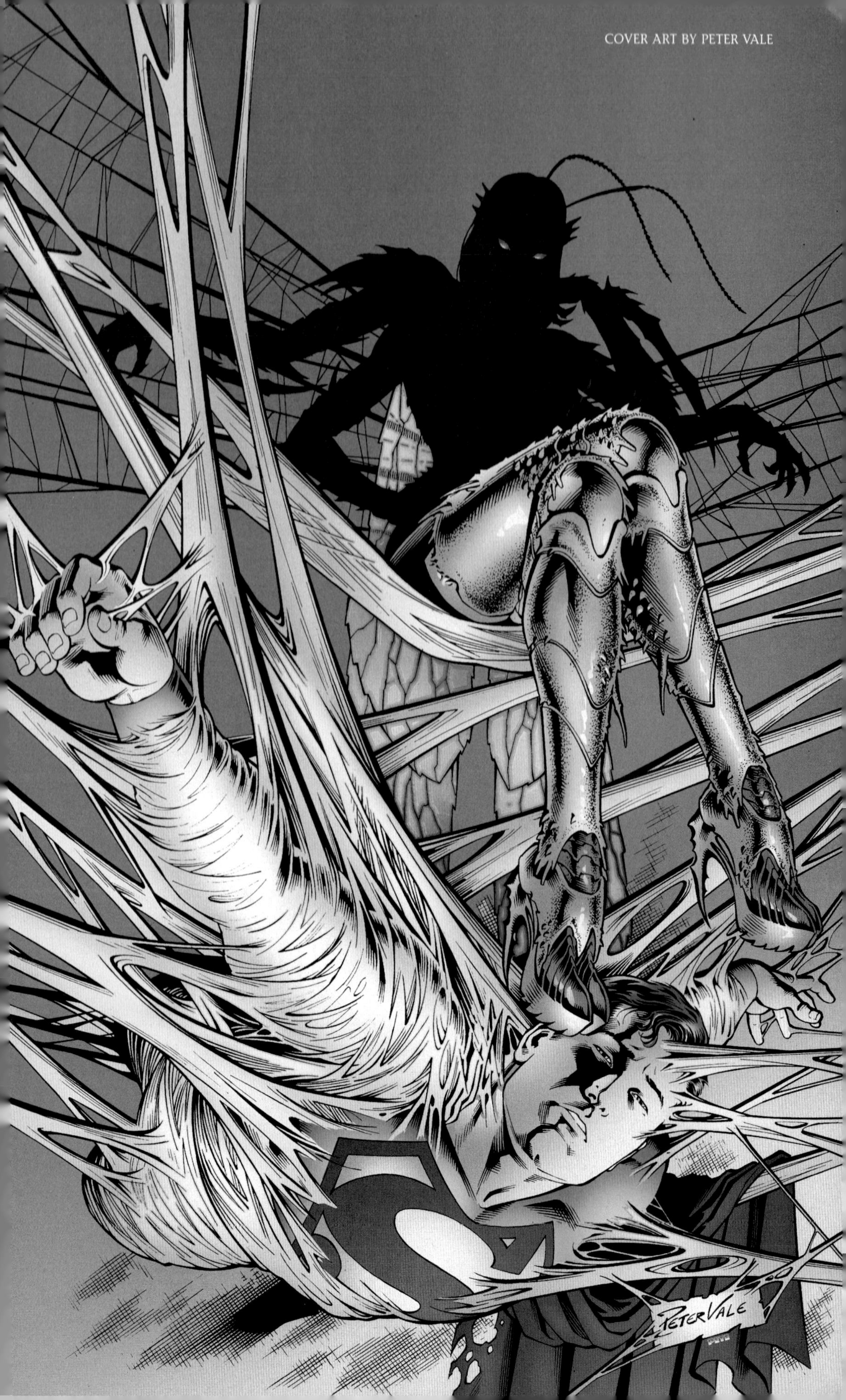
PETER VALE
COVER ART BY PETER VALE

INSECT QUEEN
PART TWO:

GOSSAMER WINGS

ART BY **PETER VALE** & **WELLINGTON DIAS**
COLORS BY **KANILA TRIPP**

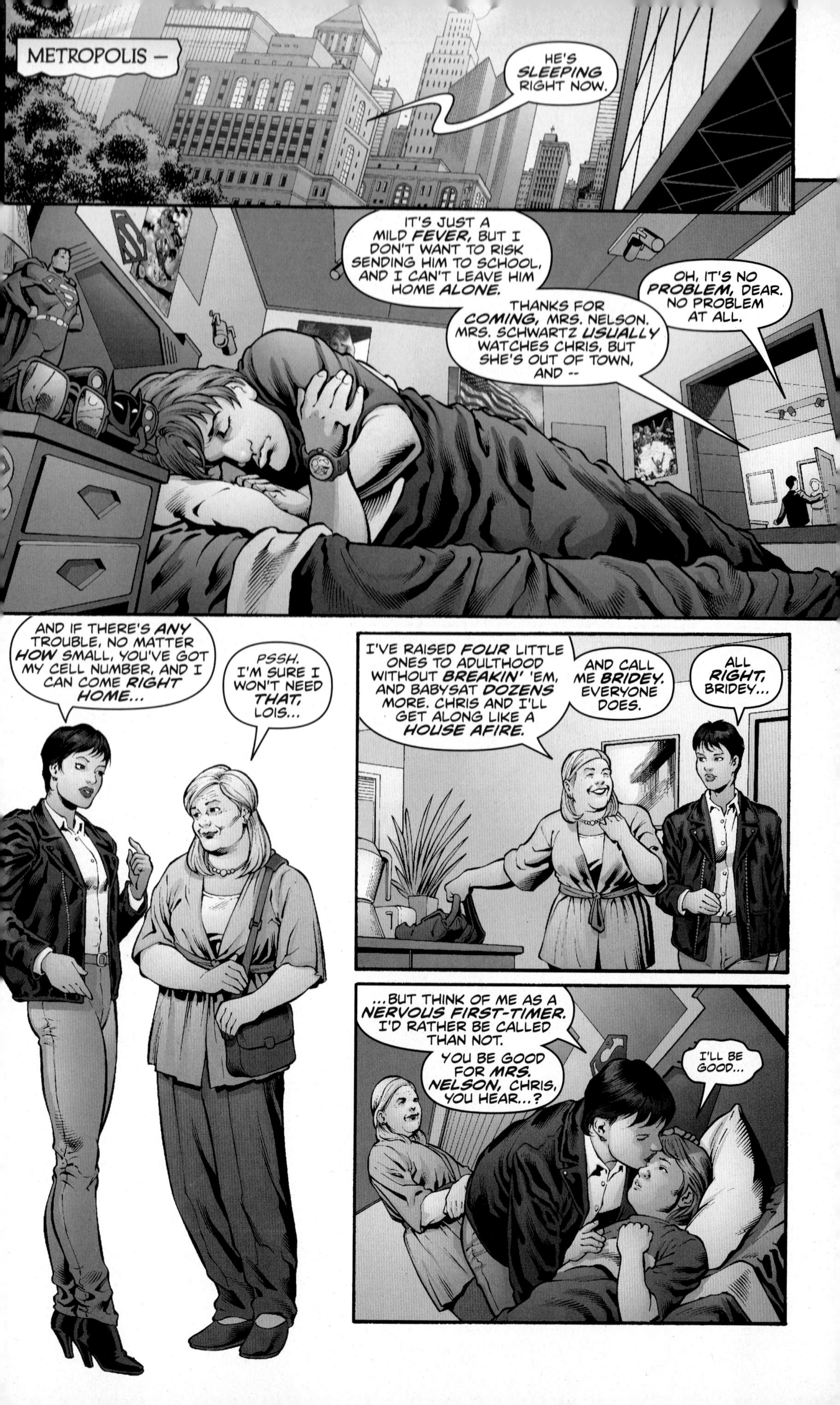
METROPOLIS —
HE'S SLEEPING RIGHT NOW.
IT'S JUST A MILD FEVER, BUT I DON'T WANT TO RISK SENDING HIM TO SCHOOL, AND I CAN'T LEAVE HIM HOME ALONE.
THANKS FOR COMING, MRS. NELSON. MRS. SCHWARTZ USUALLY WATCHES CHRIS, BUT SHE'S OUT OF TOWN, AND --
OH, IT'S NO PROBLEM, DEAR. NO PROBLEM AT ALL.
AND IF THERE'S ANY TROUBLE, NO MATTER HOW SMALL, YOU'VE GOT MY CELL NUMBER, AND I CAN COME RIGHT HOME...
PSSH. I'M SURE I WON'T NEED THAT, LOIS...
I'VE RAISED FOUR LITTLE ONES TO ADULTHOOD WITHOUT BREAKIN' 'EM, AND BABYSAT DOZENS MORE. CHRIS AND I'LL GET ALONG LIKE A HOUSE AFIRE.
AND CALL ME BRIDEY. EVERYONE DOES.
ALL RIGHT, BRIDEY...
...BUT THINK OF ME AS A NERVOUS FIRST-TIMER. I'D RATHER BE CALLED THAN NOT.
YOU BE GOOD FOR MRS. NELSON, CHRIS, YOU HEAR...?
I'LL BE GOOD...

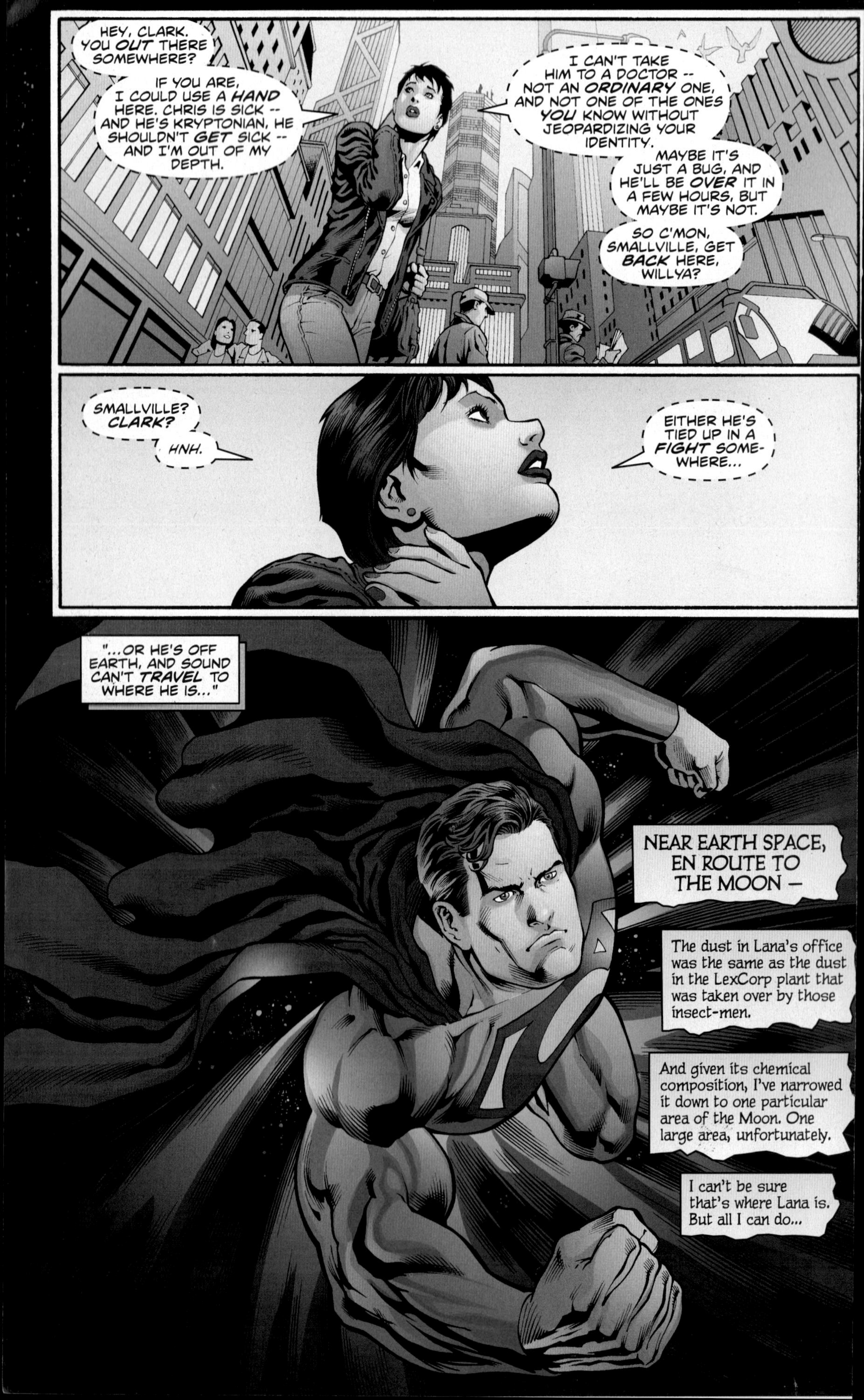
HEY, CLARK. YOU OUT THERE SOMEWHERE?
IF YOU ARE, I COULD USE A HAND HERE. CHRIS IS SICK -- AND HE'S KRYPTONIAN, HE SHOULDN'T GET SICK -- AND I'M OUT OF MY DEPTH.
I CAN'T TAKE HIM TO A DOCTOR -- NOT AN ORDINARY ONE, AND NOT ONE OF THE ONES YOU KNOW WITHOUT JEOPARDIZING YOUR IDENTITY.
MAYBE IT'S JUST A BUG, AND HE'LL BE OVER IT IN A FEW HOURS, BUT MAYBE IT'S NOT.
SO C'MON, SMALLVILLE, GET BACK HERE, WILLYA?
SMALLVILLE? CLARK?
HNH.
EITHER HE'S TIED UP IN A FIGHT SOMEWHERE...
"...OR HE'S OFF EARTH, AND SOUND CAN'T TRAVEL TO WHERE HE IS..."
NEAR EARTH SPACE, EN ROUTE TO THE MOON –
The dust in Lana's office was the same as the dust in the LexCorp plant that was taken over by those insect-men.
And given its chemical composition, I've narrowed it down to one particular area of the Moon. One large area, unfortunately.
I can't be sure that's where Lana is. But all I can do...

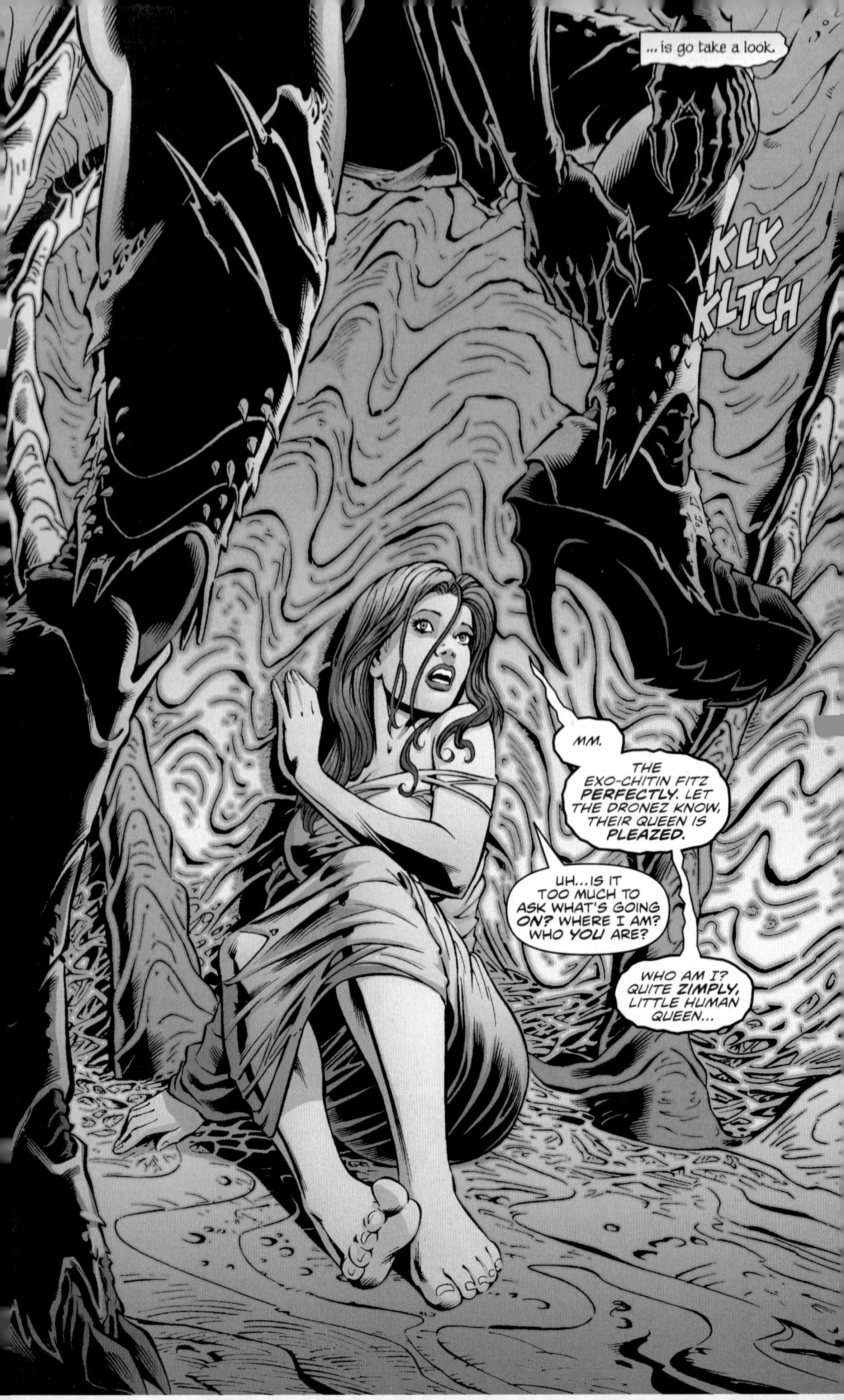
...is go take a look.
KLK KLTCH
MM.
THE EXO-CHITIN FITZ PERFECTLY. LET THE DRONEZ KNOW, THEIR QUEEN IS PLEAZED.
UH...IS IT TOO MUCH TO ASK WHAT'S GOING ON? WHERE I AM? WHO YOU ARE?
WHO AM I? QUITE ZIMPLY, LITTLE HUMAN QUEEN...

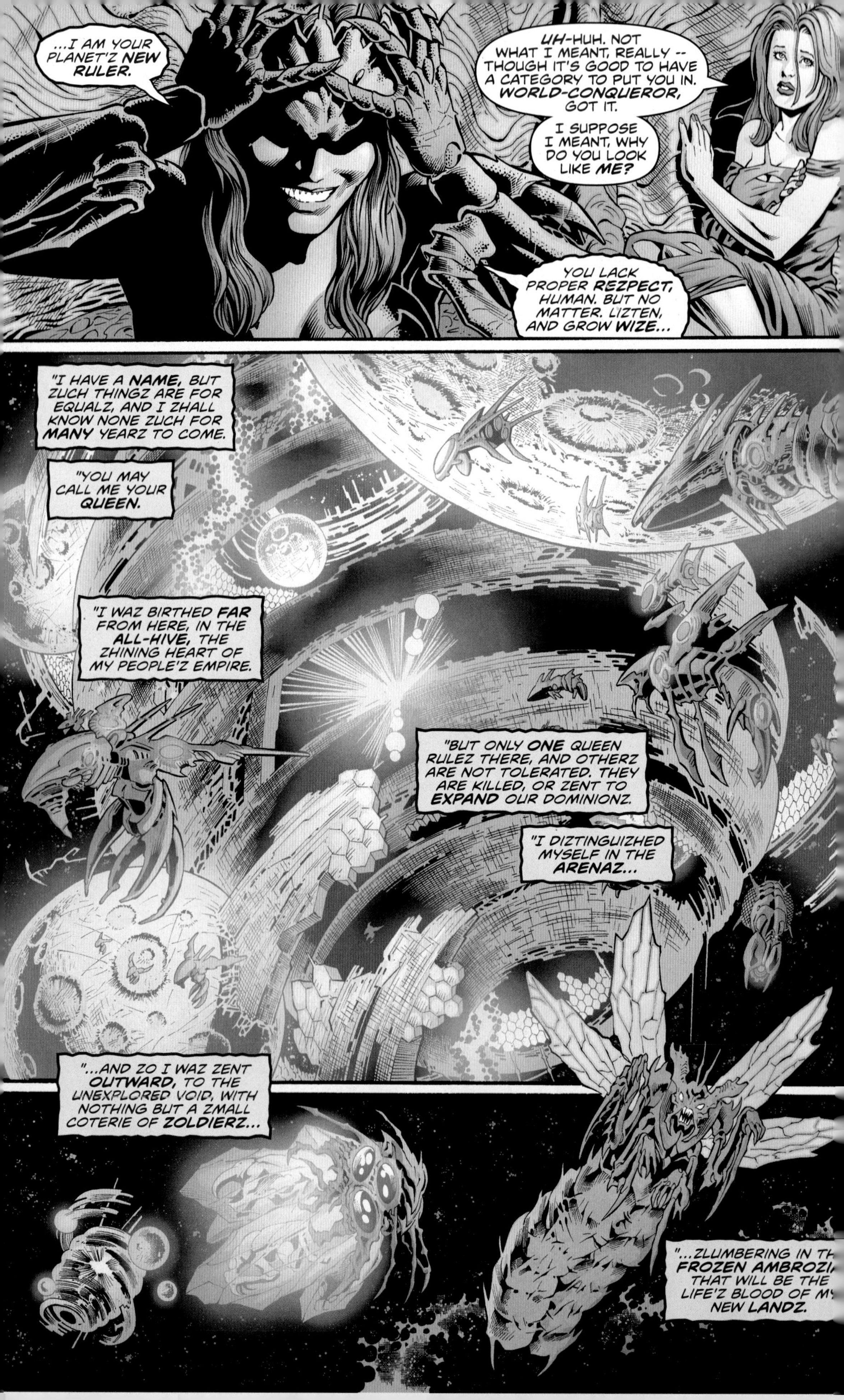
...I AM YOUR PLANET'Z NEW RULER.
UH-HUH. NOT WHAT I MEANT, REALLY -- THOUGH IT'S GOOD TO HAVE A CATEGORY TO PUT YOU IN. WORLD-CONQUEROR, GOT IT.
I SUPPOSE I MEANT, WHY DO YOU LOOK LIKE ME?
YOU LACK PROPER REZPECT, HUMAN. BUT NO MATTER. LIZTEN, AND GROW WIZE...
"I HAVE A NAME, BUT ZUCH THINGZ ARE FOR EQUALZ, AND I ZHALL KNOW NONE ZUCH FOR MANY YEARZ TO COME.
"YOU MAY CALL ME YOUR QUEEN.
"I WAZ BIRTHED FAR FROM HERE, IN THE ALL-HIVE, THE ZHINING HEART OF MY PEOPLE'Z EMPIRE.
"BUT ONLY ONE QUEEN RULEZ THERE, AND OTHERZ ARE NOT TOLERATED. THEY ARE KILLED, OR ZENT TO EXPAND OUR DOMINIONZ.
"I DIZTINGUIZHED MYSELF IN THE ARENAZ...
"...AND ZO I WAZ ZENT OUTWARD, TO THE UNEXPLORED VOID, WITH NOTHING BUT A ZMALL COTERIE OF ZOLDIERZ...
"...ZLUMBERING IN TH FROZEN AMBROZI THAT WILL BE THE LIFE'Z BLOOD OF MY NEW LANDZ.

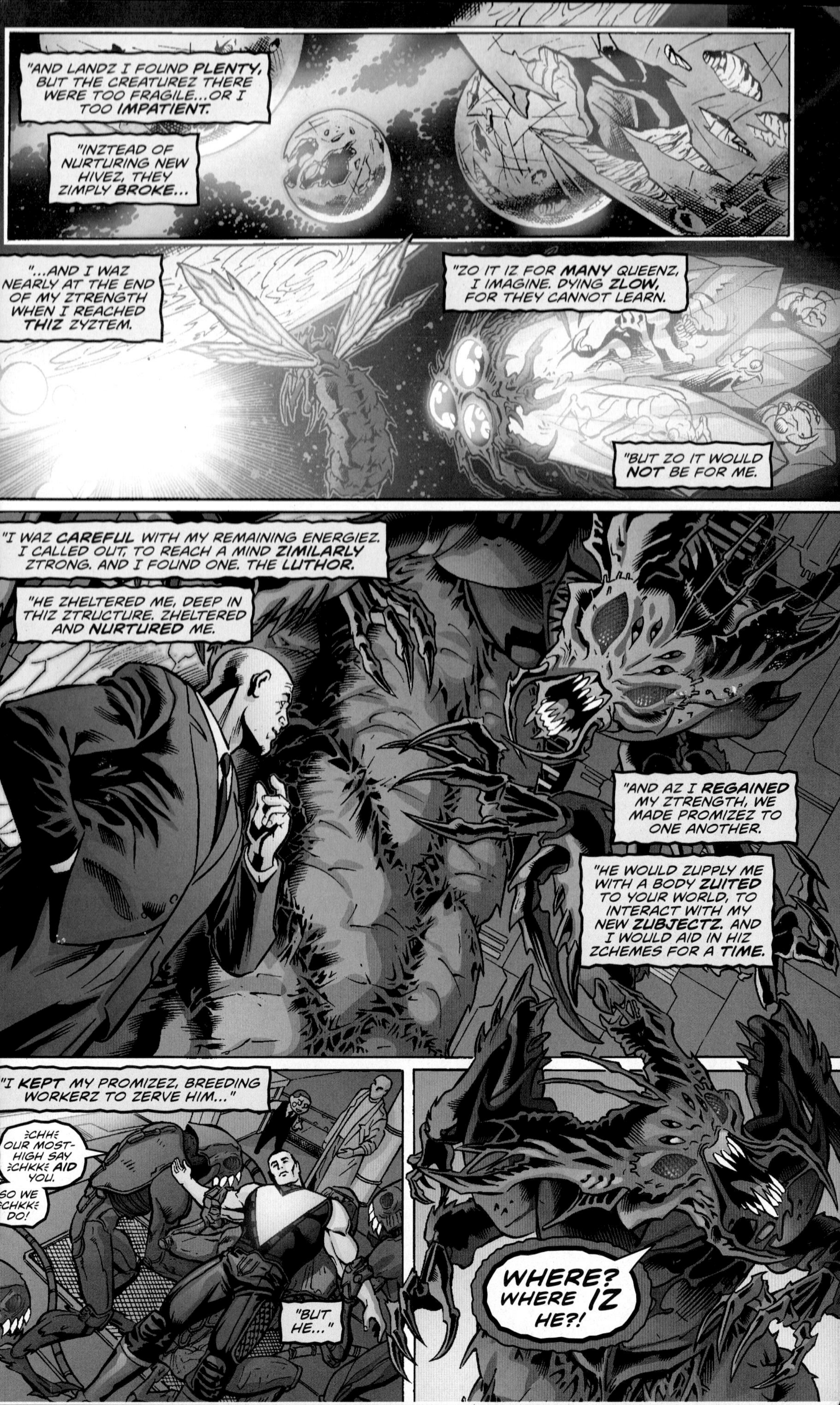
"AND LANDZ I FOUND PLENTY, BUT THE CREATUREZ THERE WERE TOO FRAGILE...OR I TOO IMPATIENT.
"INZTEAD OF NURTURING NEW HIVEZ, THEY ZIMPLY BROKE...
"...AND I WAZ NEARLY AT THE END OF MY ZTRENGTH WHEN I REACHED THIZ ZYZTEM.
"ZO IT IZ FOR MANY QUEENZ, I IMAGINE. DYING ZLOW, FOR THEY CANNOT LEARN.
"BUT ZO IT WOULD NOT BE FOR ME.
"I WAZ CAREFUL WITH MY REMAINING ENERGIEZ. I CALLED OUT, TO REACH A MIND ZIMILARLY ZTRONG. AND I FOUND ONE. THE LUTHOR.
"HE ZHELTERED ME, DEEP IN THIZ ZTRUCTURE. ZHELTERED AND NURTURED ME.
"AND AZ I REGAINED MY ZTRENGTH, WE MADE PROMIZEZ TO ONE ANOTHER.
"HE WOULD ZUPPLY ME WITH A BODY ZUITED TO YOUR WORLD, TO INTERACT WITH MY NEW ZUBJECTZ. AND I WOULD AID IN HIZ ZCHEMES FOR A TIME.
"I KEPT MY PROMIZEZ, BREEDING WORKERZ TO ZERVE HIM..."
ZCHHZ OUR MOST-HIGH SAY ZCHKKZ AID YOU.
SO WE ZCHKKZ DO!
"BUT HE..."
WHERE? WHERE IZ HE?!

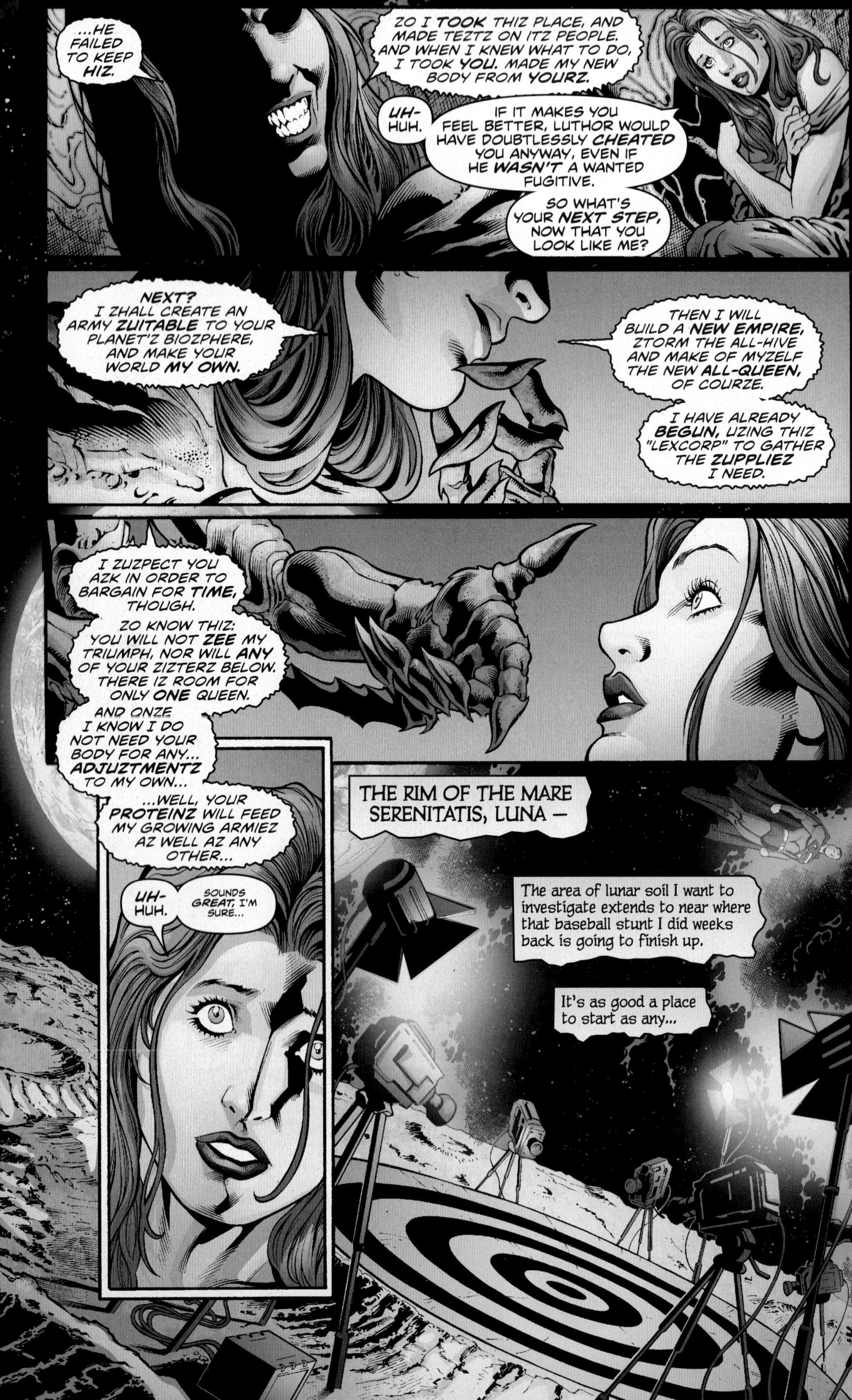
...HE FAILED TO KEEP HIZ.
ZO I TOOK THIZ PLACE, AND MADE TEZTZ ON ITZ PEOPLE. AND WHEN I KNEW WHAT TO DO, I TOOK YOU. MADE MY NEW BODY FROM YOURZ.
UH-HUH.
IF IT MAKES YOU FEEL BETTER, LUTHOR WOULD HAVE DOUBTLESSLY CHEATED YOU ANYWAY, EVEN IF HE WASN'T A WANTED FUGITIVE.
SO WHAT'S YOUR NEXT STEP, NOW THAT YOU LOOK LIKE ME?
NEXT? I ZHALL CREATE AN ARMY ZUITABLE TO YOUR PLANET'Z BIOZPHERE, AND MAKE YOUR WORLD MY OWN.
THEN I WILL BUILD A NEW EMPIRE, ZTORM THE ALL-HIVE AND MAKE OF MYZELF THE NEW ALL-QUEEN, OF COURZE.
I HAVE ALREADY BEGUN, UZING THIZ "LEXCORP" TO GATHER THE ZUPPLIEZ I NEED.
I ZUZPECT YOU AZK IN ORDER TO BARGAIN FOR TIME, THOUGH.
ZO KNOW THIZ: YOU WILL NOT ZEE MY TRIUMPH, NOR WILL ANY OF YOUR ZIZTERZ BELOW. THERE IZ ROOM FOR ONLY ONE QUEEN.
AND ONZE I KNOW I DO NOT NEED YOUR BODY FOR ANY... ADJUZTMENTZ TO MY OWN...
...WELL, YOUR PROTEINZ WILL FEED MY GROWING ARMIEZ AZ WELL AZ ANY OTHER...
UH-HUH.
SOUNDS GREAT, I'M SURE...
THE RIM OF THE MARE SERENITATIS, LUNA —
The area of lunar soil I want to investigate extends to near where that baseball stunt I did weeks back is going to finish up.
It's as good a place to start as any...

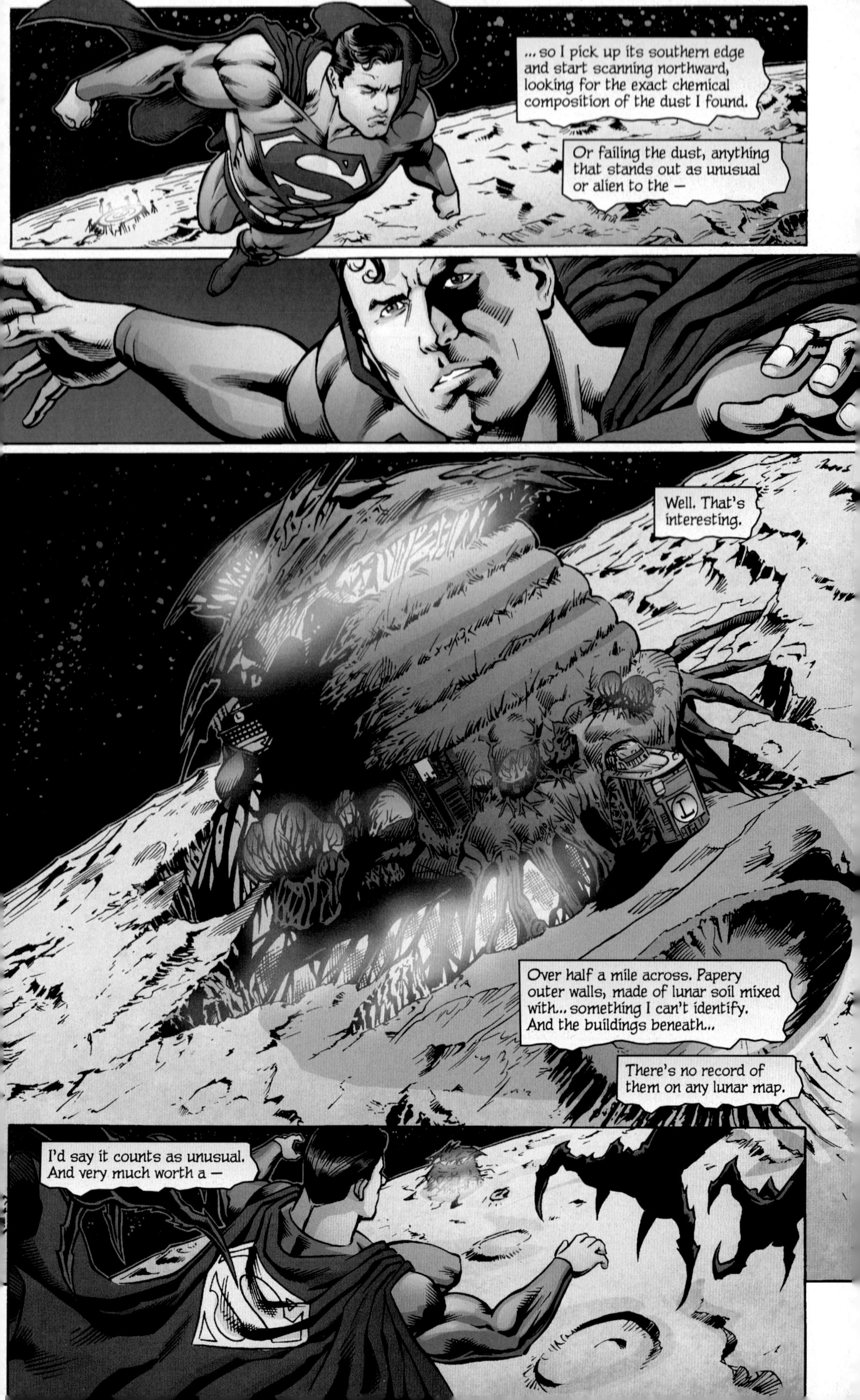
...so I pick up its southern edge and start scanning northward, looking for the exact chemical composition of the dust I found.
Or failing the dust, anything that stands out as unusual or alien to the —
Well. That's interesting.
Over half a mile across. Papery outer walls, made of lunar soil mixed with... something I can't identify. And the buildings beneath...
There's no record of them on any lunar map.
I'd say it counts as unusual. And very much worth a —

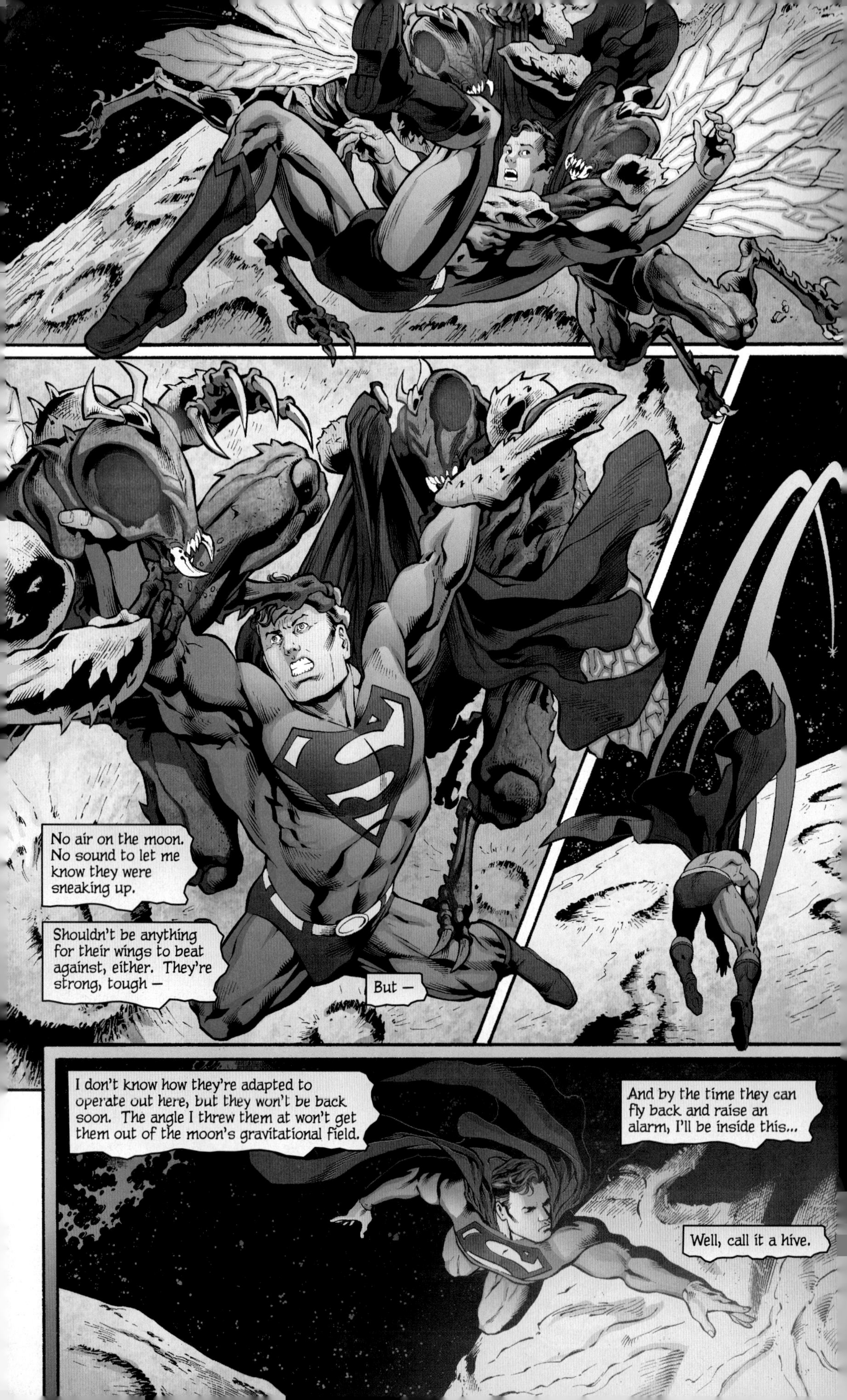
No air on the moon. No sound to let me know they were sneaking up.
Shouldn't be anything for their wings to beat against, either. They're strong, tough —
But —
I don't know how they're adapted to operate out here, but they won't be back soon. The angle I threw them at won't get them out of the moon's gravitational field.
And by the time they can fly back and raise an alarm, I'll be inside this...
Well, call it a hive.

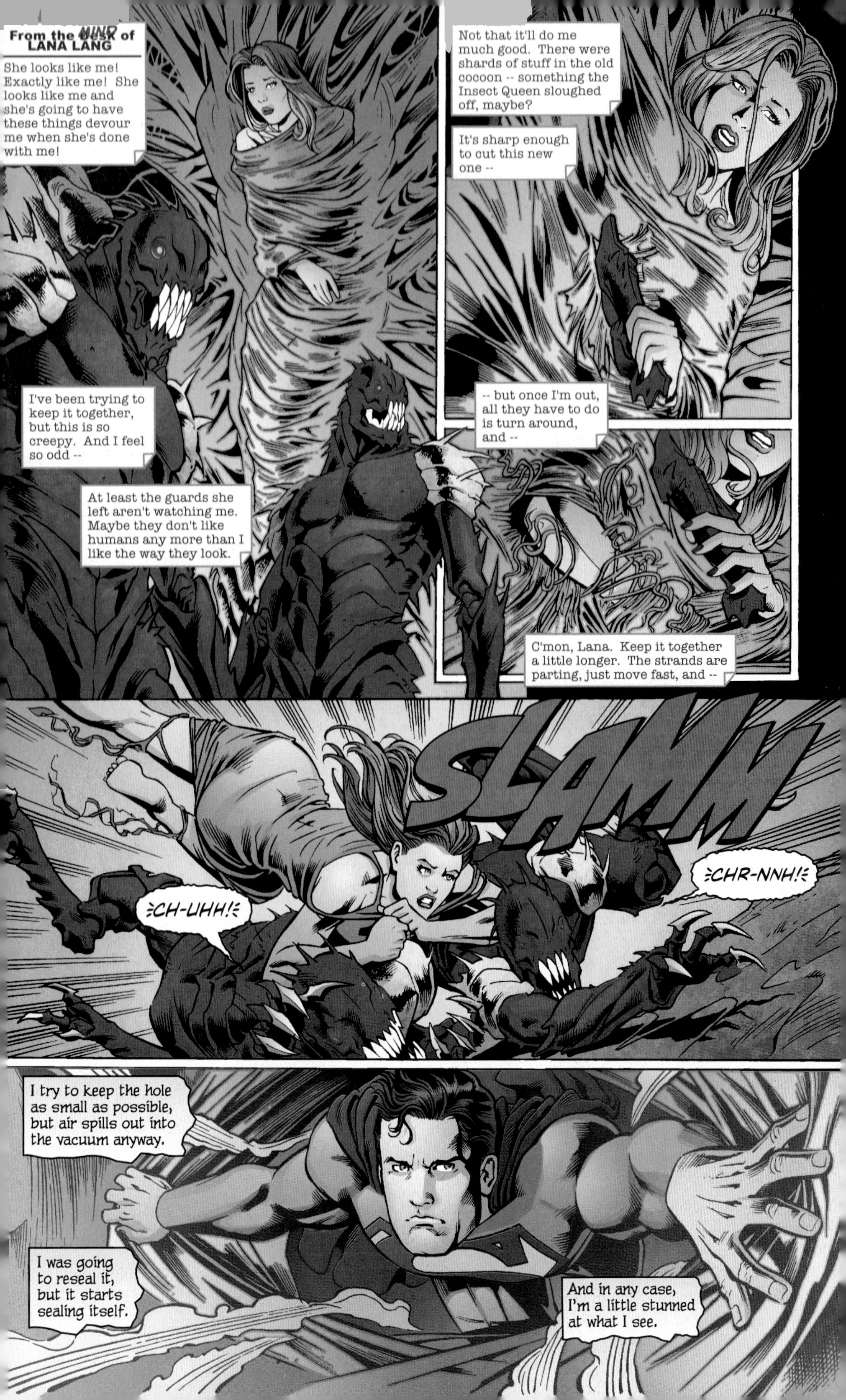
From the Desk of MIND LANA LANG
She looks like me! Exactly like me! She looks like me and she's going to have these things devour me when she's done with me!
I've been trying to keep it together, but this is so creepy. And I feel so odd --
At least the guards she left aren't watching me. Maybe they don't like humans any more than I like the way they look.
Not that it'll do me much good. There were shards of stuff in the old cocoon -- something the Insect Queen sloughed off, maybe?
It's sharp enough to cut this new one --
-- but once I'm out, all they have to do is turn around, and --
C'mon, Lana. Keep it together a little longer. The strands are parting, just move fast, and --
SLAMM
CH-UHH!
CHR-NNH!
I try to keep the hole as small as possible, but air spills out into the vacuum anyway.
I was going to reseal it, but it starts sealing itself.
And in any case, I'm a little stunned at what I see.

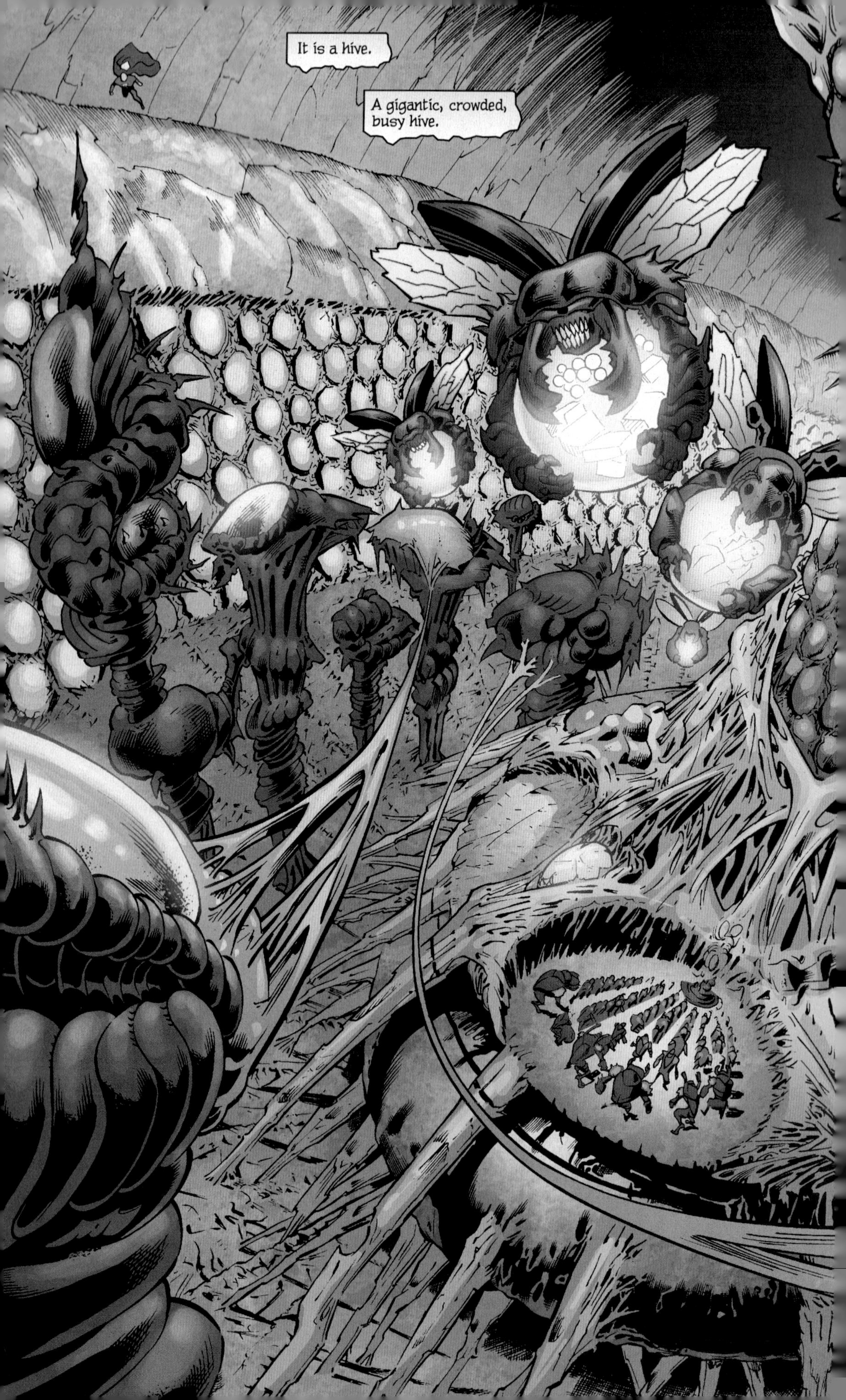
It is a hive.
A gigantic, crowded, busy hive.

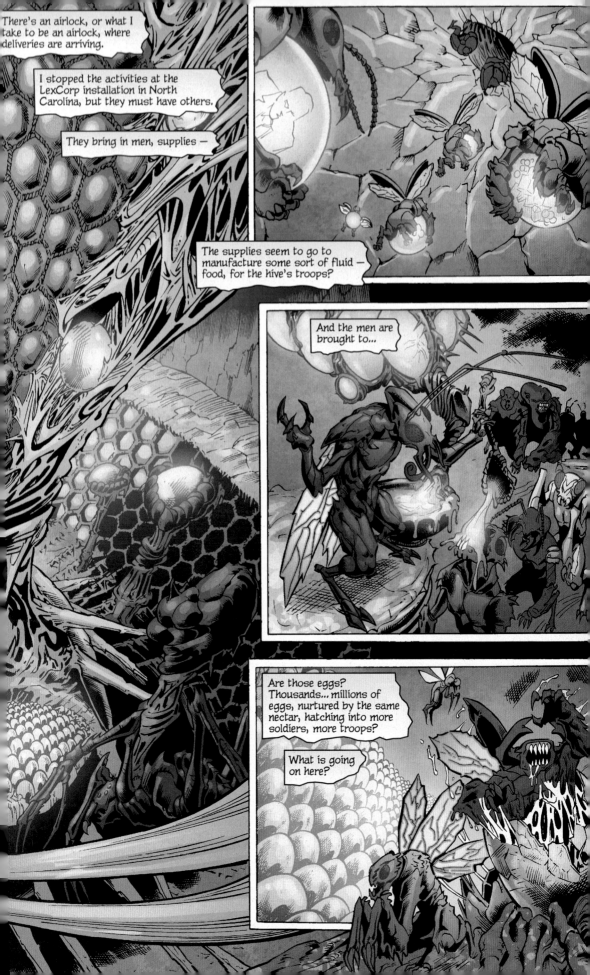

There's an airlock, or what I take to be an airlock, where deliveries are arriving.

I stopped the activities at the LexCorp installation in North Carolina, but they must have others.

They bring in men, supplies —

The supplies seem to go to manufacture some sort of fluid — food, for the hive's troops?

And the men are brought to...

Are those eggs? Thousands... millions of eggs, nurtured by the same nectar, hatching into more soldiers, more troops?

What is going on here?

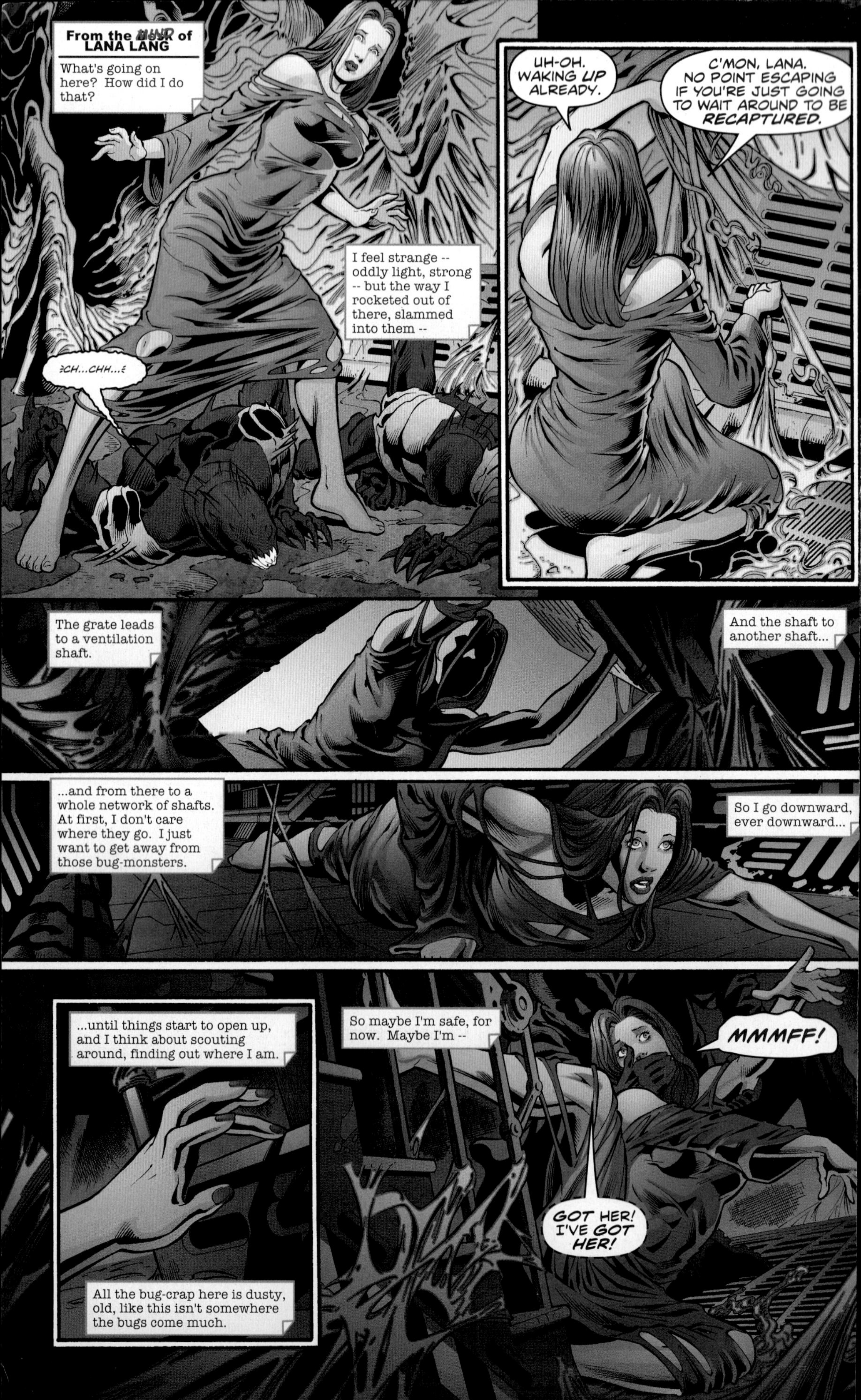
From the ~~desk~~ MIND of LANA LANG
What's going on here? How did I do that?
I feel strange -- oddly light, strong -- but the way I rocketed out of there, slammed into them --
ƎCH...CHH...Ǝ
UH-OH. WAKING UP ALREADY.
C'MON, LANA. NO POINT ESCAPING IF YOU'RE JUST GOING TO WAIT AROUND TO BE RECAPTURED.
The grate leads to a ventilation shaft.
And the shaft to another shaft...
...and from there to a whole network of shafts. At first, I don't care where they go. I just want to get away from those bug-monsters.
So I go downward, ever downward...
...until things start to open up, and I think about scouting around, finding out where I am.
All the bug-crap here is dusty, old, like this isn't somewhere the bugs come much.
So maybe I'm safe, for now. Maybe I'm --
MMMFF!
GOT HER! I'VE GOT HER!

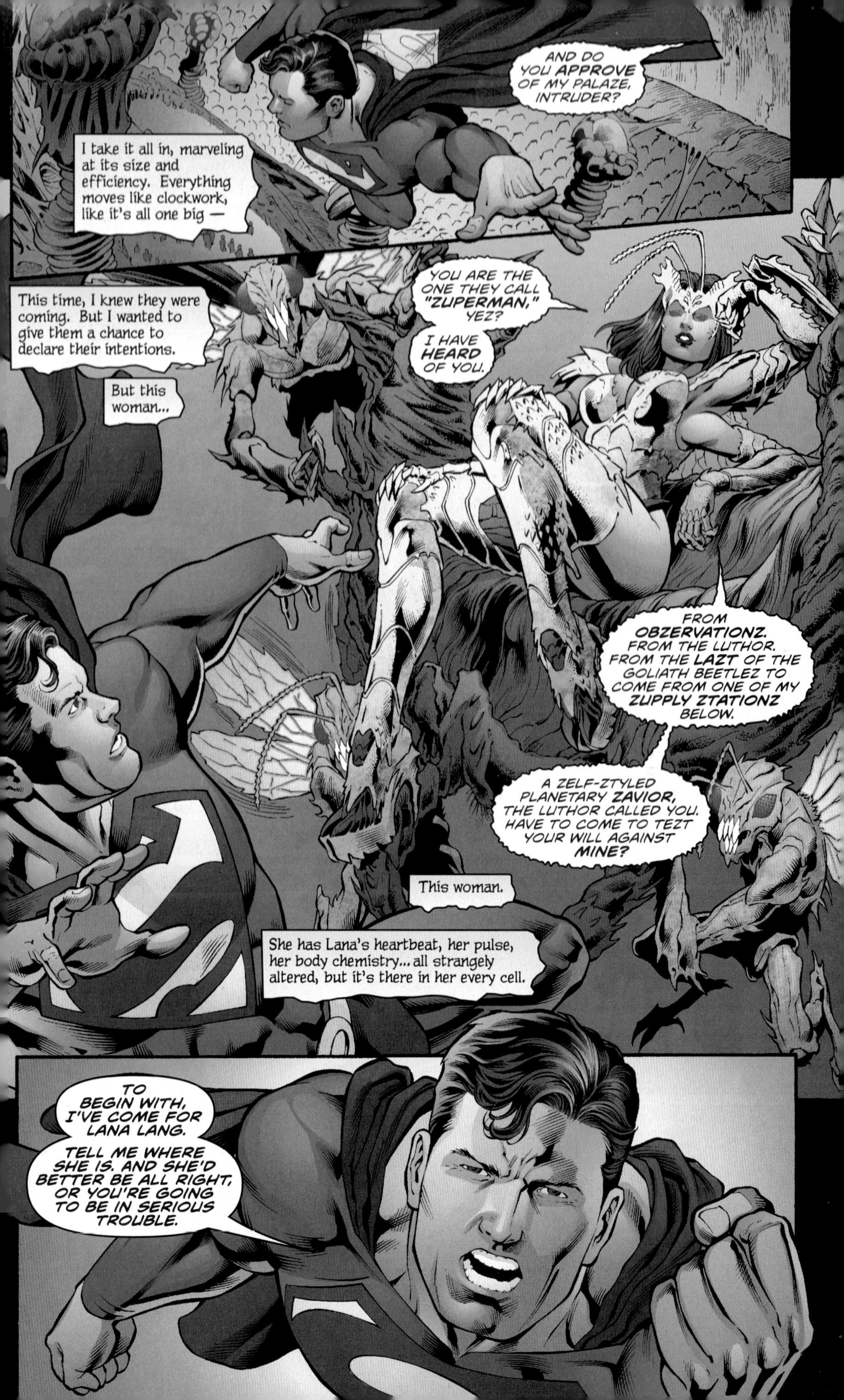
AND DO YOU APPROVE OF MY PALAZE, INTRUDER?
I take it all in, marveling at its size and efficiency. Everything moves like clockwork, like it's all one big —
This time, I knew they were coming. But I wanted to give them a chance to declare their intentions.
But this woman...
YOU ARE THE ONE THEY CALL "ZUPERMAN," YEZ?
I HAVE HEARD OF YOU.
FROM OBZERVATIONZ. FROM THE LUTHOR. FROM THE LAZT OF THE GOLIATH BEETLEZ TO COME FROM ONE OF MY ZUPPLY ZTATIONZ BELOW.
A ZELF-ZTYLED PLANETARY ZAVIOR, THE LUTHOR CALLED YOU. HAVE TO COME TO TEZT YOUR WILL AGAINST MINE?
This woman.
She has Lana's heartbeat, her pulse, her body chemistry... all strangely altered, but it's there in her every cell.
TO BEGIN WITH, I'VE COME FOR LANA LANG.
TELL ME WHERE SHE IS. AND SHE'D BETTER BE ALL RIGHT, OR YOU'RE GOING TO BE IN SERIOUS TROUBLE.

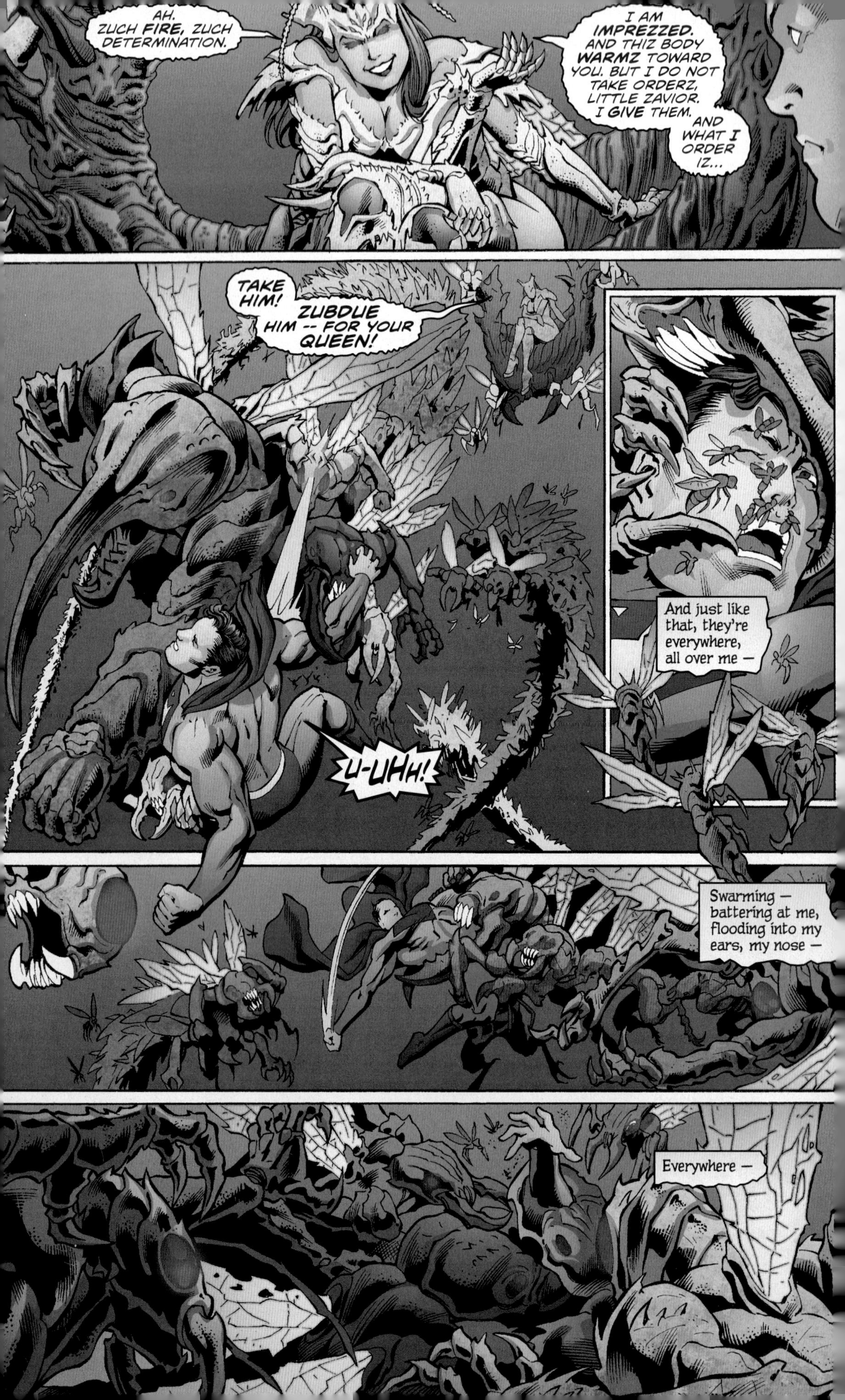
AH. ZUCH FIRE, ZUCH DETERMINATION.
I AM IMPREZZED. AND THIZ BODY WARMZ TOWARD YOU. BUT I DO NOT TAKE ORDERZ, LITTLE ZAVIOR. I GIVE THEM.
AND WHAT I ORDER IZ...
TAKE HIM!
ZUBDUE HIM -- FOR YOUR QUEEN!
U-UHH!
And just like that, they're everywhere, all over me —
Swarming — battering at me, flooding into my ears, my nose —
Everywhere —

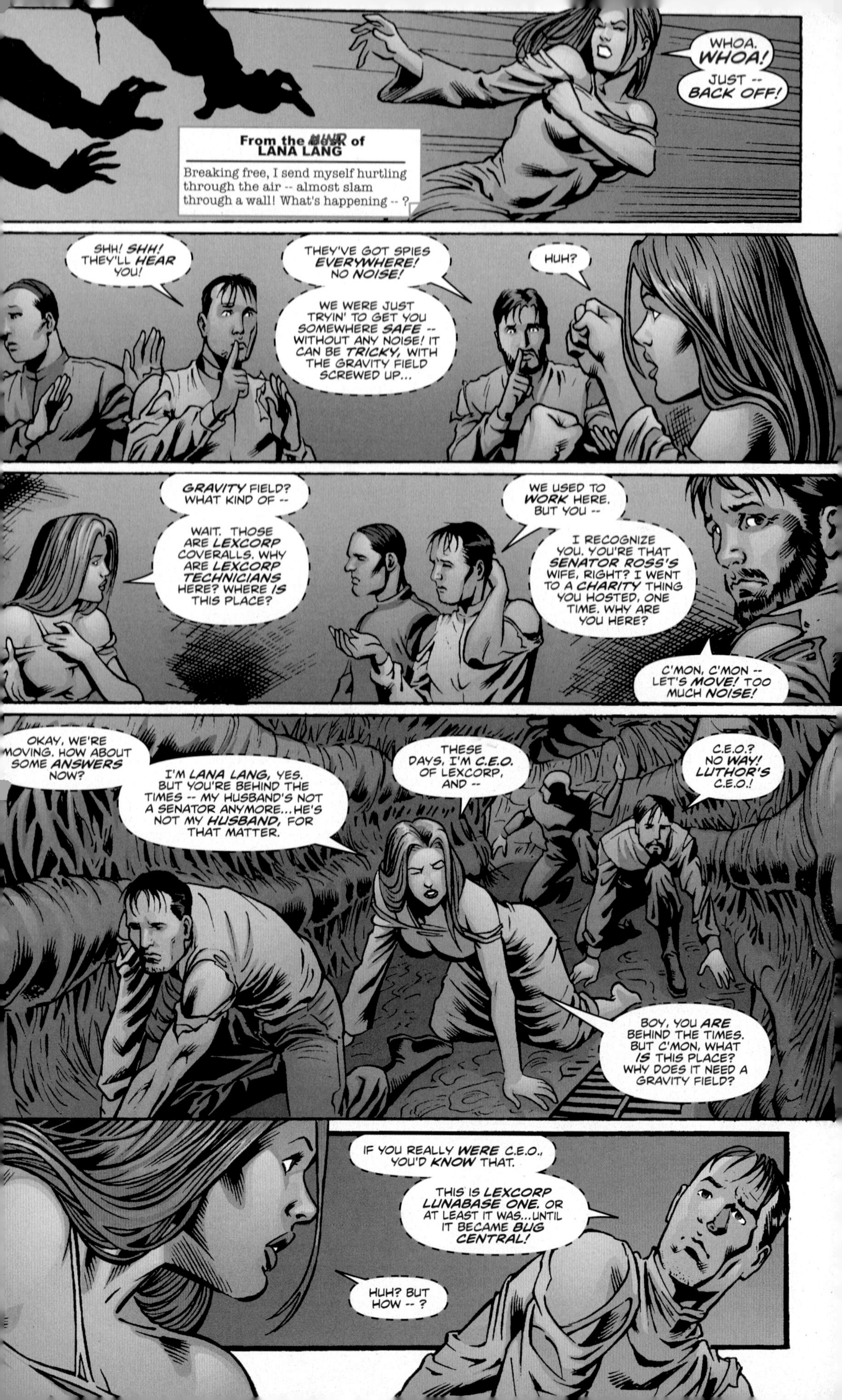
WHOA. WHOA! JUST -- BACK OFF!
From the MIND of LANA LANG
Breaking free, I send myself hurtling through the air -- almost slam through a wall! What's happening -- ?
SHH! SHH! THEY'LL HEAR YOU!
THEY'VE GOT SPIES EVERYWHERE! NO NOISE!
WE WERE JUST TRYIN' TO GET YOU SOMEWHERE SAFE -- WITHOUT ANY NOISE! IT CAN BE TRICKY, WITH THE GRAVITY FIELD SCREWED UP...
HUH?
GRAVITY FIELD? WHAT KIND OF --
WAIT. THOSE ARE LEXCORP COVERALLS. WHY ARE LEXCORP TECHNICIANS HERE? WHERE IS THIS PLACE?
WE USED TO WORK HERE. BUT YOU --
I RECOGNIZE YOU. YOU'RE THAT SENATOR ROSS'S WIFE, RIGHT? I WENT TO A CHARITY THING YOU HOSTED, ONE TIME. WHY ARE YOU HERE?
C'MON, C'MON -- LET'S MOVE! TOO MUCH NOISE!
OKAY, WE'RE MOVING. HOW ABOUT SOME ANSWERS NOW?
I'M LANA LANG, YES. BUT YOU'RE BEHIND THE TIMES -- MY HUSBAND'S NOT A SENATOR ANYMORE... HE'S NOT MY HUSBAND, FOR THAT MATTER.
THESE DAYS, I'M C.E.O. OF LEXCORP, AND --
C.E.O.? NO WAY! LUTHOR'S C.E.O.!
BOY, YOU ARE BEHIND THE TIMES. BUT C'MON, WHAT IS THIS PLACE? WHY DOES IT NEED A GRAVITY FIELD?
IF YOU REALLY WERE C.E.O., YOU'D KNOW THAT.
THIS IS LEXCORP LUNABASE ONE. OR AT LEAST IT WAS... UNTIL IT BECAME BUG CENTRAL!
HUH? BUT HOW -- ?

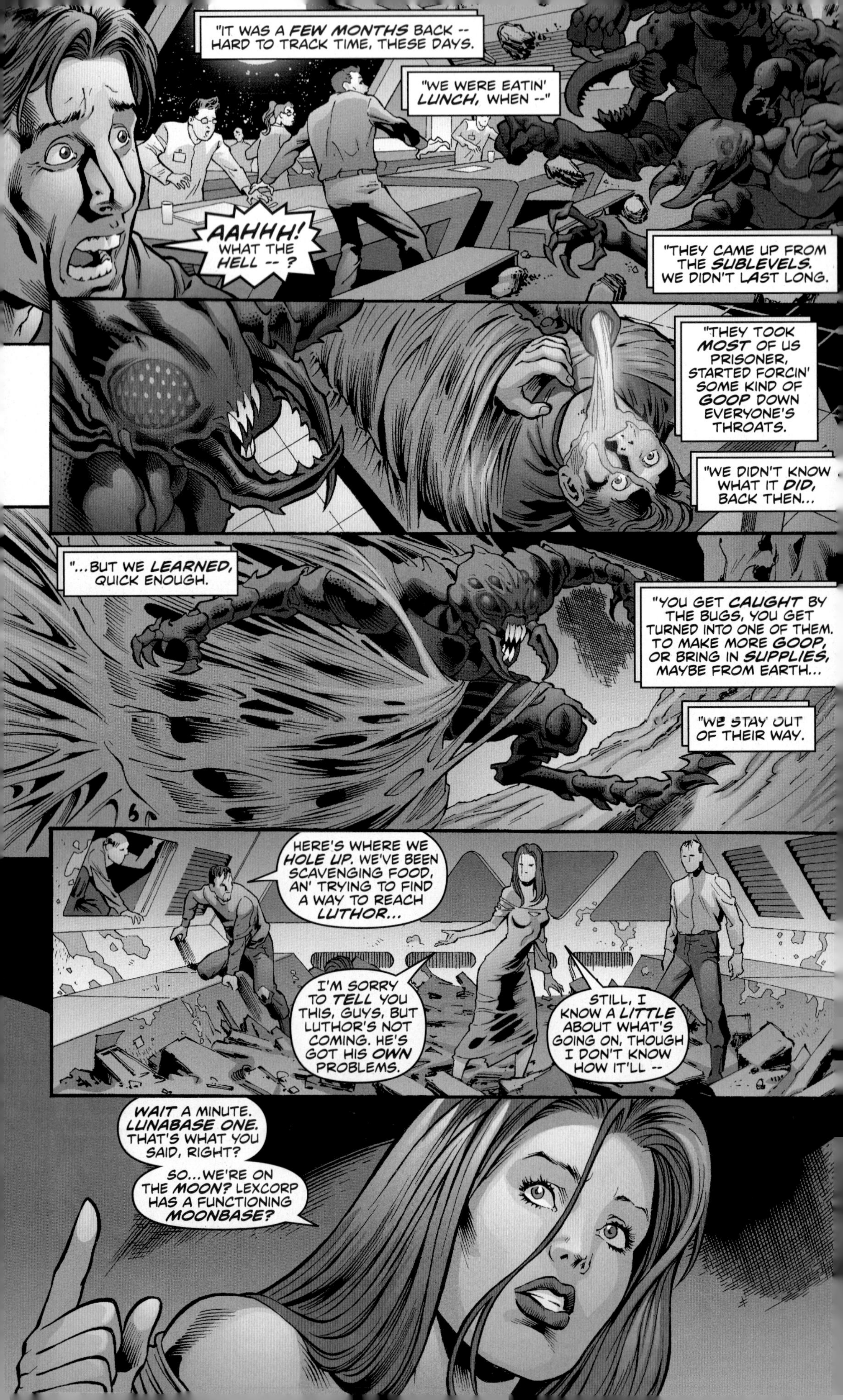
"IT WAS A FEW MONTHS BACK -- HARD TO TRACK TIME, THESE DAYS.
"WE WERE EATIN' LUNCH, WHEN --"
AAHHH! WHAT THE HELL -- ?
"THEY CAME UP FROM THE SUBLEVELS. WE DIDN'T LAST LONG.
"THEY TOOK MOST OF US PRISONER, STARTED FORCIN' SOME KIND OF GOOP DOWN EVERYONE'S THROATS.
"WE DIDN'T KNOW WHAT IT DID, BACK THEN...
"...BUT WE LEARNED, QUICK ENOUGH.
"YOU GET CAUGHT BY THE BUGS, YOU GET TURNED INTO ONE OF THEM. TO MAKE MORE GOOP, OR BRING IN SUPPLIES, MAYBE FROM EARTH...
"WE STAY OUT OF THEIR WAY.
HERE'S WHERE WE HOLE UP. WE'VE BEEN SCAVENGING FOOD, AN' TRYING TO FIND A WAY TO REACH LUTHOR...
I'M SORRY TO TELL YOU THIS, GUYS, BUT LUTHOR'S NOT COMING. HE'S GOT HIS OWN PROBLEMS.
STILL, I KNOW A LITTLE ABOUT WHAT'S GOING ON, THOUGH I DON'T KNOW HOW IT'LL --
WAIT A MINUTE. LUNABASE ONE. THAT'S WHAT YOU SAID, RIGHT?
SO...WE'RE ON THE MOON? LEXCORP HAS A FUNCTIONING MOONBASE?

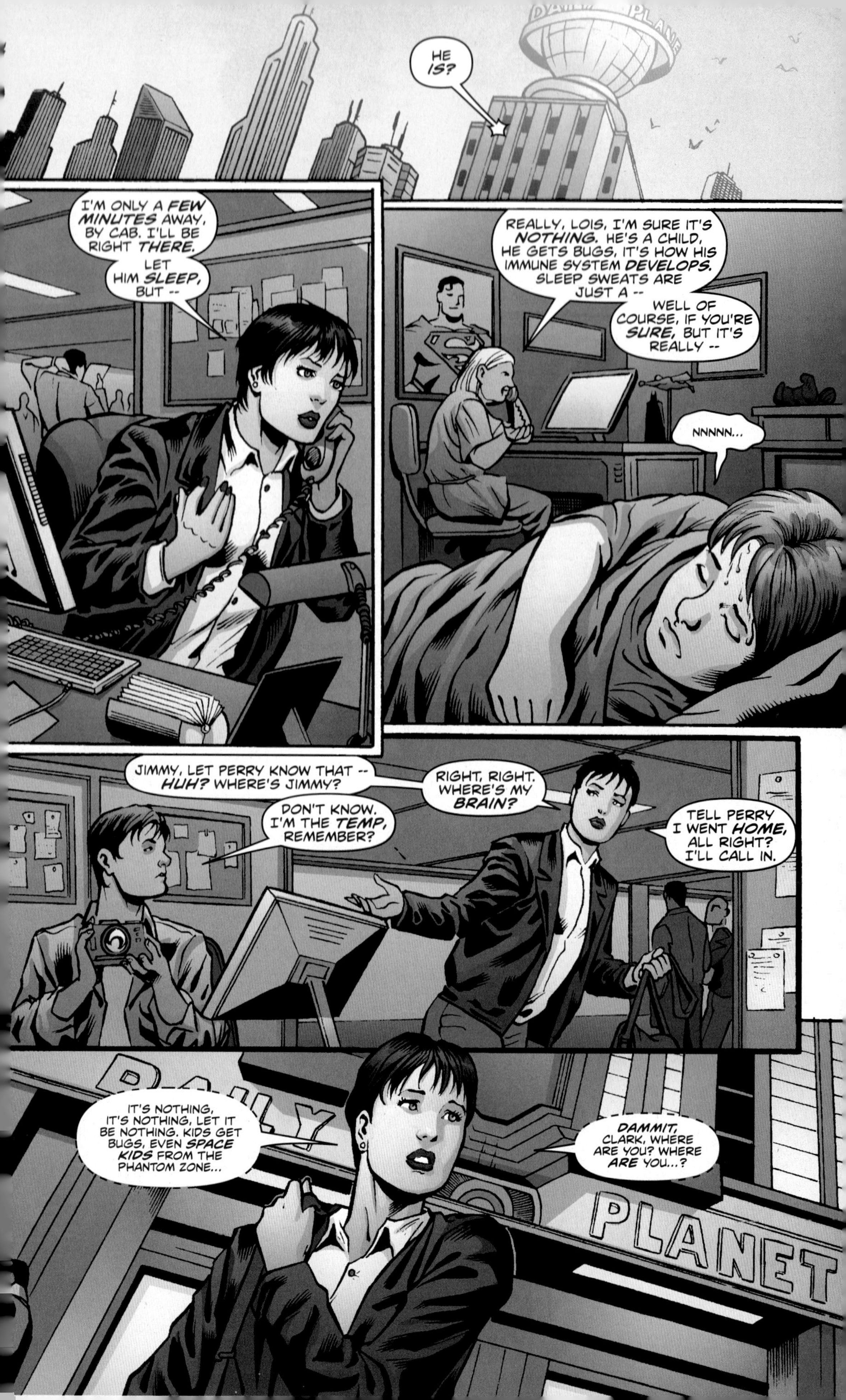
HE IS?
I'M ONLY A FEW MINUTES AWAY, BY CAB. I'LL BE RIGHT THERE.
LET HIM SLEEP, BUT --
REALLY, LOIS, I'M SURE IT'S NOTHING. HE'S A CHILD, HE GETS BUGS, IT'S HOW HIS IMMUNE SYSTEM DEVELOPS. SLEEP SWEATS ARE JUST A --
WELL OF COURSE, IF YOU'RE SURE, BUT IT'S REALLY --
NNNNN...
JIMMY, LET PERRY KNOW THAT -- HUH? WHERE'S JIMMY?
DON'T KNOW. I'M THE TEMP, REMEMBER?
RIGHT, RIGHT. WHERE'S MY BRAIN?
TELL PERRY I WENT HOME, ALL RIGHT? I'LL CALL IN.
IT'S NOTHING, IT'S NOTHING, LET IT BE NOTHING. KIDS GET BUGS, EVEN SPACE KIDS FROM THE PHANTOM ZONE...
DAMMIT, CLARK, WHERE ARE YOU? WHERE ARE YOU...?
PLANET

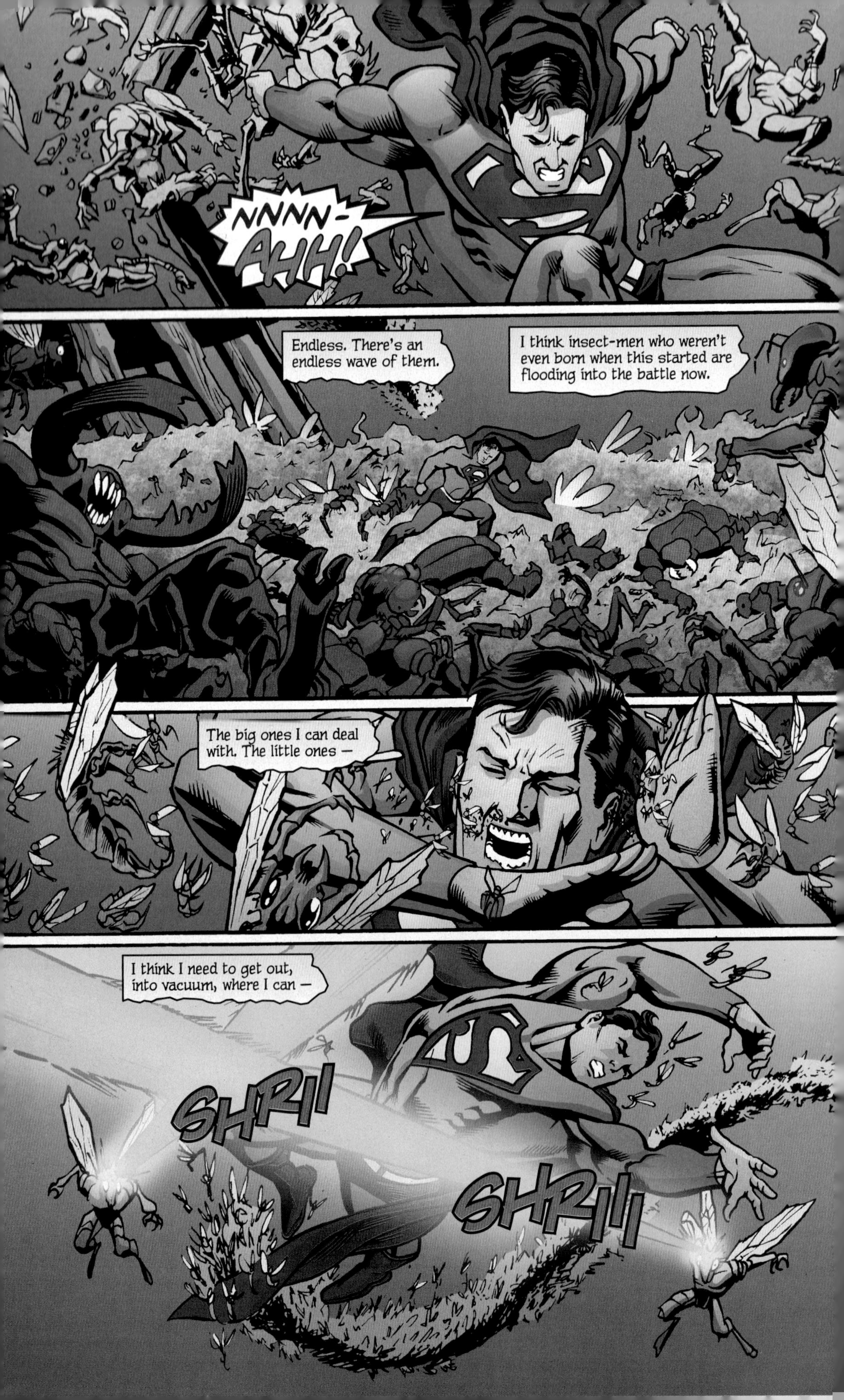
NNNN-AHH!
Endless. There's an endless wave of them.
I think insect-men who weren't even born when this started are flooding into the battle now.
The big ones I can deal with. The little ones —
I think I need to get out, into vacuum, where I can —
SHRII
SHRIII

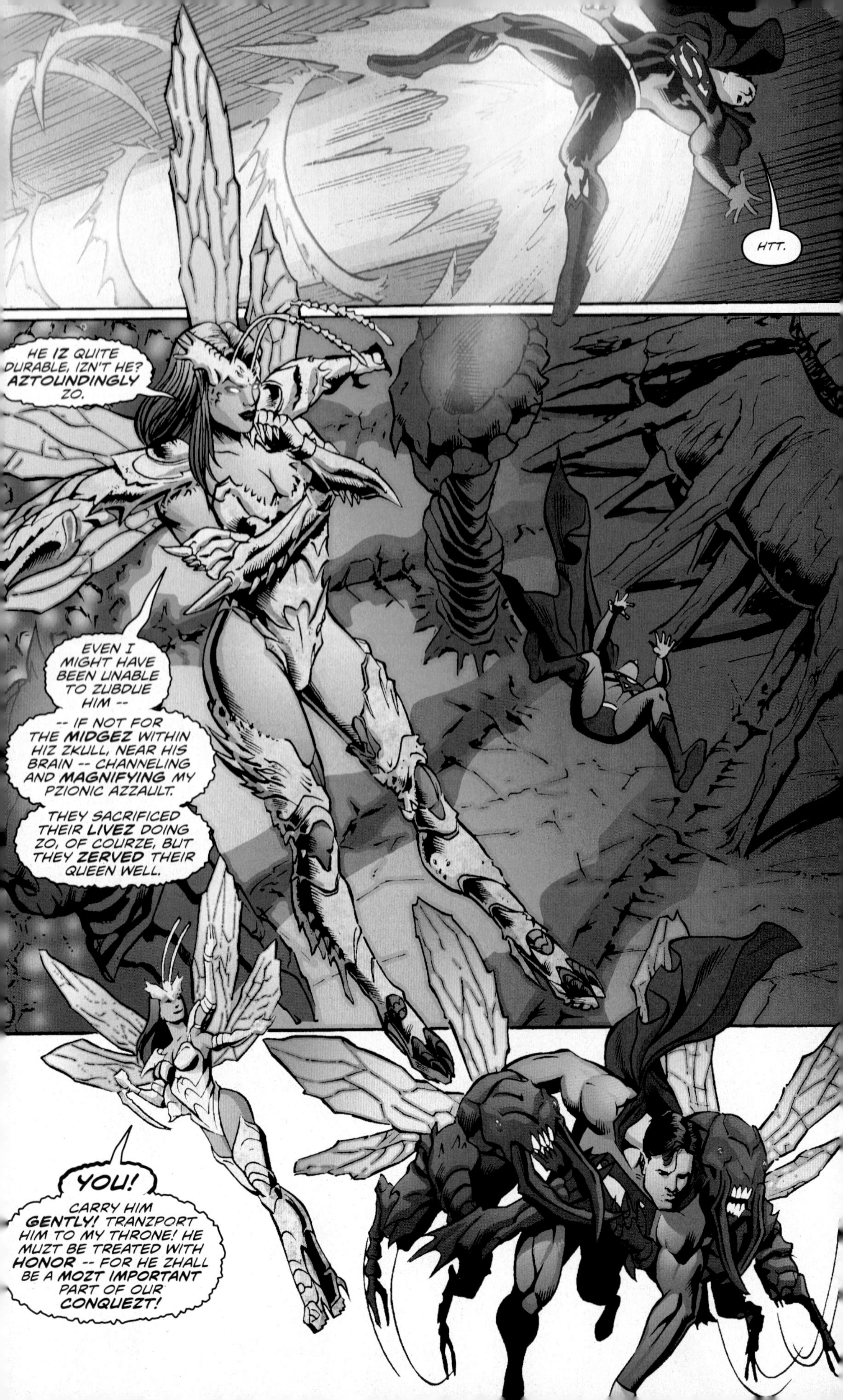
HTT.
HE IZ QUITE DURABLE, IZN'T HE? AZTOUNDINGLY ZO.
EVEN I MIGHT HAVE BEEN UNABLE TO ZUBDUE HIM --
-- IF NOT FOR THE MIDGEZ WITHIN HIZ ZKULL, NEAR HIS BRAIN -- CHANNELING AND MAGNIFYING MY PZIONIC AZZAULT.
THEY SACRIFICED THEIR LIVEZ DOING ZO, OF COURZE, BUT THEY ZERVED THEIR QUEEN WELL.
YOU!
CARRY HIM GENTLY! TRANZPORT HIM TO MY THRONE! HE MUZT BE TREATED WITH HONOR -- FOR HE ZHALL BE A MOZT IMPORTANT PART OF OUR CONQUEZT!

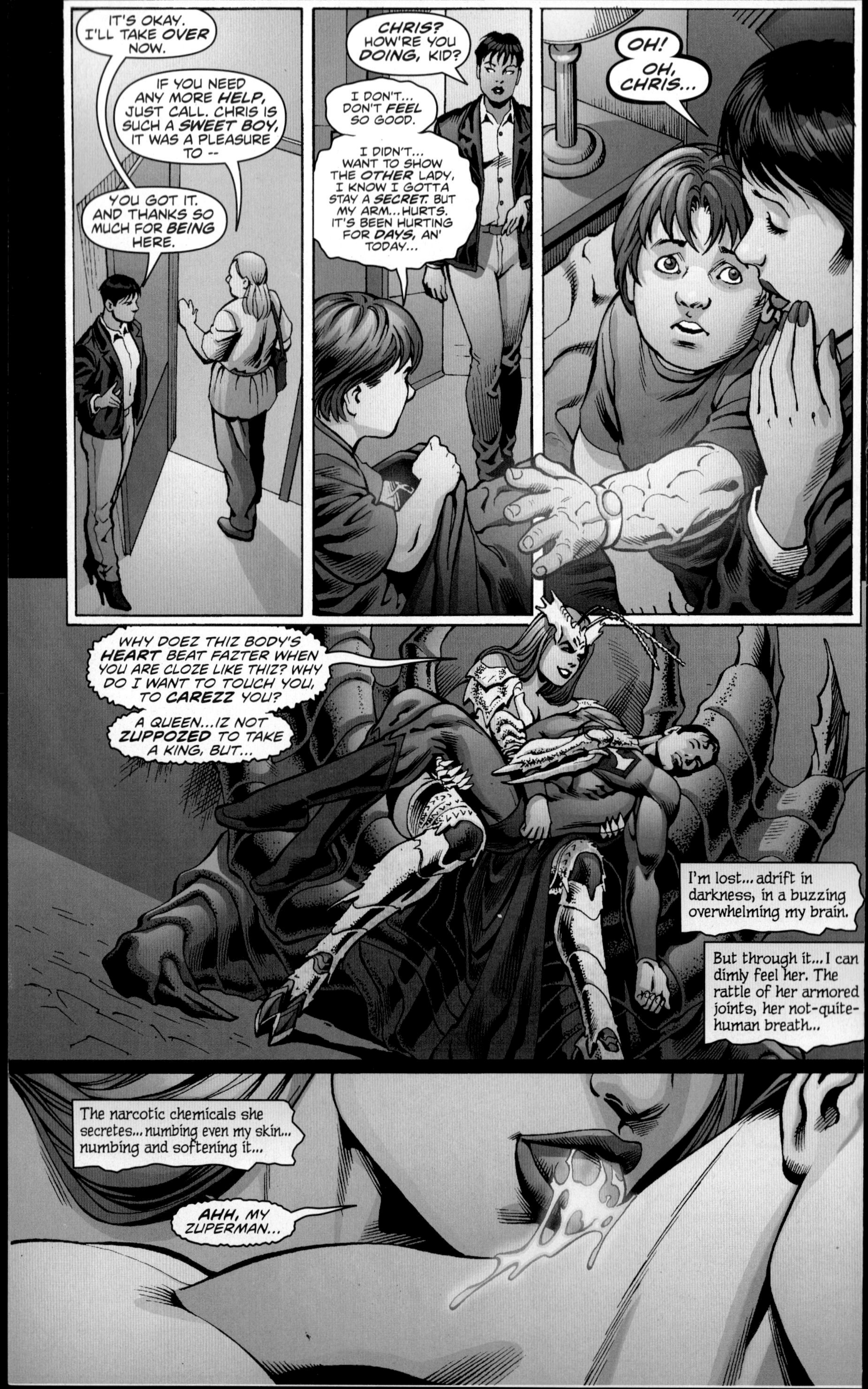
IT'S OKAY. I'LL TAKE OVER NOW.
IF YOU NEED ANY MORE HELP, JUST CALL. CHRIS IS SUCH A SWEET BOY, IT WAS A PLEASURE TO --
YOU GOT IT. AND THANKS SO MUCH FOR BEING HERE.
CHRIS? HOW'RE YOU DOING, KID?
I DON'T... DON'T FEEL SO GOOD.
I DIDN'T... WANT TO SHOW THE OTHER LADY, I KNOW I GOTTA STAY A SECRET. BUT MY ARM... HURTS. IT'S BEEN HURTING FOR DAYS, AN' TODAY...
OH! OH, CHRIS...
WHY DOEZ THIZ BODY'S HEART BEAT FAZTER WHEN YOU ARE CLOZE LIKE THIZ? WHY DO I WANT TO TOUCH YOU, TO CAREZZ YOU?
A QUEEN...IZ NOT ZUPPOZED TO TAKE A KING, BUT...
I'm lost... adrift in darkness, in a buzzing overwhelming my brain.
But through it... I can dimly feel her. The rattle of her armored joints, her not-quite-human breath...
The narcotic chemicals she secretes... numbing even my skin... numbing and softening it...
AHH, MY ZUPERMAN...

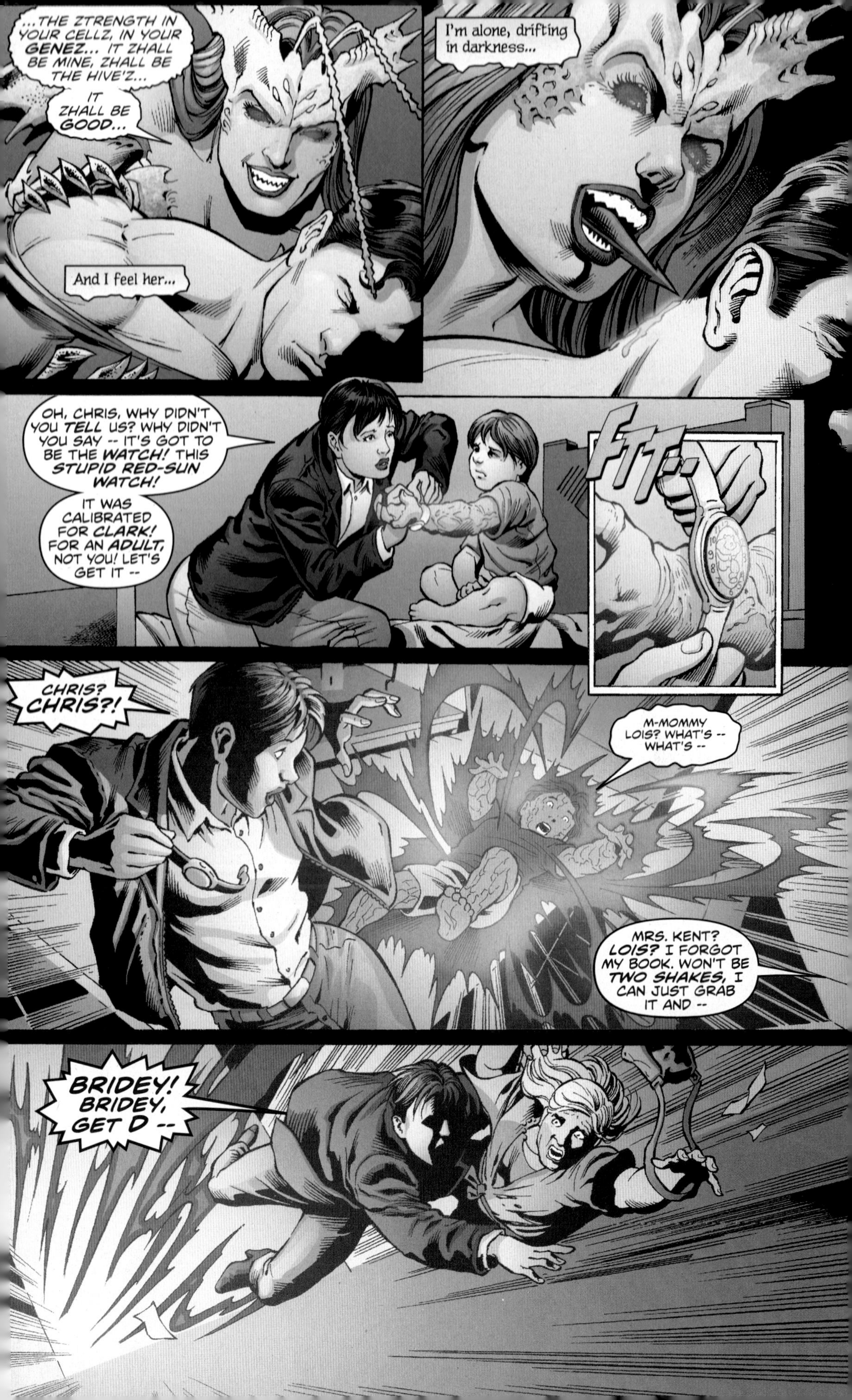
...THE ZTRENGTH IN YOUR CELLZ, IN YOUR GENEZ... IT ZHALL BE MINE, ZHALL BE THE HIVE'Z...
IT ZHALL BE GOOD...
And I feel her...
I'm alone, drifting in darkness...
OH, CHRIS, WHY DIDN'T YOU TELL US? WHY DIDN'T YOU SAY -- IT'S GOT TO BE THE WATCH! THIS STUPID RED-SUN WATCH!
IT WAS CALIBRATED FOR CLARK! FOR AN ADULT, NOT YOU! LET'S GET IT --
FTT..
CHRIS? CHRIS?!
M-MOMMY LOIS? WHAT'S -- WHAT'S --
MRS. KENT? LOIS? I FORGOT MY BOOK. WON'T BE TWO SHAKES, I CAN JUST GRAB IT AND --
BRIDEY! BRIDEY, GET D --

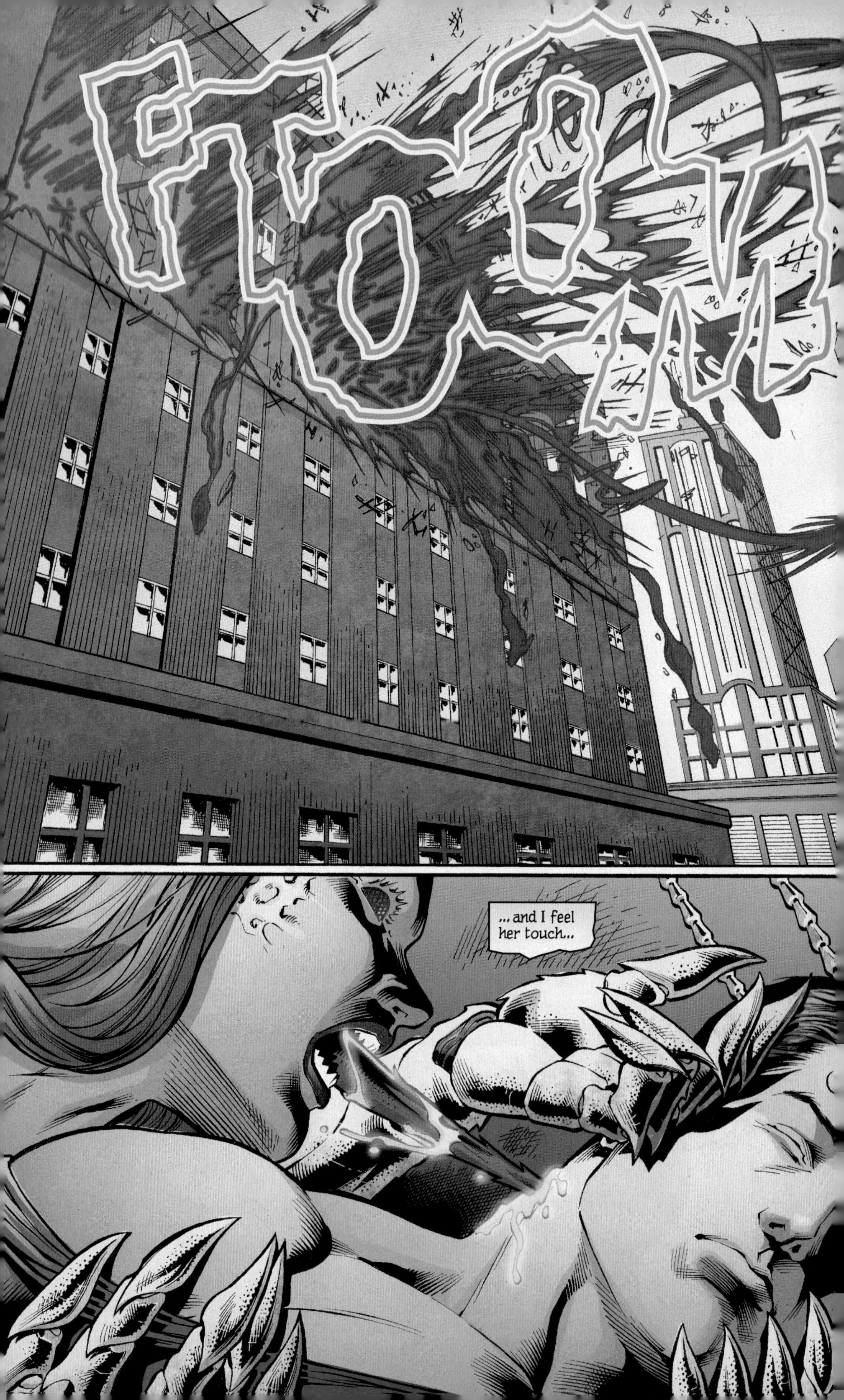
...and I feel her touch...

COVER ART BY PETER VALE & WELLINGTON DIAS

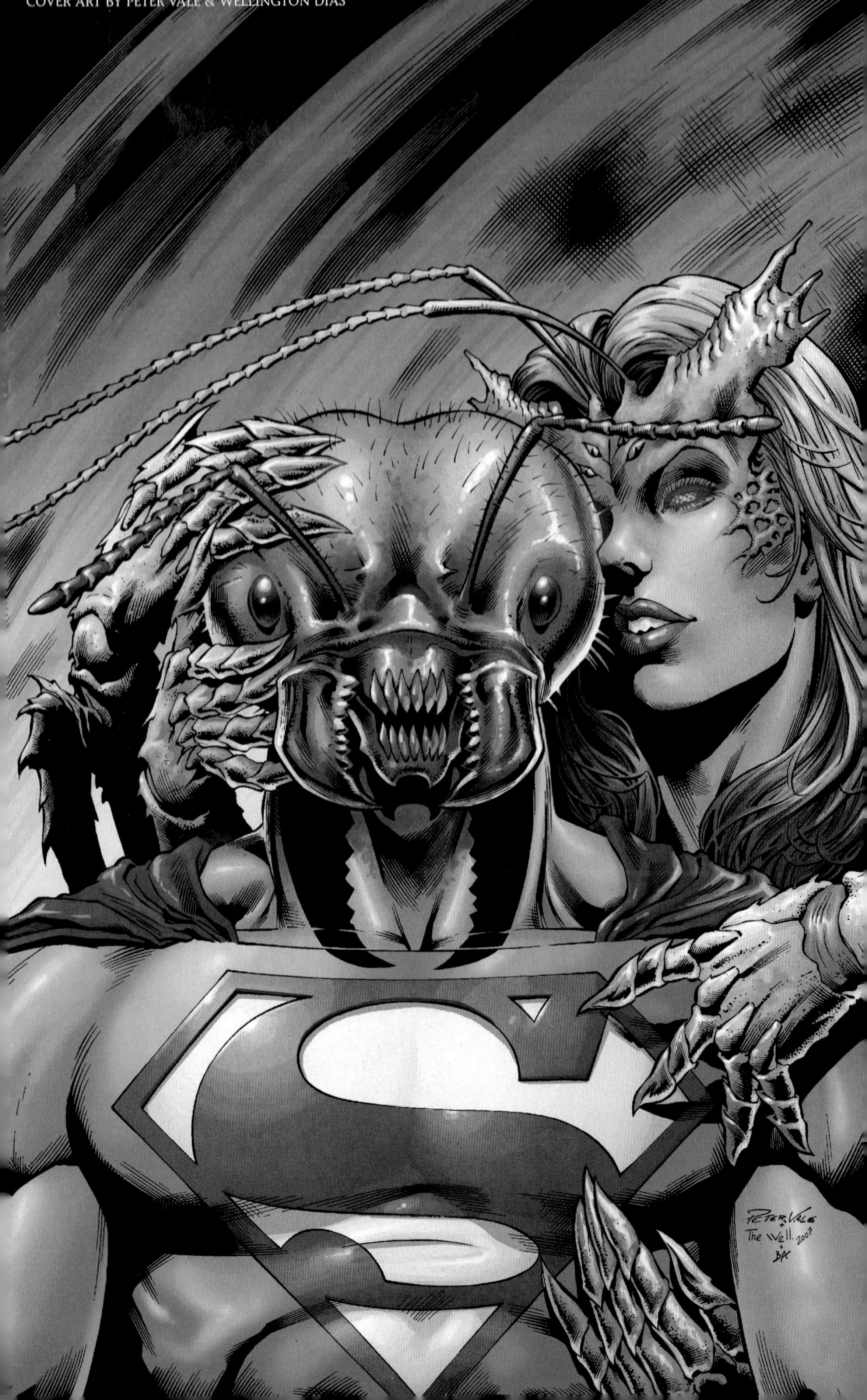

INSECT QUEEN
PART THREE:

MOONLIGHT & VICTORY

ART BY **JESÚS MERINO** COLORS BY **KANILA TRIPP**

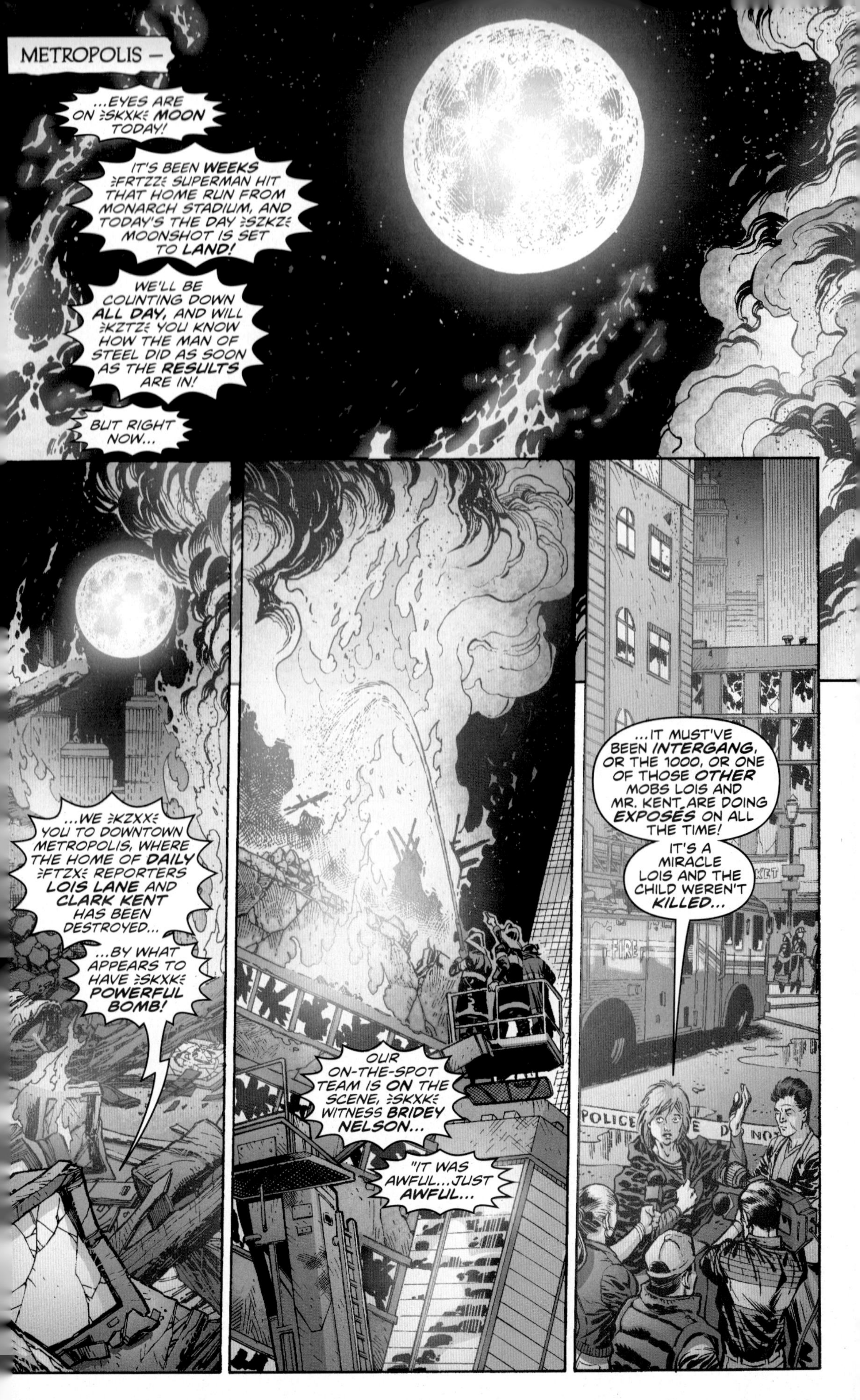
METROPOLIS —
...EYES ARE ON ≡SKXK≡ MOON TODAY!
IT'S BEEN WEEKS ≡FRTZZ≡ SUPERMAN HIT THAT HOME RUN FROM MONARCH STADIUM, AND TODAY'S THE DAY ≡SZKZ≡ MOONSHOT IS SET TO LAND!
WE'LL BE COUNTING DOWN ALL DAY, AND WILL ≡KZTZ≡ YOU KNOW HOW THE MAN OF STEEL DID AS SOON AS THE RESULTS ARE IN!
BUT RIGHT NOW...
...WE ≡KZXX≡ YOU TO DOWNTOWN METROPOLIS, WHERE THE HOME OF DAILY ≡FTZX≡ REPORTERS LOIS LANE AND CLARK KENT HAS BEEN DESTROYED...
...BY WHAT APPEARS TO HAVE ≡SKXK≡ POWERFUL BOMB!
OUR ON-THE-SPOT TEAM IS ON THE SCENE, ≡SKXK≡ WITNESS BRIDEY NELSON...
"IT WAS AWFUL...JUST AWFUL...
...IT MUST'VE BEEN INTERGANG, OR THE 1000, OR ONE OF THOSE OTHER MOBS LOIS AND MR. KENT ARE DOING EXPOSÉS ON ALL THE TIME!
IT'S A MIRACLE LOIS AND THE CHILD WEREN'T KILLED...
FIRE
POLICE

SURE YOU DON'T **KNOW** ANYTHING, LOIS?

CAN'T EVEN GIVE YOU A PLACE TO **START**, KENNY. LORD KNOWS CLARK AND I HAVE TWEAKED OUR SHARE OF POWERFUL **NOSES** OVER THE YEARS.

LOOK, WE'VE GOT TO **GO**. I'VE GOT TO LINE UP A PLACE TO STAY, GET CHRIS FED AND INTO A **BED**. HE'S HAD A HARD TIME.

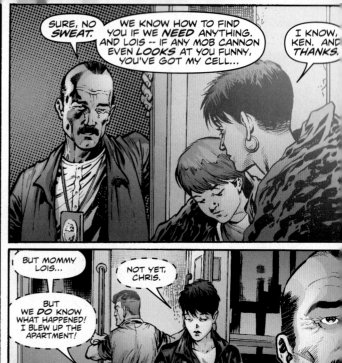

SURE, NO **SWEAT**.

WE KNOW HOW TO FIND YOU IF WE **NEED** ANYTHING. AND LOIS -- IF ANY MOB CANNON EVEN **LOOKS** AT YOU FUNNY, YOU'VE GOT MY CELL...

I KNOW, KEN. AND **THANKS**.

BUT MOMMY LOIS...

NOT YET, CHRIS.

BUT WE **DO** KNOW WHAT HAPPENED! I BLEW UP THE APARTMENT!

I HAD ALL THAT **ENERGY** BUILT UP IN ME 'CAUSE OF THE RED-SUN WATCH, AN' IT ALL CAME OUT **AT ONCE**, AND --

IT'S OKAY, CHRIS. IT'S **OKAY**.

LOOK, AS A REPORTER AND A FOSTER MOTHER, I DON'T ADVOCATE **LYING**, BUT FOR SECRET I.D. STUFF, "I DON'T **KNOW**" IS ALMOST **ALWAYS** A GOOD ANSWER.

PEOPLE GENERALLY FIGURE OUT SOME WORKABLE STORY ON THEIR **OWN** -- THEY'RE **GOOD** AT THAT.

NOBODY WAS **HURT**, THANK GOD, AND DADDY CLARK WILL SHORE UP ANY STRUCTURAL DAMAGE TO THE BUILDING AS SOON AS HE'S **BACK**, YOU'LL SEE.

YEAH...

WHEN HE... WHEN HE GETS BACK...

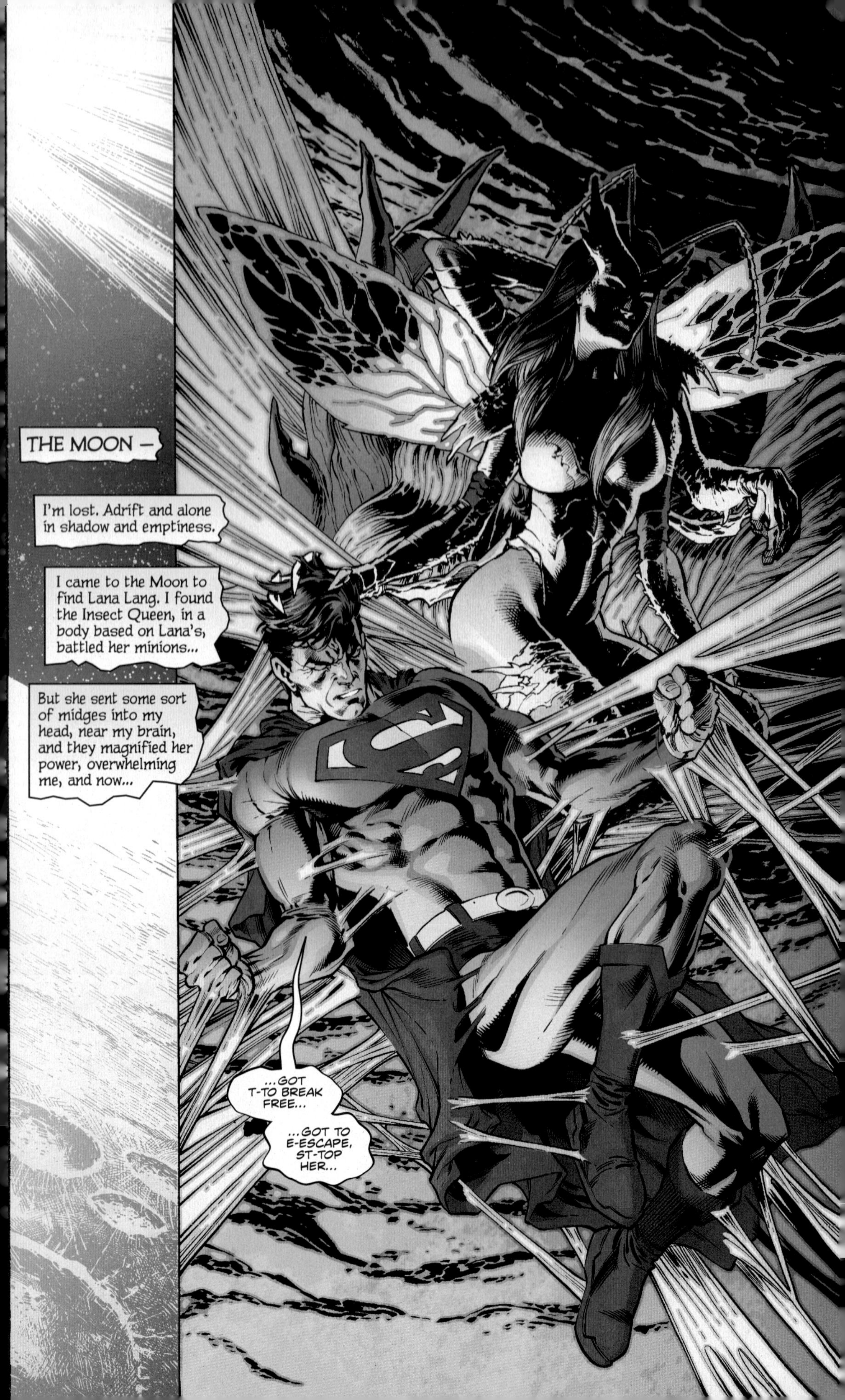
THE MOON —
I'm lost. Adrift and alone in shadow and emptiness.
I came to the Moon to find Lana Lang. I found the Insect Queen, in a body based on Lana's, battled her minions...
But she sent some sort of midges into my head, near my brain, and they magnified her power, overwhelming me, and now...
...GOT T-TO BREAK FREE...
...GOT TO E-ESCAPE, ST-TOP HER...

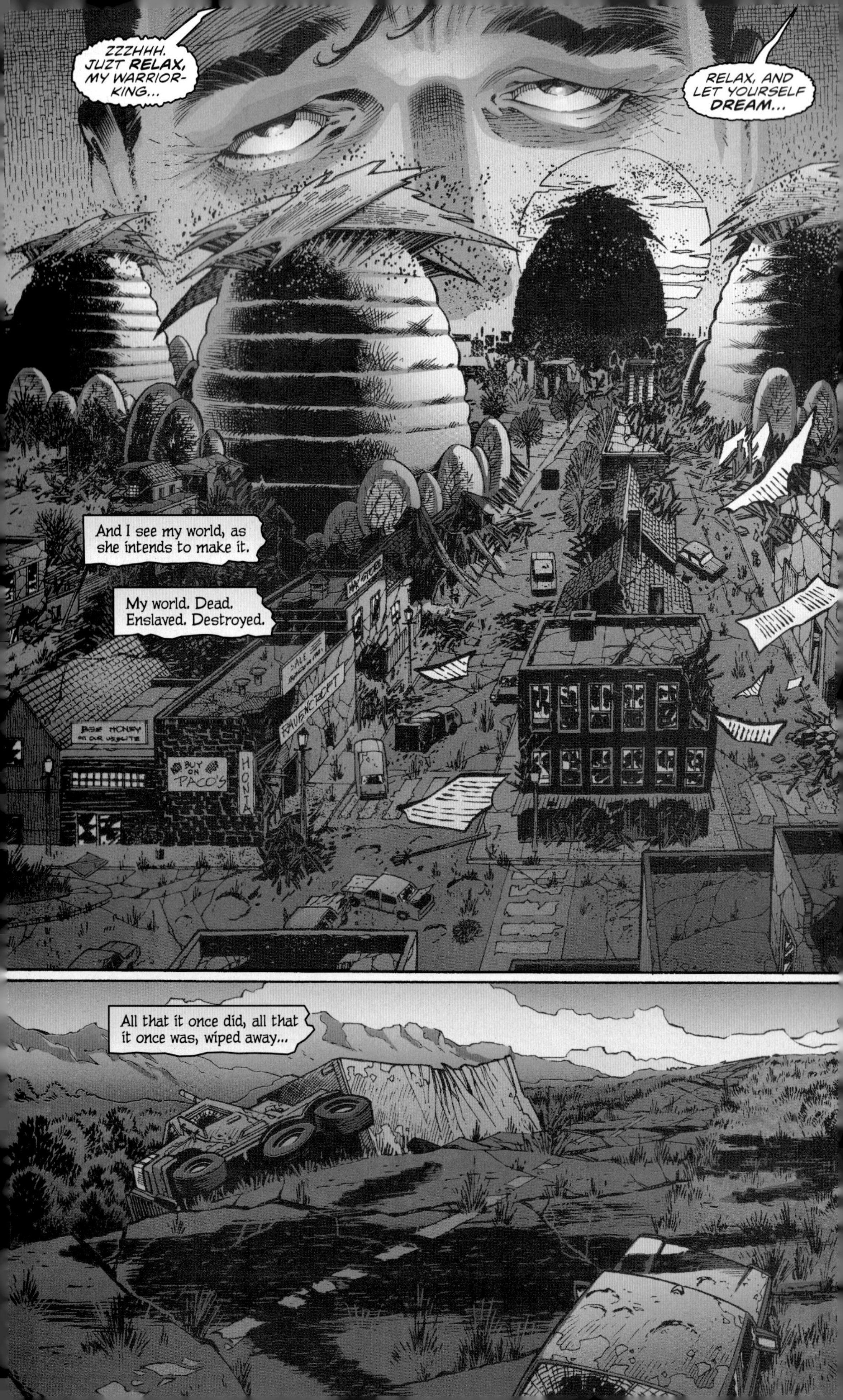
ZZZHHH. JUZT **RELAX,** MY WARRIOR-KING...
RELAX, AND LET YOURSELF **DREAM...**
And I see my world, as she intends to make it.
My world. Dead. Enslaved. Destroyed.
All that it once did, all that it once was, wiped away...

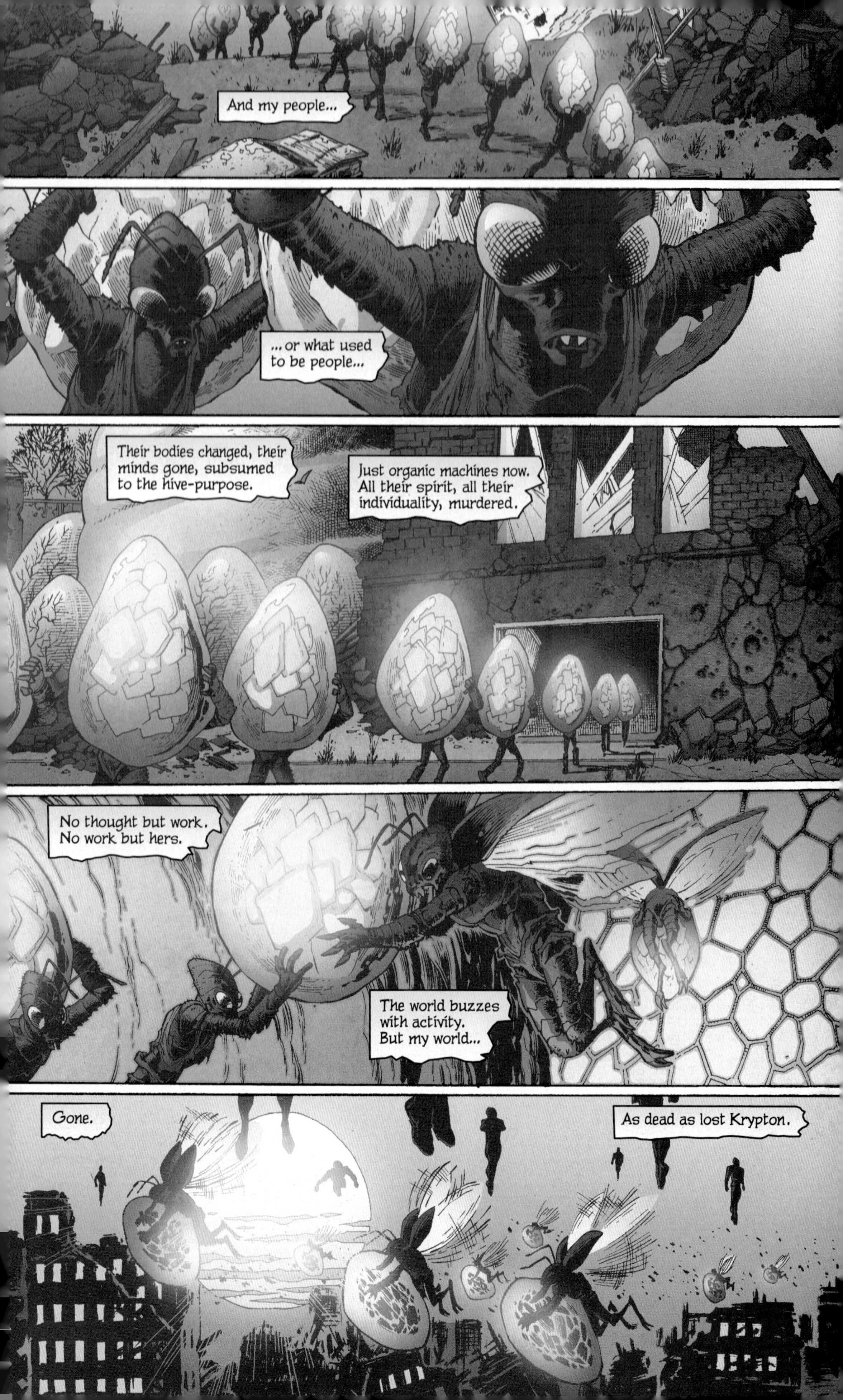

And my people...
...or what used to be people...
Their bodies changed, their minds gone, subsumed to the hive-purpose.
Just organic machines now. All their spirit, all their individuality, murdered.
No thought but work. No work but hers.
The world buzzes with activity. But my world...
Gone.
As dead as lost Krypton.

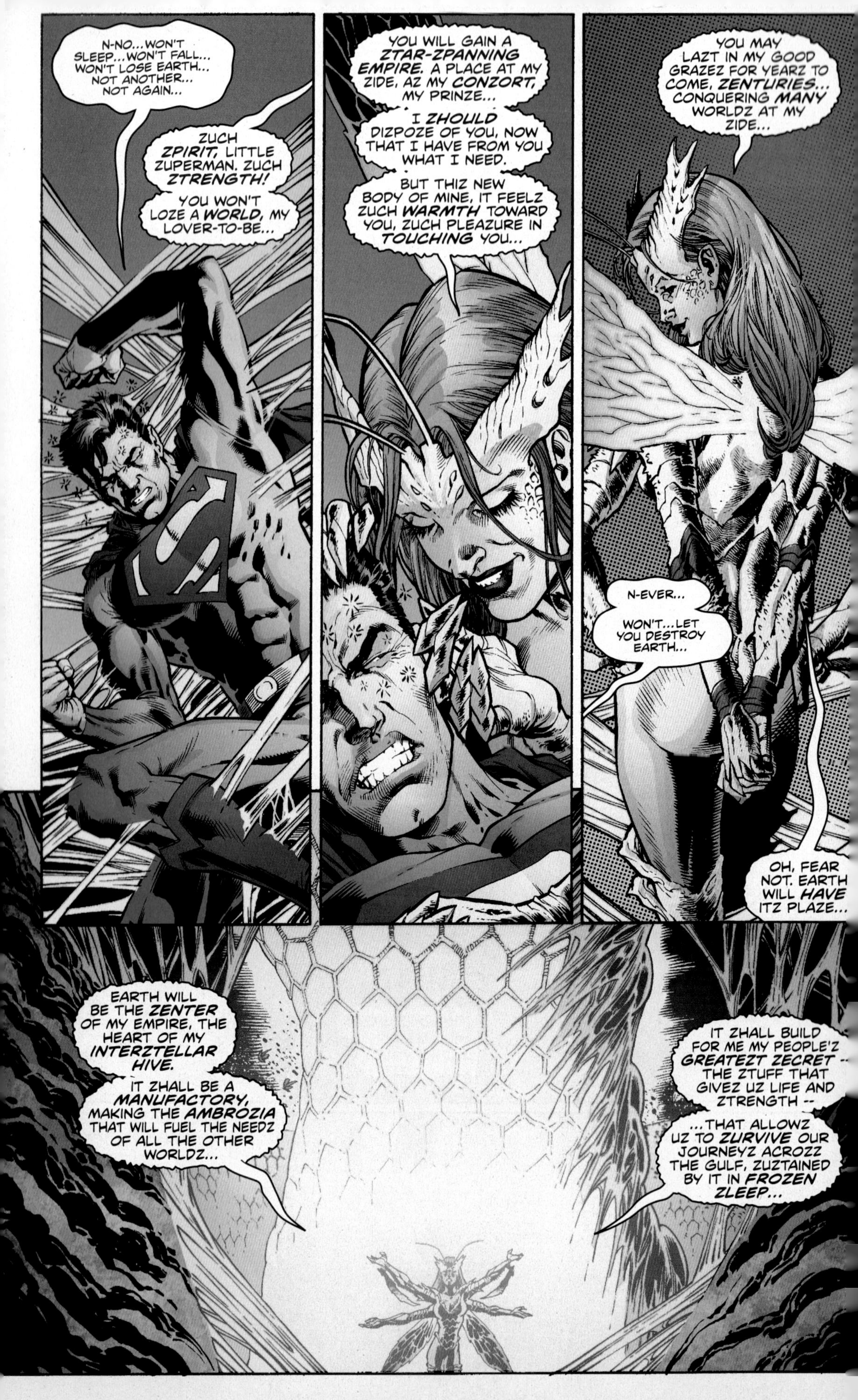
N-NO...WON'T SLEEP...WON'T FALL... WON'T LOSE EARTH... NOT ANOTHER... NOT AGAIN...
ZUCH ZPIRIT, LITTLE ZUPERMAN. ZUCH ZTRENGTH!
YOU WON'T LOZE A WORLD, MY LOVER-TO-BE...
YOU WILL GAIN A ZTAR-ZPANNING EMPIRE. A PLACE AT MY ZIDE, AZ MY CONZORT, MY PRINZE...
I ZHOULD DIZPOZE OF YOU, NOW THAT I HAVE FROM YOU WHAT I NEED.
BUT THIZ NEW BODY OF MINE, IT FEELZ ZUCH WARMTH TOWARD YOU, ZUCH PLEAZURE IN TOUCHING YOU...
YOU MAY LAZT IN MY GOOD GRAZEZ FOR YEARZ TO COME, ZENTURIES... CONQUERING MANY WORLDZ AT MY ZIDE...
N-EVER...
WON'T...LET YOU DESTROY EARTH...
OH, FEAR NOT. EARTH WILL HAVE ITZ PLAZE...
EARTH WILL BE THE ZENTER OF MY EMPIRE, THE HEART OF MY INTERZTELLAR HIVE.
IT ZHALL BE A MANUFACTORY, MAKING THE AMBROZIA THAT WILL FUEL THE NEEDZ OF ALL THE OTHER WORLDZ...
IT ZHALL BUILD FOR ME MY PEOPLE'Z GREATEZT ZECRET -- THE ZTUFF THAT GIVEZ UZ LIFE AND ZTRENGTH --
...THAT ALLOWZ UZ TO ZURVIVE OUR JOURNEYZ ACROZZ THE GULF, ZUZTAINED BY IT IN FROZEN ZLEEP...

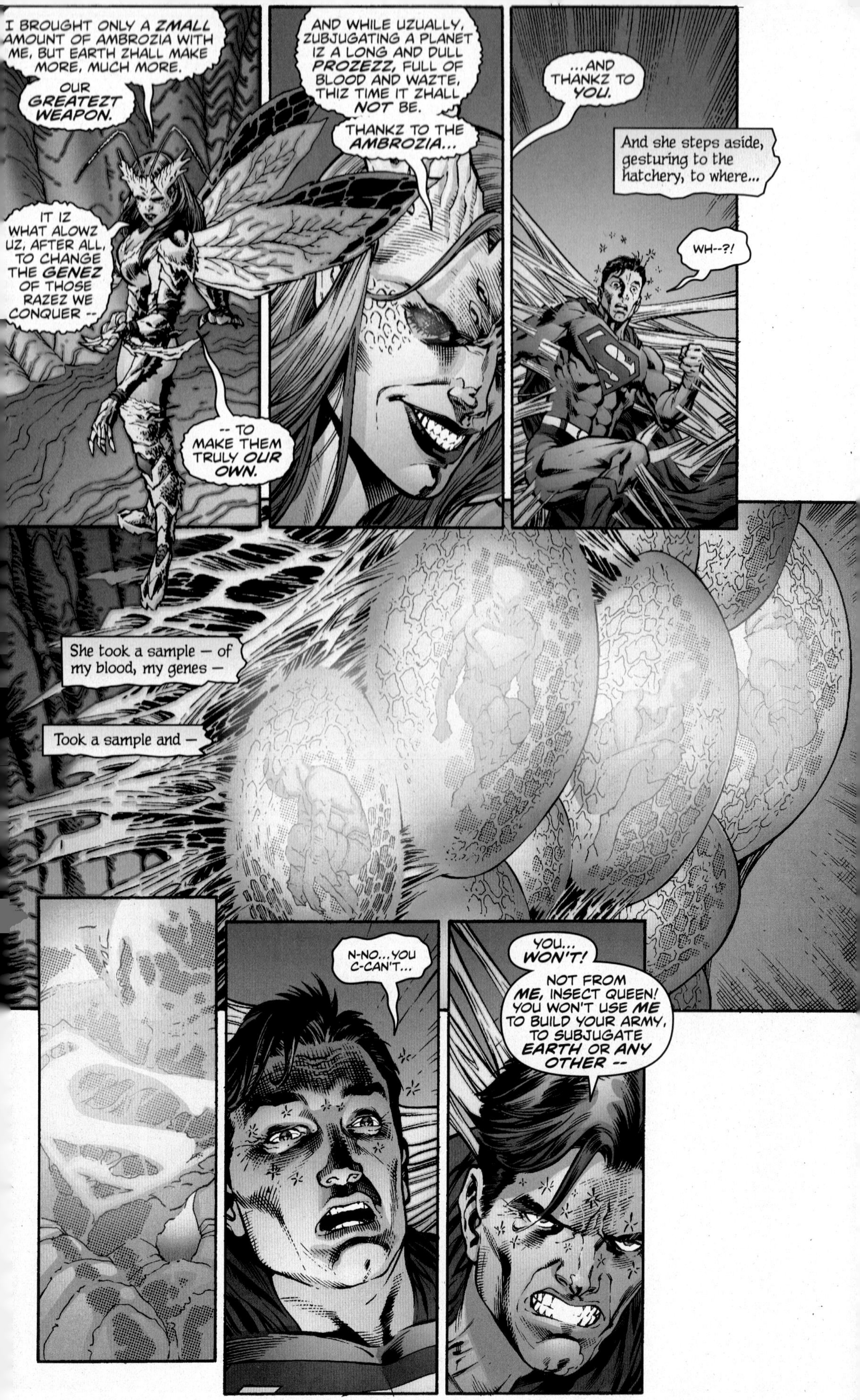
I BROUGHT ONLY A ZMALL AMOUNT OF AMBROZIA WITH ME, BUT EARTH ZHALL MAKE MORE, MUCH MORE.
OUR GREATEZT WEAPON.
IT IZ WHAT ALOWZ UZ, AFTER ALL, TO CHANGE THE GENEZ OF THOSE RAZEZ WE CONQUER --
-- TO MAKE THEM TRULY OUR OWN.
AND WHILE UZUALLY, ZUBJUGATING A PLANET IZ A LONG AND DULL PROZEZZ, FULL OF BLOOD AND WAZTE, THIZ TIME IT ZHALL NOT BE.
THANKZ TO THE AMBROZIA...
...AND THANKZ TO YOU.
And she steps aside, gesturing to the hatchery, to where...
WH--?!
She took a sample — of my blood, my genes —
Took a sample and —
N-NO...YOU C-CAN'T...
YOU... WON'T!
NOT FROM ME, INSECT QUEEN! YOU WON'T USE ME TO BUILD YOUR ARMY, TO SUBJUGATE EARTH OR ANY OTHER --

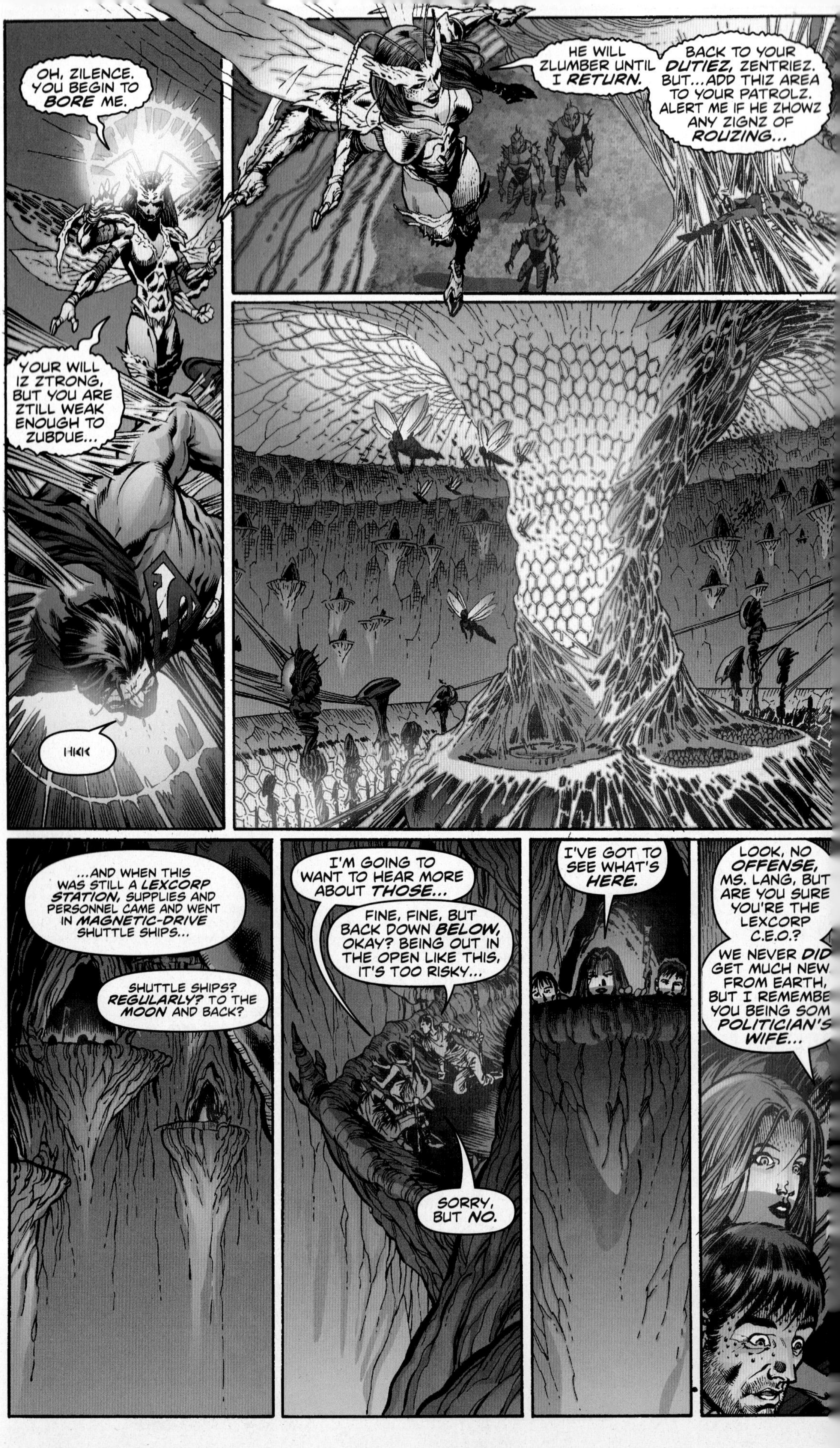

OH, ZILENCE. YOU BEGIN TO BORE ME.
HE WILL ZLUMBER UNTIL I RETURN.
BACK TO YOUR DUTIEZ, ZENTRIEZ. BUT...ADD THIZ AREA TO YOUR PATROLZ. ALERT ME IF HE ZHOWZ ANY ZIGNZ OF ROUZING...
YOUR WILL IZ ZTRONG, BUT YOU ARE ZTILL WEAK ENOUGH TO ZUBDUE...
HKK
...AND WHEN THIS WAS STILL A LEXCORP STATION, SUPPLIES AND PERSONNEL CAME AND WENT IN MAGNETIC-DRIVE SHUTTLE SHIPS...
SHUTTLE SHIPS? REGULARLY? TO THE MOON AND BACK?
I'M GOING TO WANT TO HEAR MORE ABOUT THOSE...
FINE, FINE, BUT BACK DOWN BELOW, OKAY? BEING OUT IN THE OPEN LIKE THIS, IT'S TOO RISKY...
SORRY, BUT NO.
I'VE GOT TO SEE WHAT'S HERE.
LOOK, NO OFFENSE, MS. LANG, BUT ARE YOU SURE YOU'RE THE LEXCORP C.E.O.?
WE NEVER DID GET MUCH NEW FROM EARTH, BUT I REMEMBE YOU BEING SOM POLITICIAN'S WIFE...

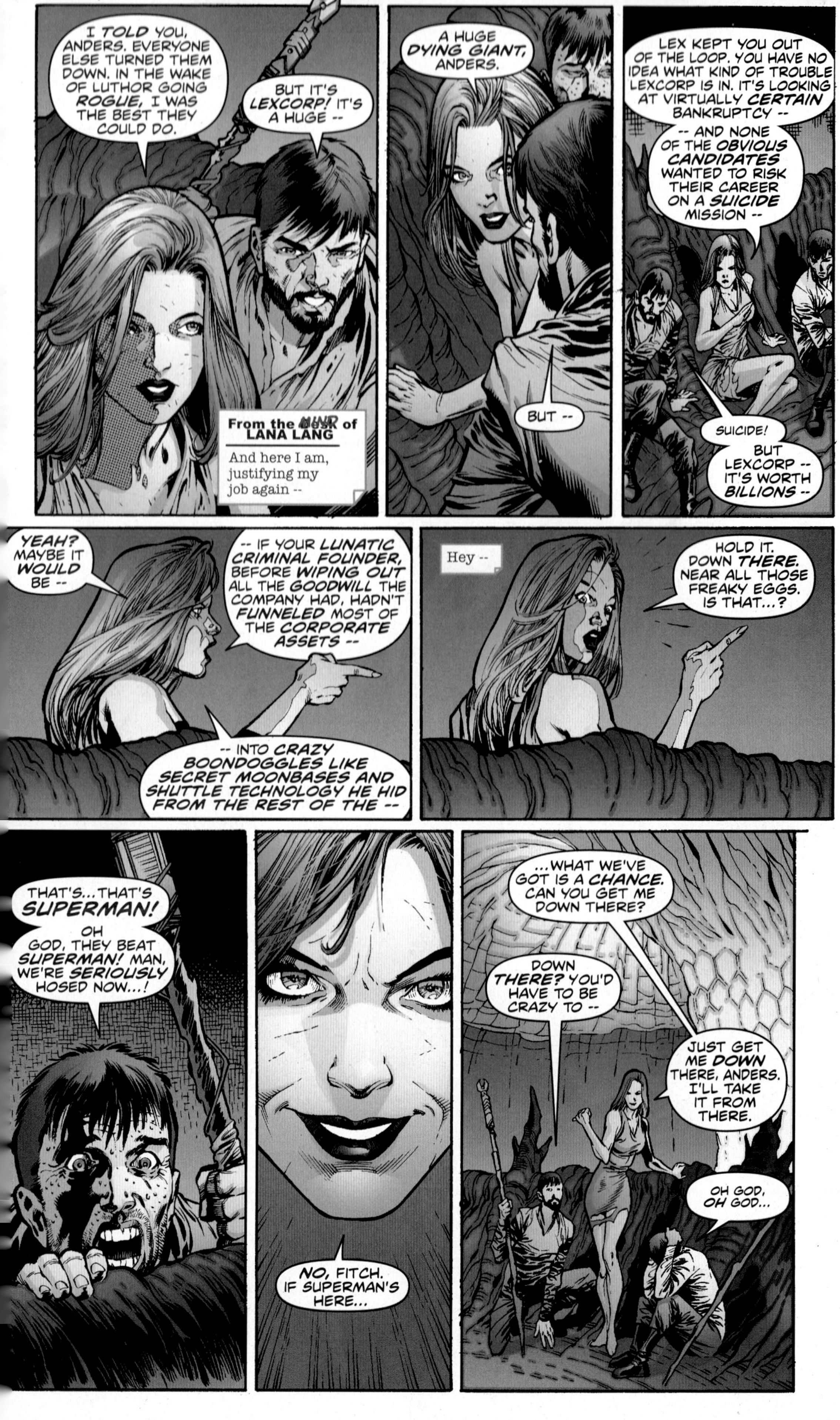
I TOLD YOU, ANDERS. EVERYONE ELSE TURNED THEM DOWN. IN THE WAKE OF LUTHOR GOING ROGUE, I WAS THE BEST THEY COULD DO.
BUT IT'S LEXCORP! IT'S A HUGE --
From the MIND Desk of LANA LANG
And here I am, justifying my job again --
A HUGE DYING GIANT, ANDERS.
BUT --
LEX KEPT YOU OUT OF THE LOOP. YOU HAVE NO IDEA WHAT KIND OF TROUBLE LEXCORP IS IN. IT'S LOOKING AT VIRTUALLY CERTAIN BANKRUPTCY --
-- AND NONE OF THE OBVIOUS CANDIDATES WANTED TO RISK THEIR CAREER ON A SUICIDE MISSION --
SUICIDE! BUT LEXCORP -- IT'S WORTH BILLIONS --
YEAH? MAYBE IT WOULD BE --
-- IF YOUR LUNATIC CRIMINAL FOUNDER, BEFORE WIPING OUT ALL THE GOODWILL THE COMPANY HAD, HADN'T FUNNELED MOST OF THE CORPORATE ASSETS --
-- INTO CRAZY BOONDOGGLES LIKE SECRET MOONBASES AND SHUTTLE TECHNOLOGY HE HID FROM THE REST OF THE --
Hey --
HOLD IT. DOWN THERE. NEAR ALL THOSE FREAKY EGGS. IS THAT...?
THAT'S...THAT'S SUPERMAN!
OH GOD, THEY BEAT SUPERMAN! MAN, WE'RE SERIOUSLY HOSED NOW...!
NO, FITCH. IF SUPERMAN'S HERE...
...WHAT WE'VE GOT IS A CHANCE. CAN YOU GET ME DOWN THERE?
DOWN THERE? YOU'D HAVE TO BE CRAZY TO --
JUST GET ME DOWN THERE, ANDERS. I'LL TAKE IT FROM THERE.
OH GOD, OH GOD...

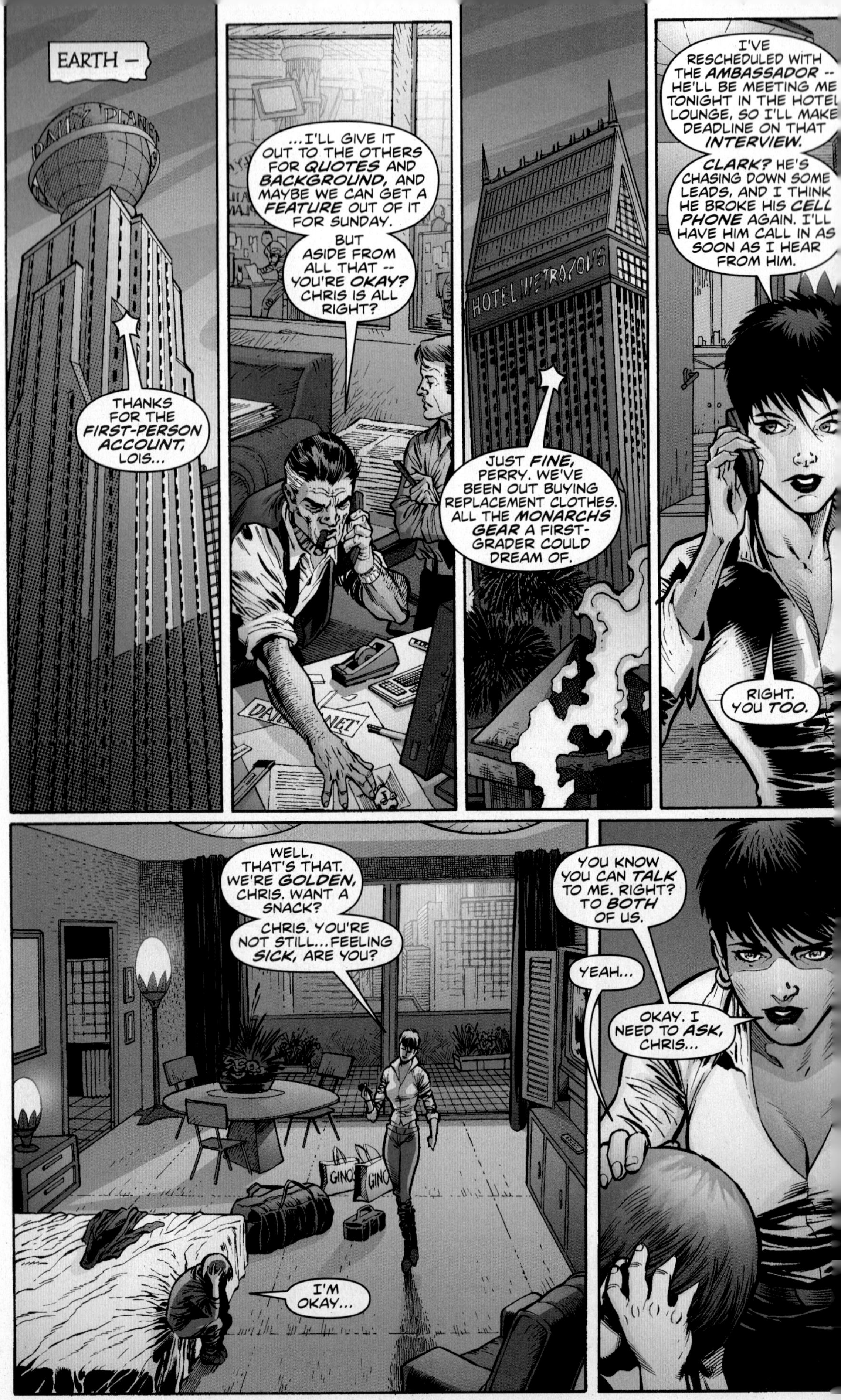

EARTH —
DAILY PLANET
THANKS FOR THE FIRST-PERSON ACCOUNT, LOIS...
...I'LL GIVE IT OUT TO THE OTHERS FOR QUOTES AND BACKGROUND, AND MAYBE WE CAN GET A FEATURE OUT OF IT FOR SUNDAY.
BUT ASIDE FROM ALL THAT -- YOU'RE OKAY? CHRIS IS ALL RIGHT?
HOTEL METROPOLIS
JUST FINE, PERRY. WE'VE BEEN OUT BUYING REPLACEMENT CLOTHES. ALL THE MONARCHS GEAR A FIRST-GRADER COULD DREAM OF.
I'VE RESCHEDULED WITH THE AMBASSADOR -- HE'LL BE MEETING ME TONIGHT IN THE HOTEL LOUNGE, SO I'LL MAKE DEADLINE ON THAT INTERVIEW.
CLARK? HE'S CHASING DOWN SOME LEADS, AND I THINK HE BROKE HIS CELL PHONE AGAIN. I'LL HAVE HIM CALL IN AS SOON AS I HEAR FROM HIM.
RIGHT. YOU TOO.
WELL, THAT'S THAT. WE'RE GOLDEN, CHRIS. WANT A SNACK?
CHRIS. YOU'RE NOT STILL...FEELING SICK, ARE YOU?
GINO'S
I'M OKAY...
YOU KNOW YOU CAN TALK TO ME. RIGHT? TO BOTH OF US.
YEAH...
OKAY. I NEED TO ASK, CHRIS...

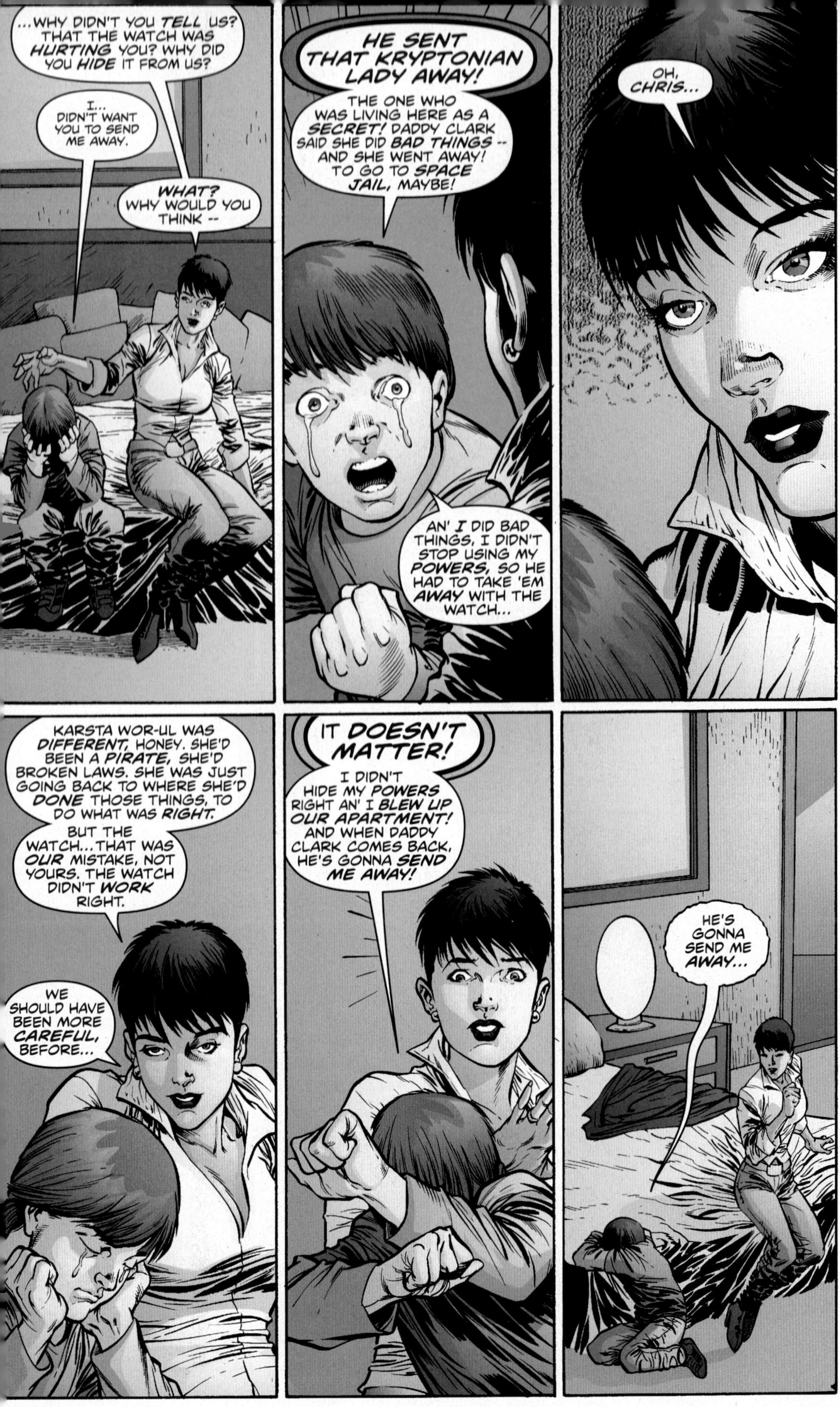
...WHY DIDN'T YOU TELL US? THAT THE WATCH WAS HURTING YOU? WHY DID YOU HIDE IT FROM US?
I... DIDN'T WANT YOU TO SEND ME AWAY.
WHAT? WHY WOULD YOU THINK --
HE SENT THAT KRYPTONIAN LADY AWAY!
THE ONE WHO WAS LIVING HERE AS A SECRET! DADDY CLARK SAID SHE DID BAD THINGS -- AND SHE WENT AWAY! TO GO TO SPACE JAIL, MAYBE!
AN' I DID BAD THINGS, I DIDN'T STOP USING MY POWERS, SO HE HAD TO TAKE 'EM AWAY WITH THE WATCH...
OH, CHRIS...
KARSTA WOR-UL WAS DIFFERENT, HONEY. SHE'D BEEN A PIRATE, SHE'D BROKEN LAWS. SHE WAS JUST GOING BACK TO WHERE SHE'D DONE THOSE THINGS, TO DO WHAT WAS RIGHT.
BUT THE WATCH...THAT WAS OUR MISTAKE, NOT YOURS. THE WATCH DIDN'T WORK RIGHT.
WE SHOULD HAVE BEEN MORE CAREFUL, BEFORE...
IT DOESN'T MATTER!
I DIDN'T HIDE MY POWERS RIGHT AN' I BLEW UP OUR APARTMENT! AND WHEN DADDY CLARK COMES BACK, HE'S GONNA SEND ME AWAY!
HE'S GONNA SEND ME AWAY...

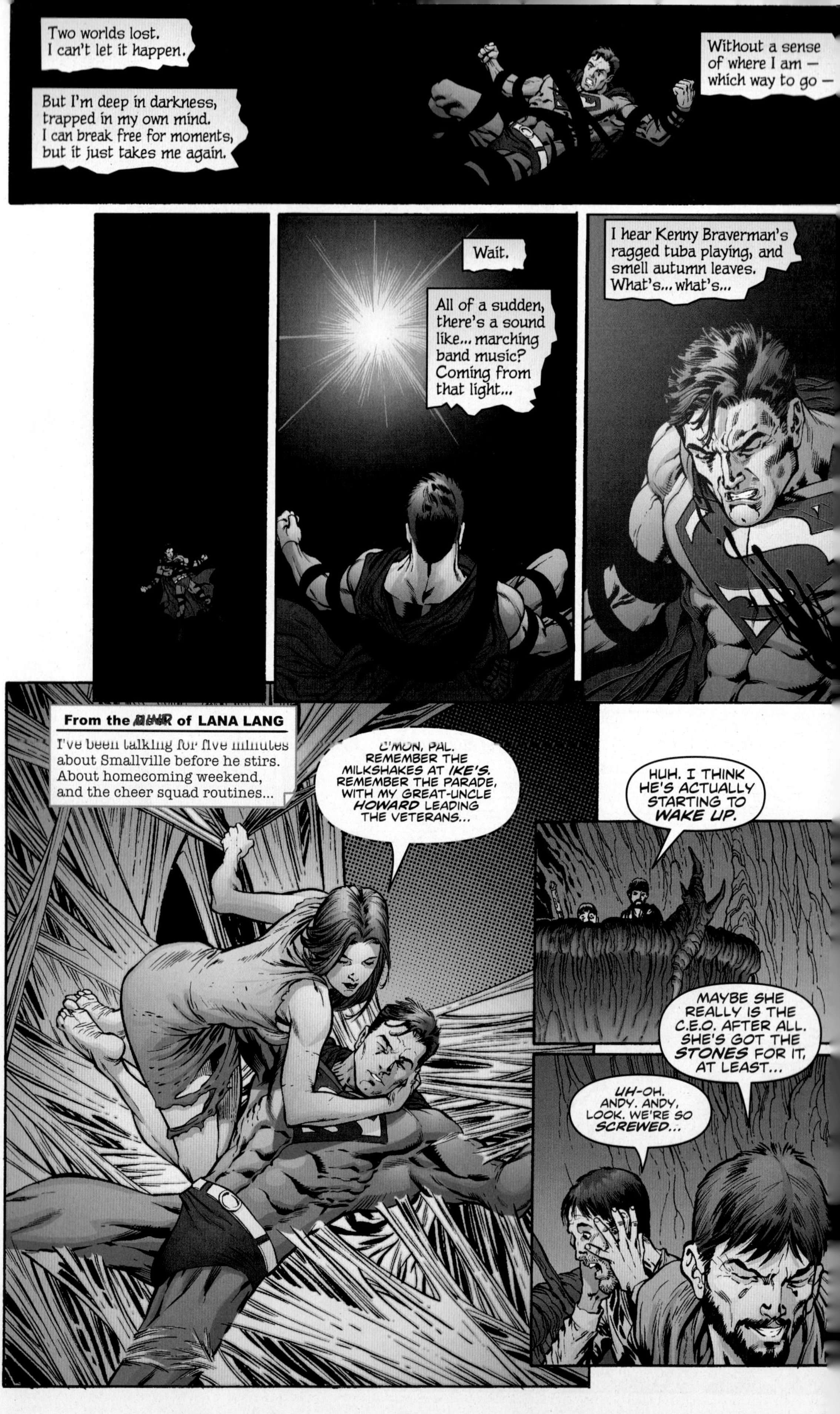

Two worlds lost.
I can't let it happen.
But I'm deep in darkness, trapped in my own mind. I can break free for moments, but it just takes me again.
Without a sense of where I am — which way to go —
Wait.
All of a sudden, there's a sound like... marching band music? Coming from that light...
I hear Kenny Braverman's ragged tuba playing, and smell autumn leaves. What's... what's...
From the MIND of LANA LANG
I've been talking for five minutes about Smallville before he stirs. About homecoming weekend, and the cheer squad routines...
C'MON, PAL. REMEMBER THE MILKSHAKES AT IKE'S. REMEMBER THE PARADE, WITH MY GREAT-UNCLE HOWARD LEADING THE VETERANS...
HUH. I THINK HE'S ACTUALLY STARTING TO WAKE UP.
MAYBE SHE REALLY IS THE C.E.O. AFTER ALL. SHE'S GOT THE STONES FOR IT, AT LEAST...
UH-OH. ANDY. ANDY, LOOK. WE'RE SO SCREWED...

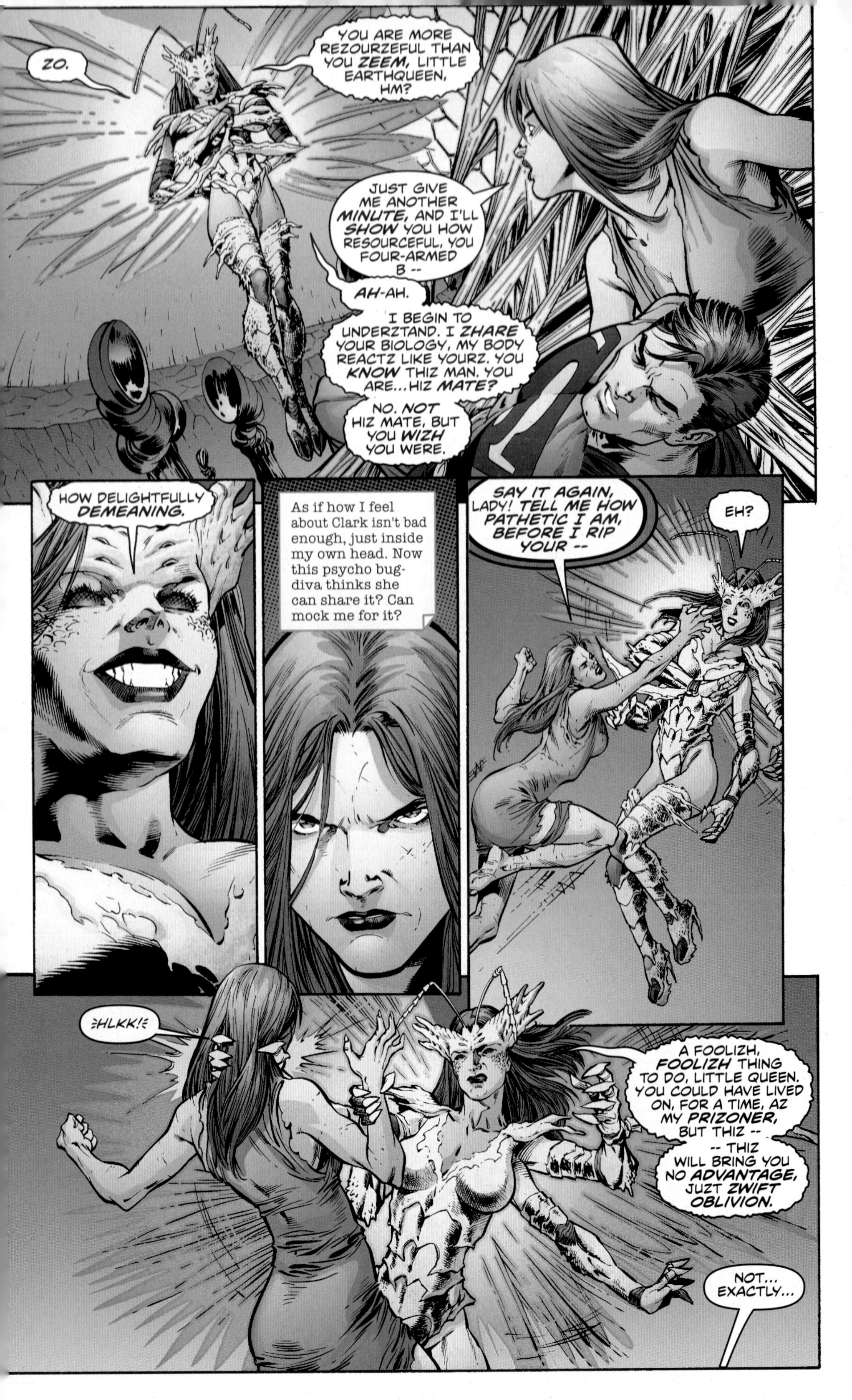
ZO.
YOU ARE MORE REZOURZEFUL THAN YOU ZEEM, LITTLE EARTHQUEEN, HM?
JUST GIVE ME ANOTHER MINUTE, AND I'LL SHOW YOU HOW RESOURCEFUL, YOU FOUR-ARMED B --
AH-AH.
I BEGIN TO UNDERZTAND. I ZHARE YOUR BIOLOGY, MY BODY REACTZ LIKE YOURZ. YOU KNOW THIZ MAN. YOU ARE...HIZ MATE?
NO. NOT HIZ MATE, BUT YOU WIZH YOU WERE.
HOW DELIGHTFULLY DEMEANING.
As if how I feel about Clark isn't bad enough, just inside my own head. Now this psycho bug-diva thinks she can share it? Can mock me for it?
SAY IT AGAIN, LADY! TELL ME HOW PATHETIC I AM, BEFORE I RIP YOUR --
EH?
HLKK!
A FOOLIZH, FOOLIZH THING TO DO, LITTLE QUEEN. YOU COULD HAVE LIVED ON, FOR A TIME, AZ MY PRIZONER, BUT THIZ --
-- THIZ WILL BRING YOU NO ADVANTAGE, JUZT ZWIFT OBLIVION.
NOT... EXACTLY...

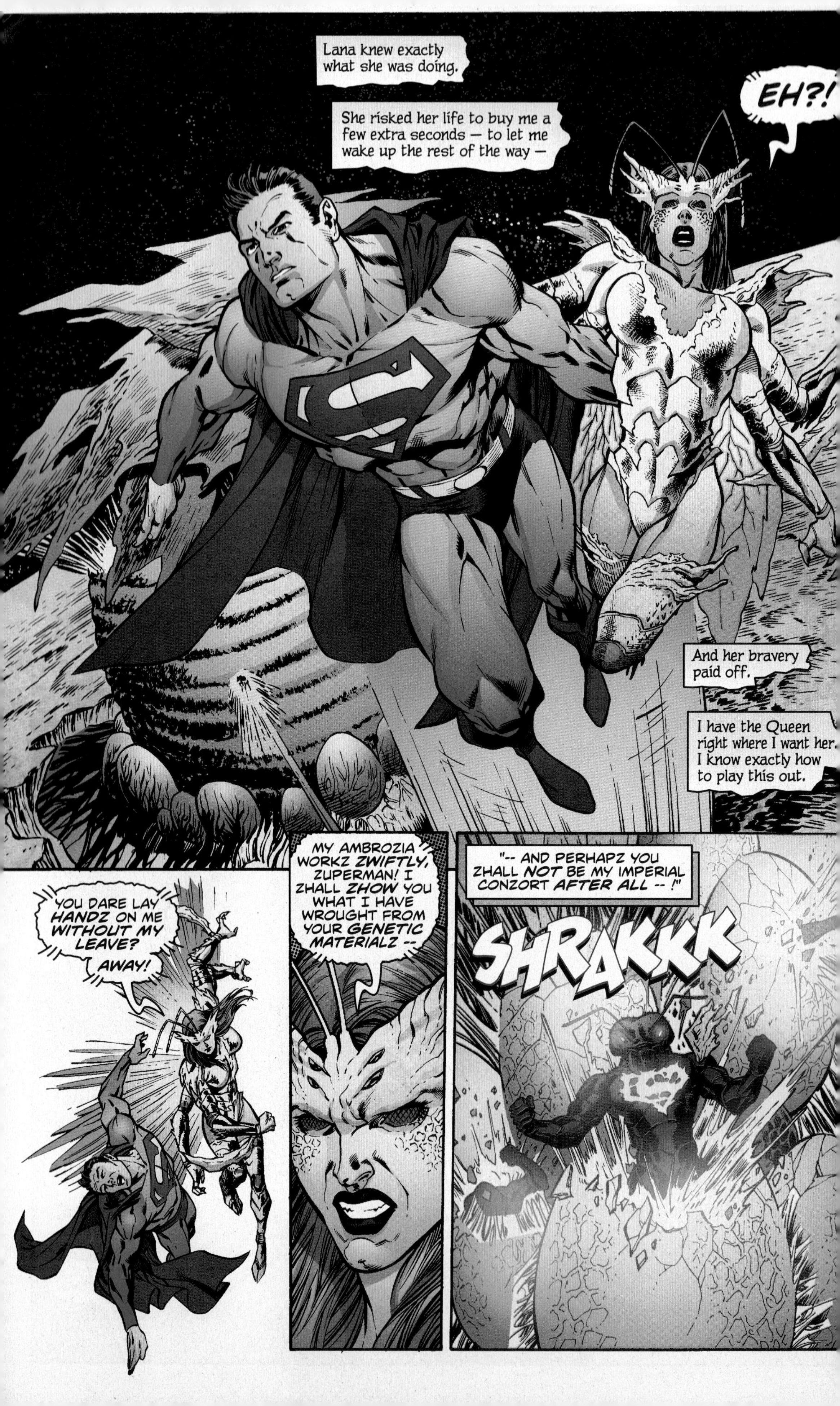
Lana knew exactly what she was doing.
She risked her life to buy me a few extra seconds — to let me wake up the rest of the way —
EH?!
And her bravery paid off.
I have the Queen right where I want her. I know exactly how to play this out.
YOU DARE LAY HANDZ ON ME WITHOUT MY LEAVE?
AWAY!
MY AMBROZIA WORKZ ZWIFTLY, ZUPERMAN! I ZHALL ZHOW YOU WHAT I HAVE WROUGHT FROM YOUR GENETIC MATERIALZ --
"-- AND PERHAPZ YOU ZHALL NOT BE MY IMPERIAL CONZORT AFTER ALL -- !"
SHRAKKK

AGAINST THOSE MONSTERS, EVEN *SUPERMAN* DOESN'T STAND A CHANCE! WE'VE GOT TO GET INTO *HIDING*, BEFORE --

WHERE'VE YOU *BEEN*, ANDERS? HE'S SUPERMAN -- OF *COURSE* HE'S GOING TO WIN.

WHAT I NEED IS FOR YOU TO TELL ME MORE ABOUT THOSE *SHUTTLES* --

From the *MIND* of LANA LANG

She's called in the cavalry. Hah! That means he's got her on the ropes...

MS. LANG! WE'VE GOT TO GET BACK TO THE *LOWER* LEVELS!

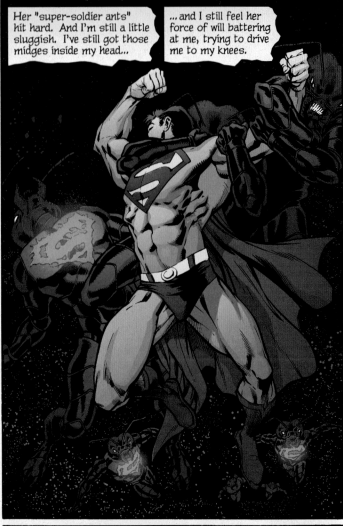

Her "super-soldier ants" hit hard. And I'm still a little sluggish. I've still got those midges inside my head...

...and I still feel her force of will battering at me, trying to drive me to my knees.

But Earth's at stake. Earth and everyone on it.

She hovers nearby, watching, gloating...

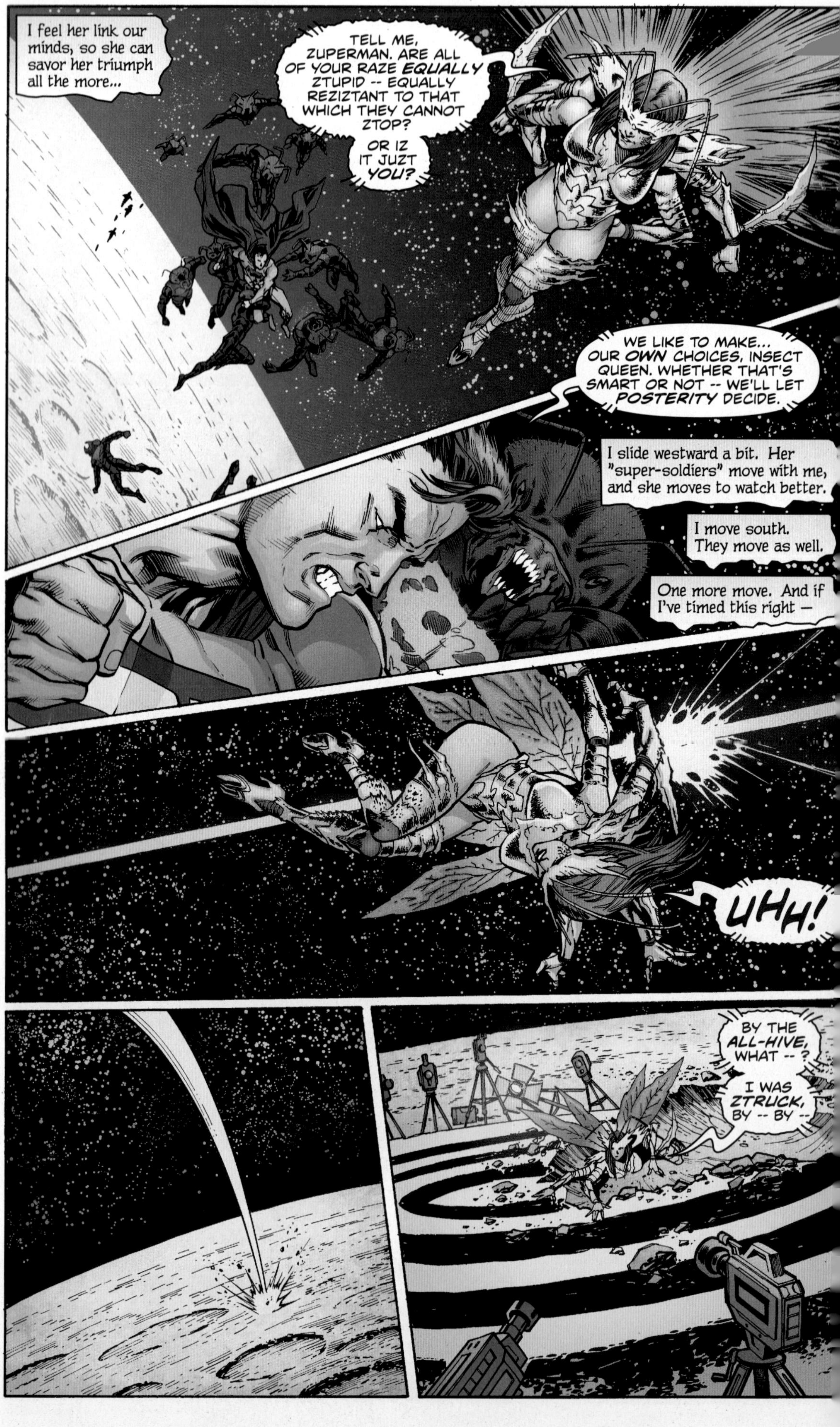
I feel her link our minds, so she can savor her triumph all the more...
TELL ME, ZUPERMAN. ARE ALL OF YOUR RAZE EQUALLY ZTUPID -- EQUALLY REZIZTANT TO THAT WHICH THEY CANNOT ZTOP?
OR IZ IT JUZT YOU?
WE LIKE TO MAKE... OUR OWN CHOICES, INSECT QUEEN. WHETHER THAT'S SMART OR NOT -- WE'LL LET POSTERITY DECIDE.
I slide westward a bit. Her "super-soldiers" move with me, and she moves to watch better.
I move south. They move as well.
One more move. And if I've timed this right —
UHH!
BY THE ALL-HIVE, WHAT -- ?
I WAS ZTRUCK, BY -- BY --

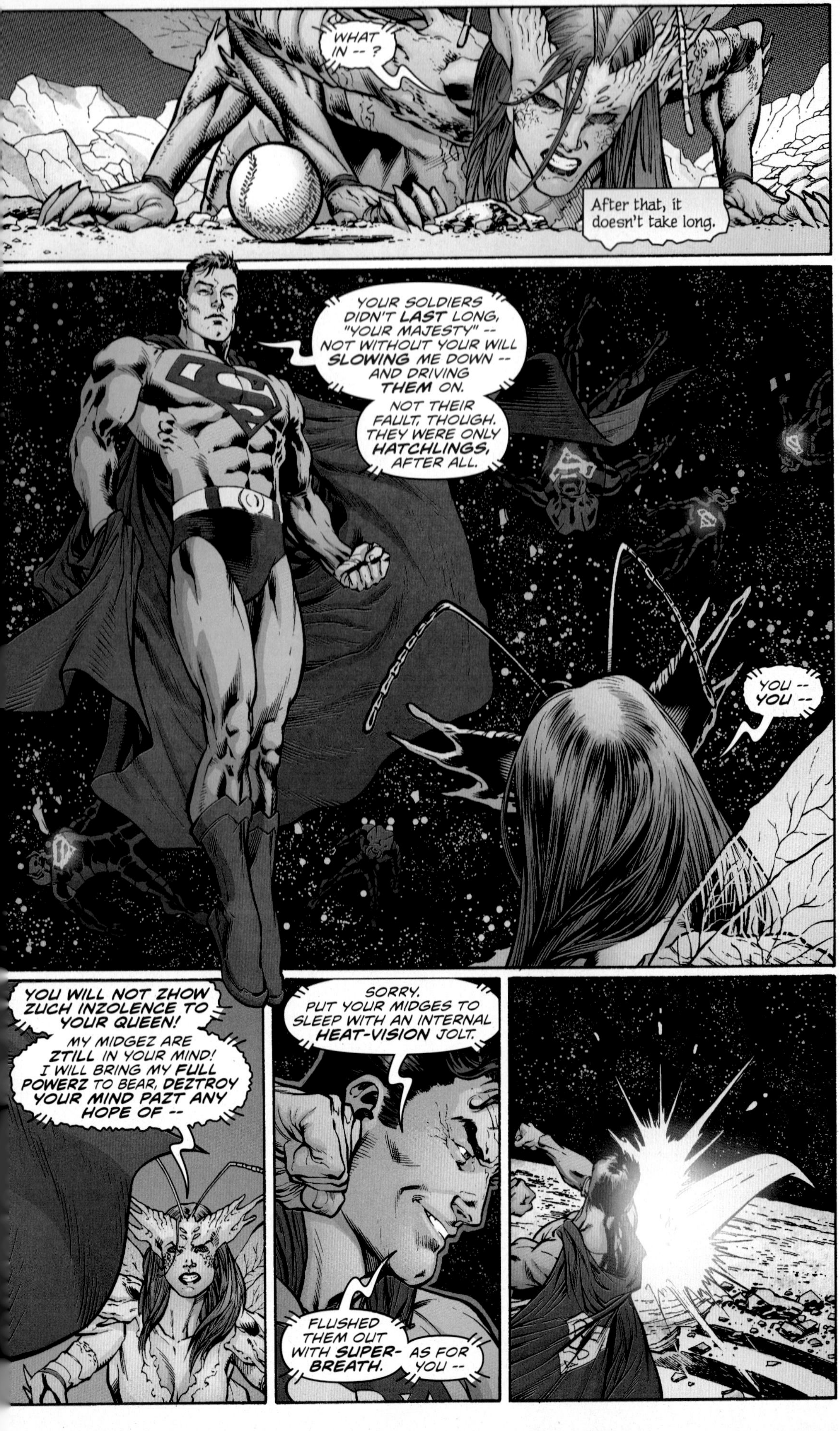
WHAT IN -- ?
After that, it doesn't take long.
YOUR SOLDIERS DIDN'T LAST LONG, "YOUR MAJESTY" -- NOT WITHOUT YOUR WILL SLOWING ME DOWN -- AND DRIVING THEM ON.
NOT THEIR FAULT, THOUGH. THEY WERE ONLY HATCHLINGS, AFTER ALL.
YOU -- YOU --
YOU WILL NOT ZHOW ZUCH INZOLENCE TO YOUR QUEEN!
MY MIDGEZ ARE ZTILL IN YOUR MIND! I WILL BRING MY FULL POWERZ TO BEAR, DEZTROY YOUR MIND PAZT ANY HOPE OF --
SORRY. PUT YOUR MIDGES TO SLEEP WITH AN INTERNAL HEAT-VISION JOLT.
FLUSHED THEM OUT WITH SUPER-BREATH.
AS FOR YOU --

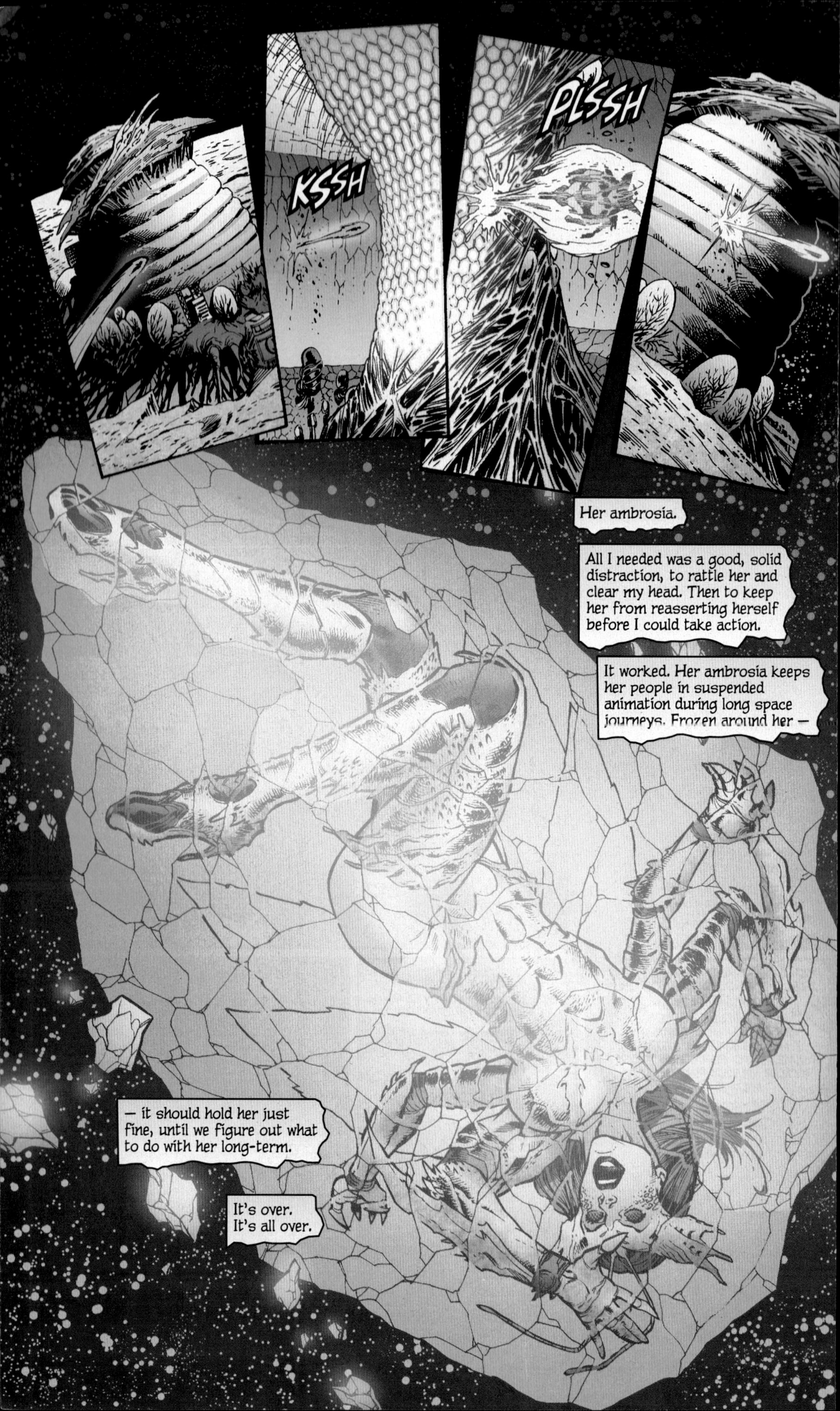
KSSH
PLSSH
Her ambrosia.
All I needed was a good, solid distraction, to rattle her and clear my head. Then to keep her from reasserting herself before I could take action.
It worked. Her ambrosia keeps her people in suspended animation during long space journeys. Frozen around her —
— it should hold her just fine, until we figure out what to do with her long-term.
It's over. It's all over.

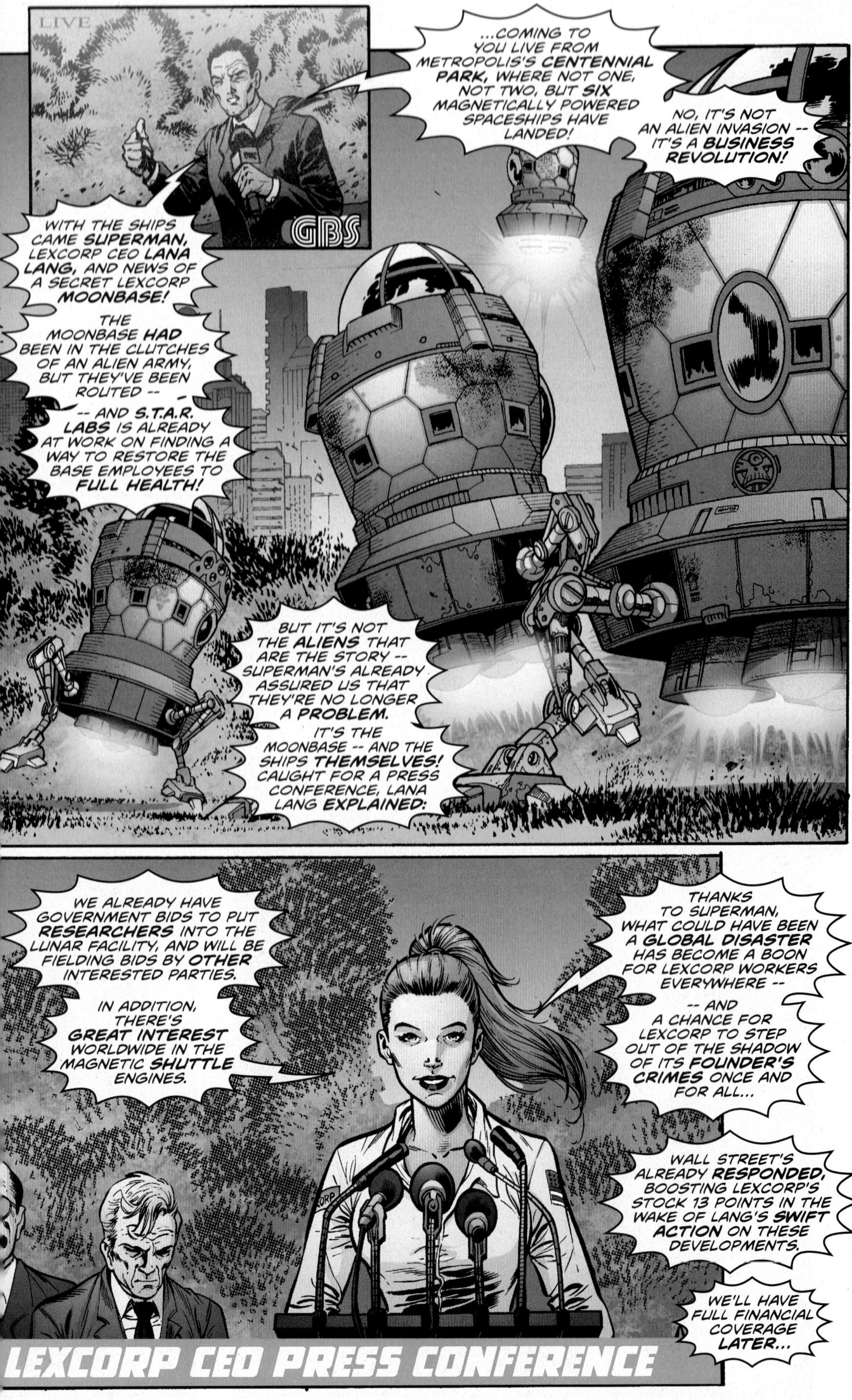
LIVE
...COMING TO YOU LIVE FROM METROPOLIS'S CENTENNIAL PARK, WHERE NOT ONE, NOT TWO, BUT SIX MAGNETICALLY POWERED SPACESHIPS HAVE LANDED!
NO, IT'S NOT AN ALIEN INVASION -- IT'S A BUSINESS REVOLUTION!
GBS
WITH THE SHIPS CAME SUPERMAN, LEXCORP CEO LANA LANG, AND NEWS OF A SECRET LEXCORP MOONBASE!
THE MOONBASE HAD BEEN IN THE CLUTCHES OF AN ALIEN ARMY, BUT THEY'VE BEEN ROUTED --
-- AND S.T.A.R. LABS IS ALREADY AT WORK ON FINDING A WAY TO RESTORE THE BASE EMPLOYEES TO FULL HEALTH!
BUT IT'S NOT THE ALIENS THAT ARE THE STORY -- SUPERMAN'S ALREADY ASSURED US THAT THEY'RE NO LONGER A PROBLEM.
IT'S THE MOONBASE -- AND THE SHIPS THEMSELVES! CAUGHT FOR A PRESS CONFERENCE, LANA LANG EXPLAINED:
WE ALREADY HAVE GOVERNMENT BIDS TO PUT RESEARCHERS INTO THE LUNAR FACILITY, AND WILL BE FIELDING BIDS BY OTHER INTERESTED PARTIES.
IN ADDITION, THERE'S GREAT INTEREST WORLDWIDE IN THE MAGNETIC SHUTTLE ENGINES.
THANKS TO SUPERMAN, WHAT COULD HAVE BEEN A GLOBAL DISASTER HAS BECOME A BOON FOR LEXCORP WORKERS EVERYWHERE --
-- AND A CHANCE FOR LEXCORP TO STEP OUT OF THE SHADOW OF ITS FOUNDER'S CRIMES ONCE AND FOR ALL...
WALL STREET'S ALREADY RESPONDED, BOOSTING LEXCORP'S STOCK 13 POINTS IN THE WAKE OF LANG'S SWIFT ACTION ON THESE DEVELOPMENTS.
WE'LL HAVE FULL FINANCIAL COVERAGE LATER...
LEXCORP CEO PRESS CONFERENCE

...AND IN *SPORTS,* TIM MCCREADY WILL COVER THE BIZARRE STORY OF THE *MOONSHOT-THAT-WASN'T.*

THAT'S *RIGHT,* BRIAN -- SUPERMAN'S LONG BALL *DIDN'T* HIT THE BULL'S-EYE AFTER ALL, THOUGH SCIENTISTS ASSURE US IT *WOULD* HAVE...

THE SPORTS HOUR   GBS

...AND LEXCORP SPOKESMEN SAY THAT UNDER THE *CIRCUMSTANCES,* THEY'LL TREAT IT AS IF IT DID, AND *TRIPLE* THE CHARITABLE CONTRIBUTION THEY'D HAVE MADE...

WELL, GOOD FOR YOU, LANA. GOOD FOR *YOU.*

AND CHRIS, YOU'VE GOT TO *UNDERSTAND.* YOU DIDN'T DO ANYTHING *WRONG.*

WHAT HAPPENED WITH THE WATCH -- THE TECHNOLOGY INSIDE IT WAS DESIGNED TO WORK ON *CLARK.* NOBODY KNEW IT WOULD AFFECT A KRYPTONIAN *CHILD* DIFFERENTLY.

I WISH YOU'D *TOLD* US ABOUT IT, BUT THAT STILL DOESN'T MEAN WE'RE GOING TO *BLAME* YOU FOR IT.

NOBODY'S GOING TO SEND YOU *AWAY...*

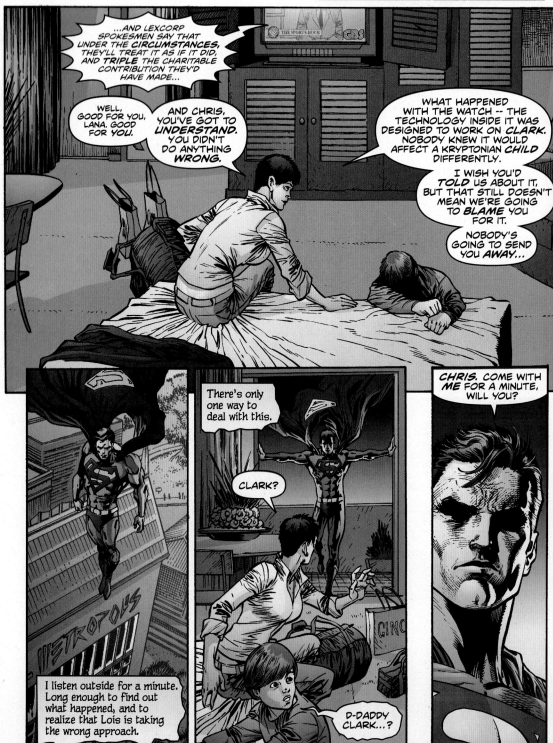

There's only one way to deal with this.

CLARK?

CHRIS. COME WITH ME FOR A MINUTE, WILL YOU?

I listen outside for a minute. Long enough to find out what happened, and to realize that Lois is taking the wrong approach.

D-DADDY CLARK...?

Lois tried to explain things to Chris logically, to make him understand why he wasn't going to be punished.

But it didn't work, because Chris is scared of things Lois has never felt, not really. Lois may have felt isolated, from time to time.

Moving around, part of a military family, she'd have felt lonely. But never as alone as Chris can feel.

Never so alone she had to question whether she even belongs on this planet. Not so alone she could really imagine losing everything.

But I've lost a world.

It makes this one feel fragile, because I know how easily I could lose it, too. But it also makes it precious beyond all measure.

That's why the Insect Queen could make me so devastated at the thought of losing Earth. Why Lana could bring me back.

And that's how Chris feels now. Scared he's going to lose it all. Everything he has.

There's still just enough air for sound to travel...

LOOK AT IT, CHRIS. TAKE A GOOD, LONG LOOK.

NOW, I WANT YOU TO LISTEN TO ME. LOIS AND I ARE YOUR FAMILY.

WE'LL NEVER SEND YOU AWAY. WE'LL NEVER LEAVE YOU. IF YOU'RE WORRIED ABOUT THAT, YOU CAN STOP, RIGHT NOW.

WE'RE A FAMILY. YOU BELONG WITH US, AND THAT'S JUST HOW IT IS. WE'LL MAKE MISTAKES, AND STUMBLE, AND FIGURE OUT HOW TO FIX IT.

BUT THERE'LL ALWAYS BE ONE THING YOU CAN COUNT ON.

WE'RE YOUR FAMILY. THERE, BELOW US, THAT'S YOUR WORLD.

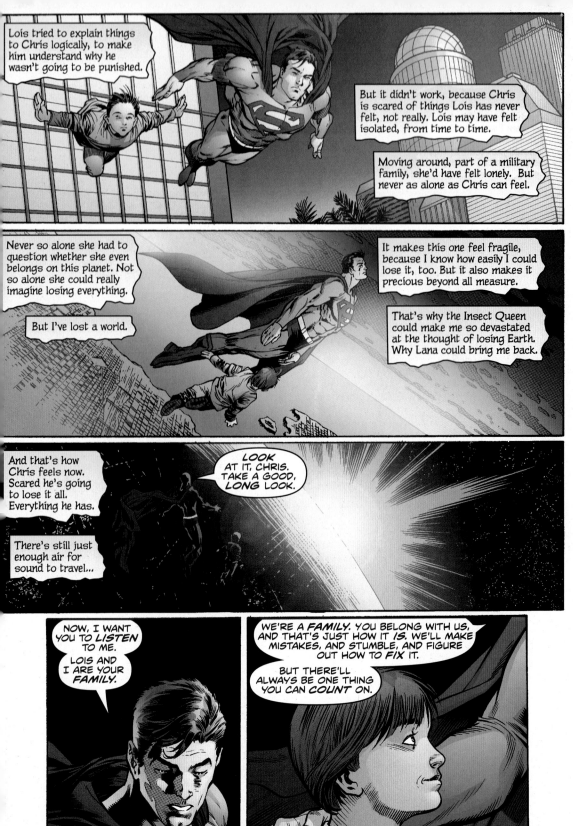

SHADOWS LINGER
PART ONE:

BRIGHT TOMORROWS

ART BY **RENATO GUEDES** & **JOSÉ WILSON MAGALHÁES**

COLORS BY **DAVID CURIEL**

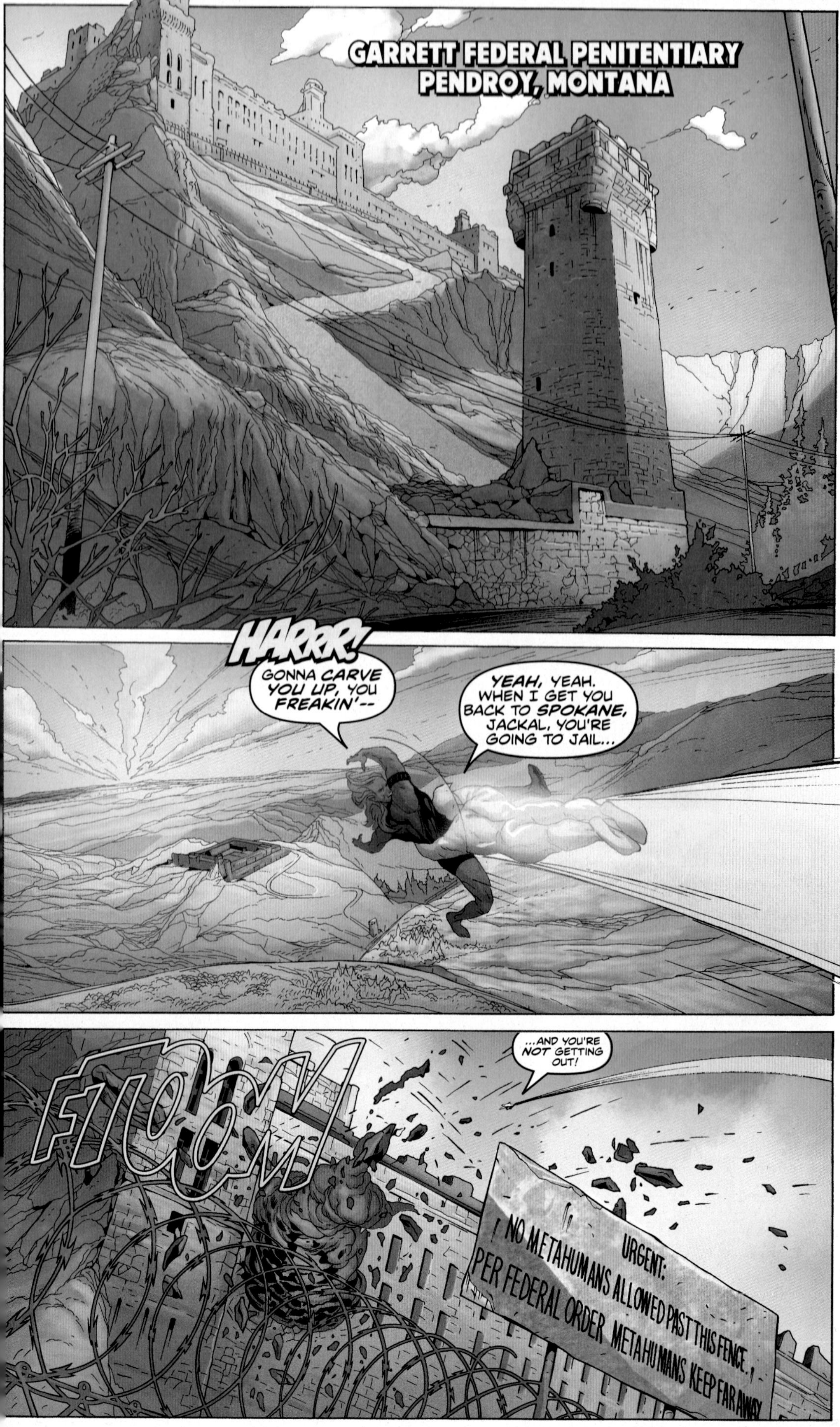
GARRETT FEDERAL PENITENTIARY
PENDROY, MONTANA
HARRR!
GONNA CARVE YOU UP, YOU FREAKIN'--
YEAH, YEAH. WHEN I GET YOU BACK TO SPOKANE, JACKAL, YOU'RE GOING TO JAIL...
FTOOM
...AND YOU'RE NOT GETTING OUT!
URGENT:
NO METAHUMANS ALLOWED PAST THIS FENCE.
PER FEDERAL ORDER METAHUMANS KEEP FAR AWAY

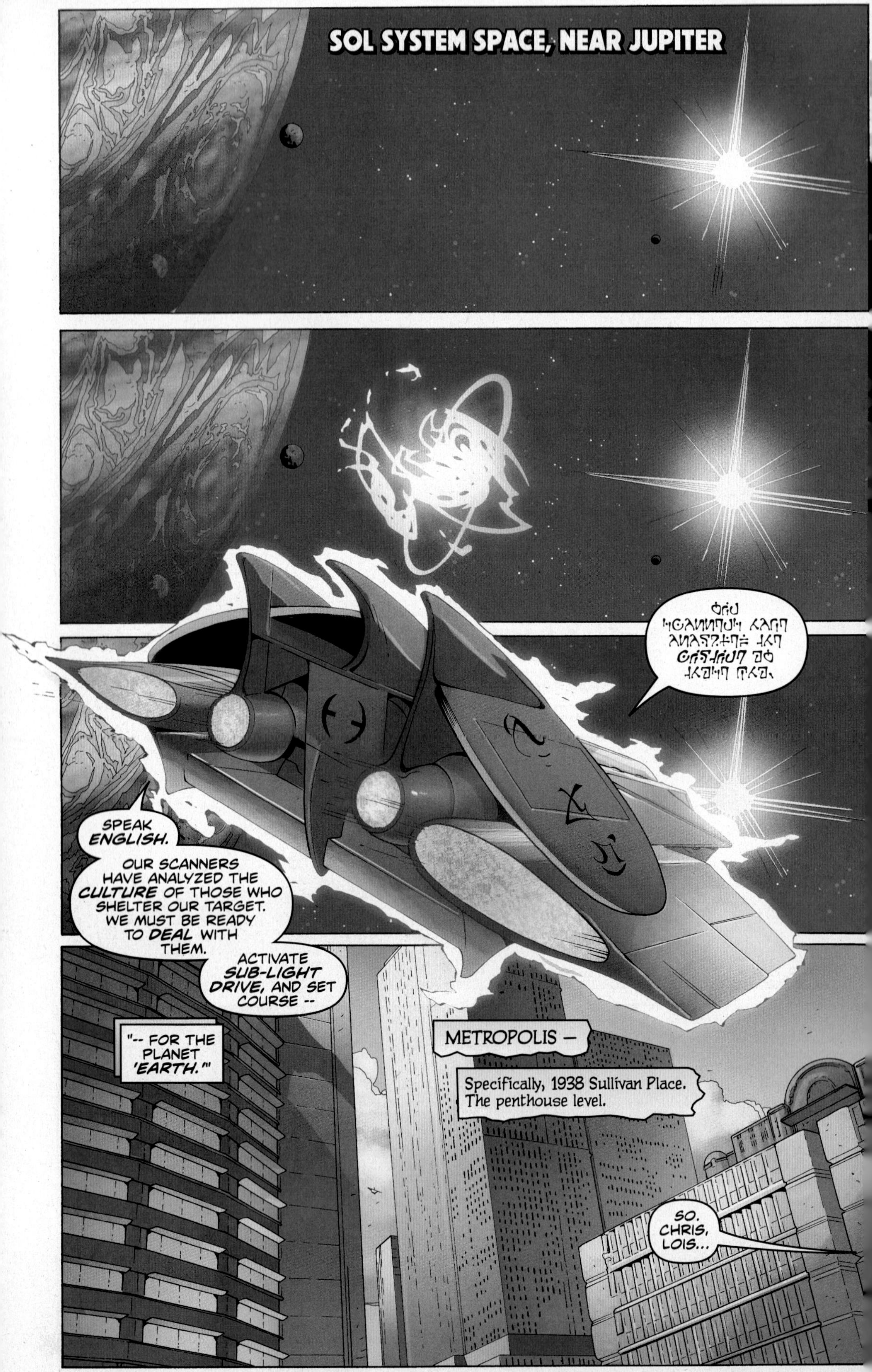
SOL SYSTEM SPACE, NEAR JUPITER
SPEAK ENGLISH.
OUR SCANNERS HAVE ANALYZED THE CULTURE OF THOSE WHO SHELTER OUR TARGET. WE MUST BE READY TO DEAL WITH THEM.
ACTIVATE SUB-LIGHT DRIVE, AND SET COURSE --
"-- FOR THE PLANET 'EARTH.'"
METROPOLIS —
Specifically, 1938 Sullivan Place. The penthouse level.
SO. CHRIS, LOIS...

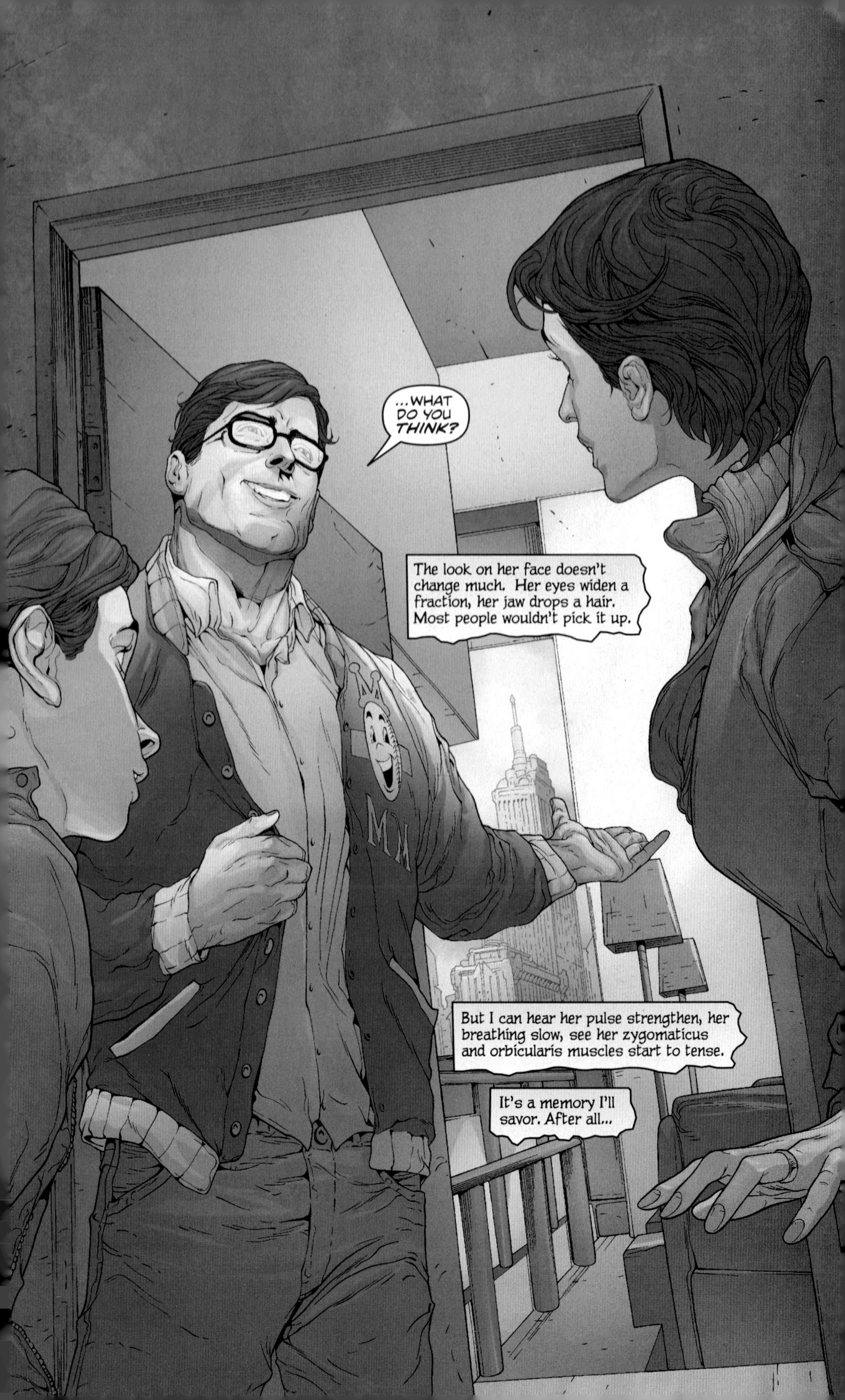
...WHAT DO YOU *THINK?*
The look on her face doesn't change much. Her eyes widen a fraction, her jaw drops a hair. Most people wouldn't pick it up.
But I can hear her pulse strengthen, her breathing slow, see her zygomaticus and orbicularis muscles start to tense.
It's a memory I'll savor. After all...

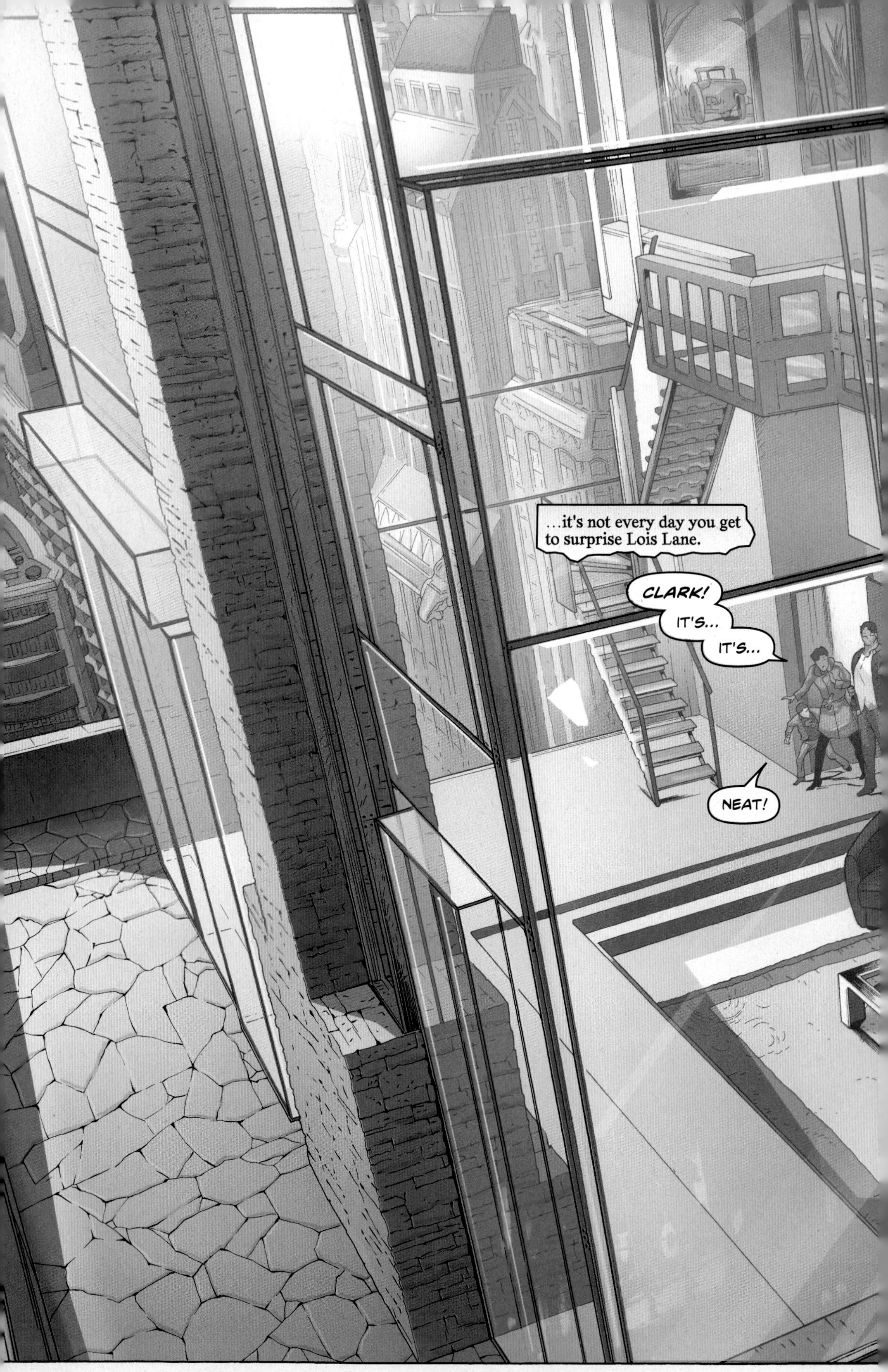
…it's not every day you get to surprise Lois Lane.
CLARK!
IT'S…
IT'S…
NEAT!

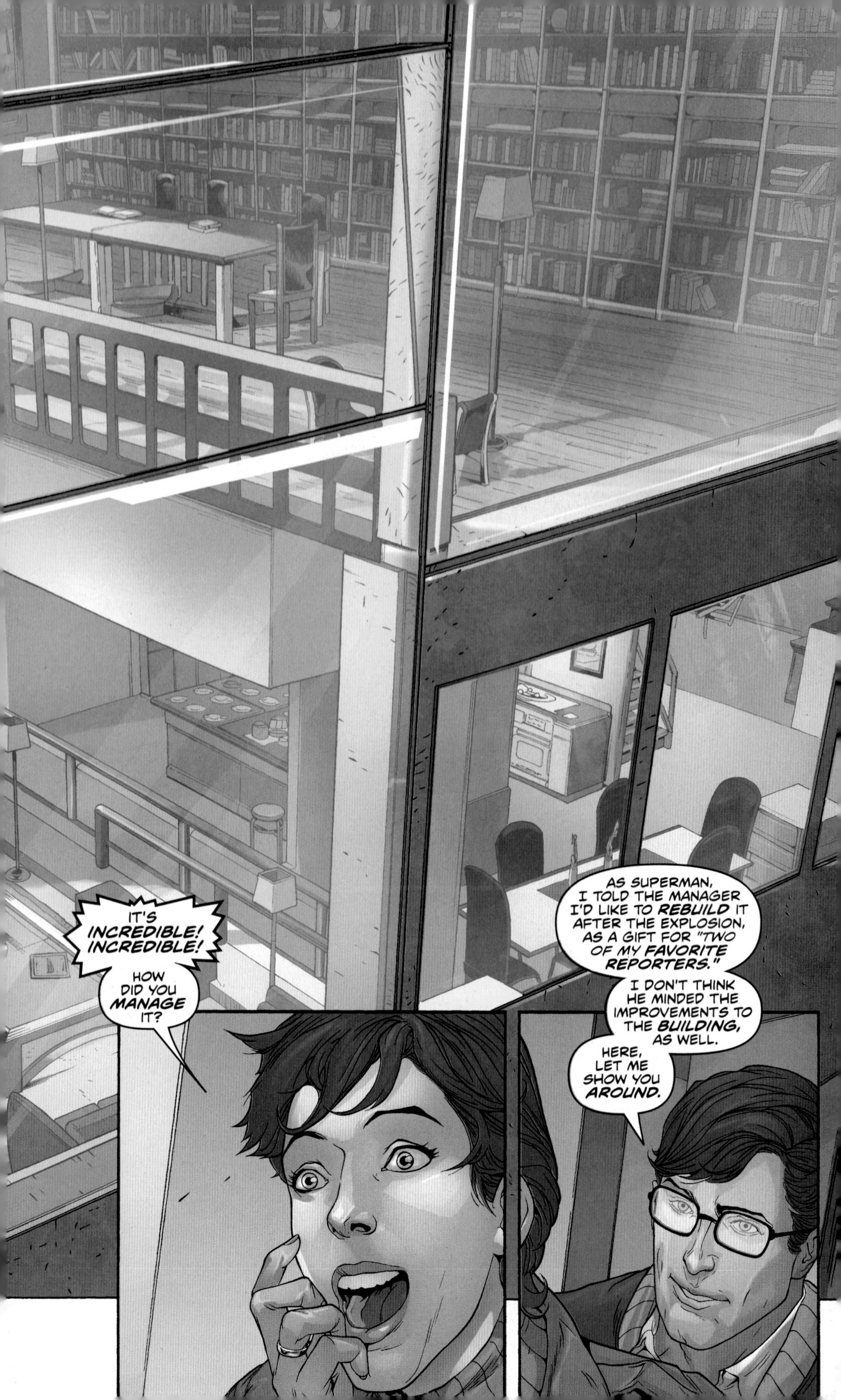

IT'S INCREDIBLE! INCREDIBLE!
HOW DID YOU MANAGE IT?
AS SUPERMAN, I TOLD THE MANAGER I'D LIKE TO REBUILD IT AFTER THE EXPLOSION, AS A GIFT FOR "TWO OF MY FAVORITE REPORTERS."
I DON'T THINK HE MINDED THE IMPROVEMENTS TO THE BUILDING, AS WELL.
HERE, LET ME SHOW YOU AROUND.

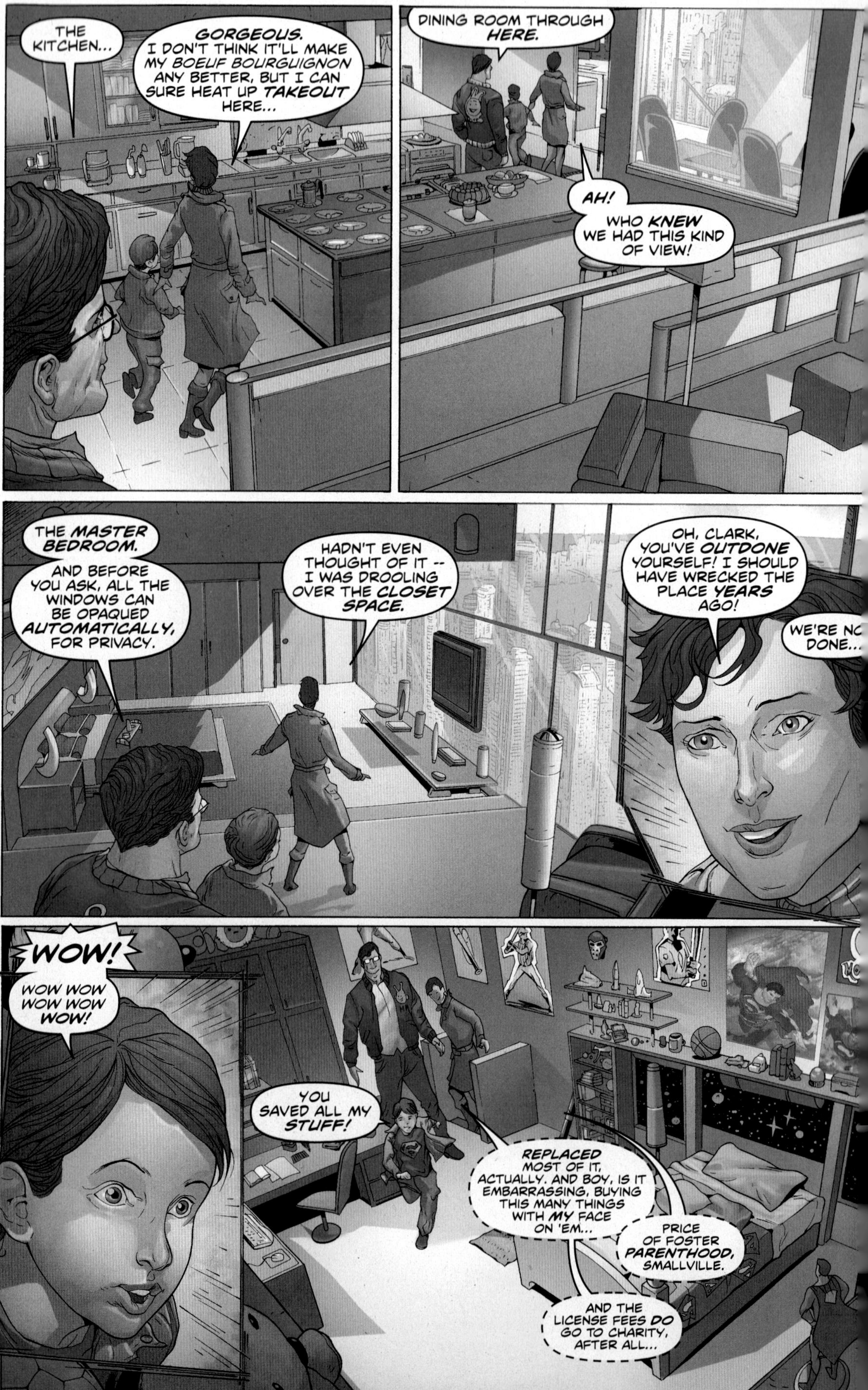
THE KITCHEN...
GORGEOUS. I DON'T THINK IT'LL MAKE MY BOEUF BOURGUIGNON ANY BETTER, BUT I CAN SURE HEAT UP TAKEOUT HERE...
DINING ROOM THROUGH HERE.
AH!
WHO KNEW WE HAD THIS KIND OF VIEW!
THE MASTER BEDROOM.
AND BEFORE YOU ASK, ALL THE WINDOWS CAN BE OPAQUED AUTOMATICALLY, FOR PRIVACY.
HADN'T EVEN THOUGHT OF IT -- I WAS DROOLING OVER THE CLOSET SPACE.
OH, CLARK, YOU'VE OUTDONE YOURSELF! I SHOULD HAVE WRECKED THE PLACE YEARS AGO!
WE'RE NO DONE...
WOW!
WOW WOW WOW WOW WOW!
YOU SAVED ALL MY STUFF!
REPLACED MOST OF IT, ACTUALLY. AND BOY, IS IT EMBARRASSING, BUYING THIS MANY THINGS WITH MY FACE ON 'EM...
PRICE OF FOSTER PARENTHOOD, SMALLVILLE.
AND THE LICENSE FEES DO GO TO CHARITY, AFTER ALL...

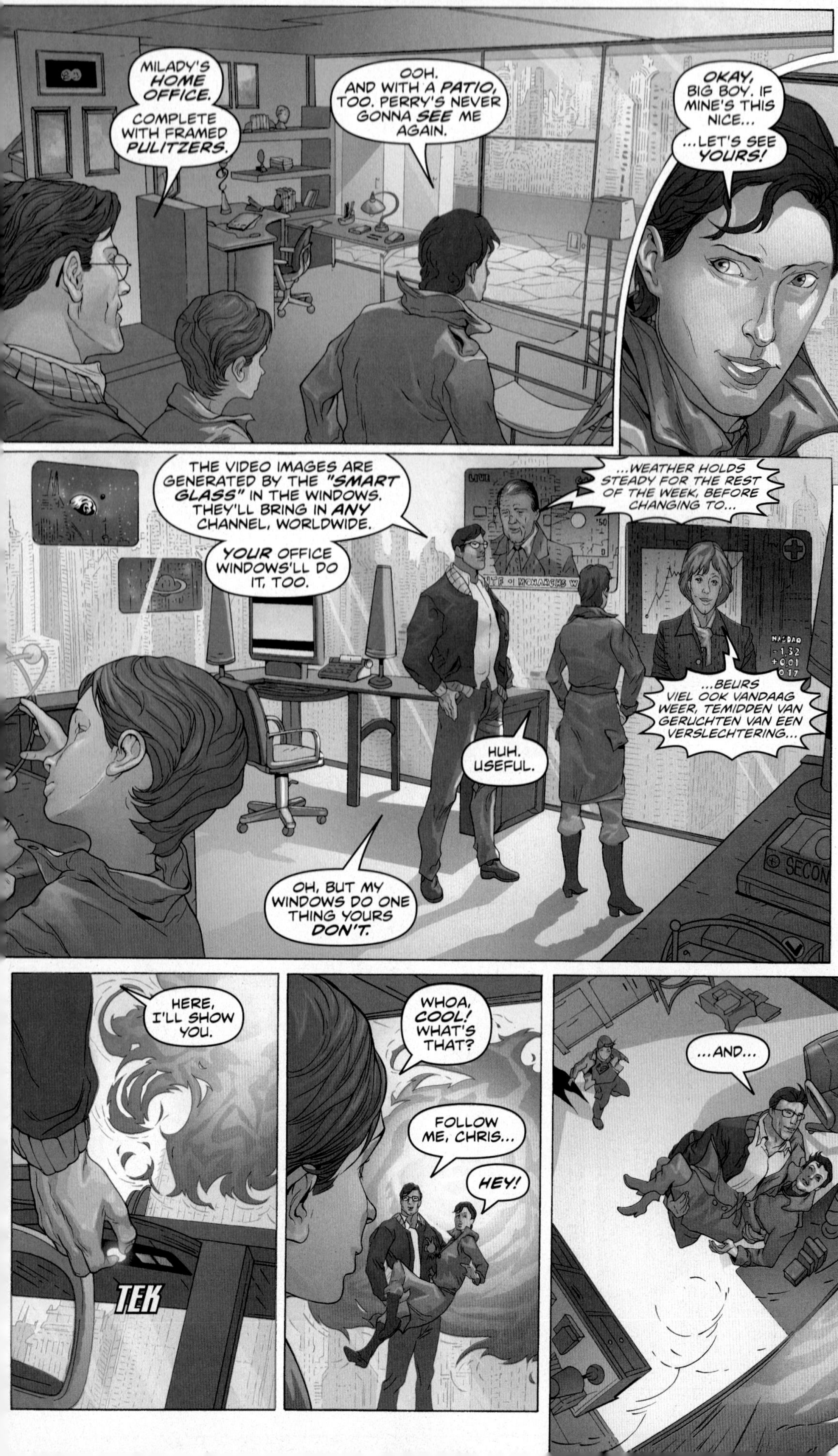
MILADY'S HOME OFFICE.
COMPLETE WITH FRAMED PULITZERS.
OOH. AND WITH A PATIO, TOO. PERRY'S NEVER GONNA SEE ME AGAIN.
OKAY, BIG BOY. IF MINE'S THIS NICE...
...LET'S SEE YOURS!
THE VIDEO IMAGES ARE GENERATED BY THE "SMART GLASS" IN THE WINDOWS. THEY'LL BRING IN ANY CHANNEL, WORLDWIDE.
YOUR OFFICE WINDOWS'LL DO IT, TOO.
...WEATHER HOLDS STEADY FOR THE REST OF THE WEEK, BEFORE CHANGING TO...
...BEURS VIEL OOK VANDAAG WEER, TEMIDDEN VAN GERUCHTEN VAN EEN VERSLECHTERING...
HUH. USEFUL.
OH, BUT MY WINDOWS DO ONE THING YOURS DON'T.
HERE, I'LL SHOW YOU.
TEK
WHOA, COOL! WHAT'S THAT?
FOLLOW ME, CHRIS...
HEY!
...AND...

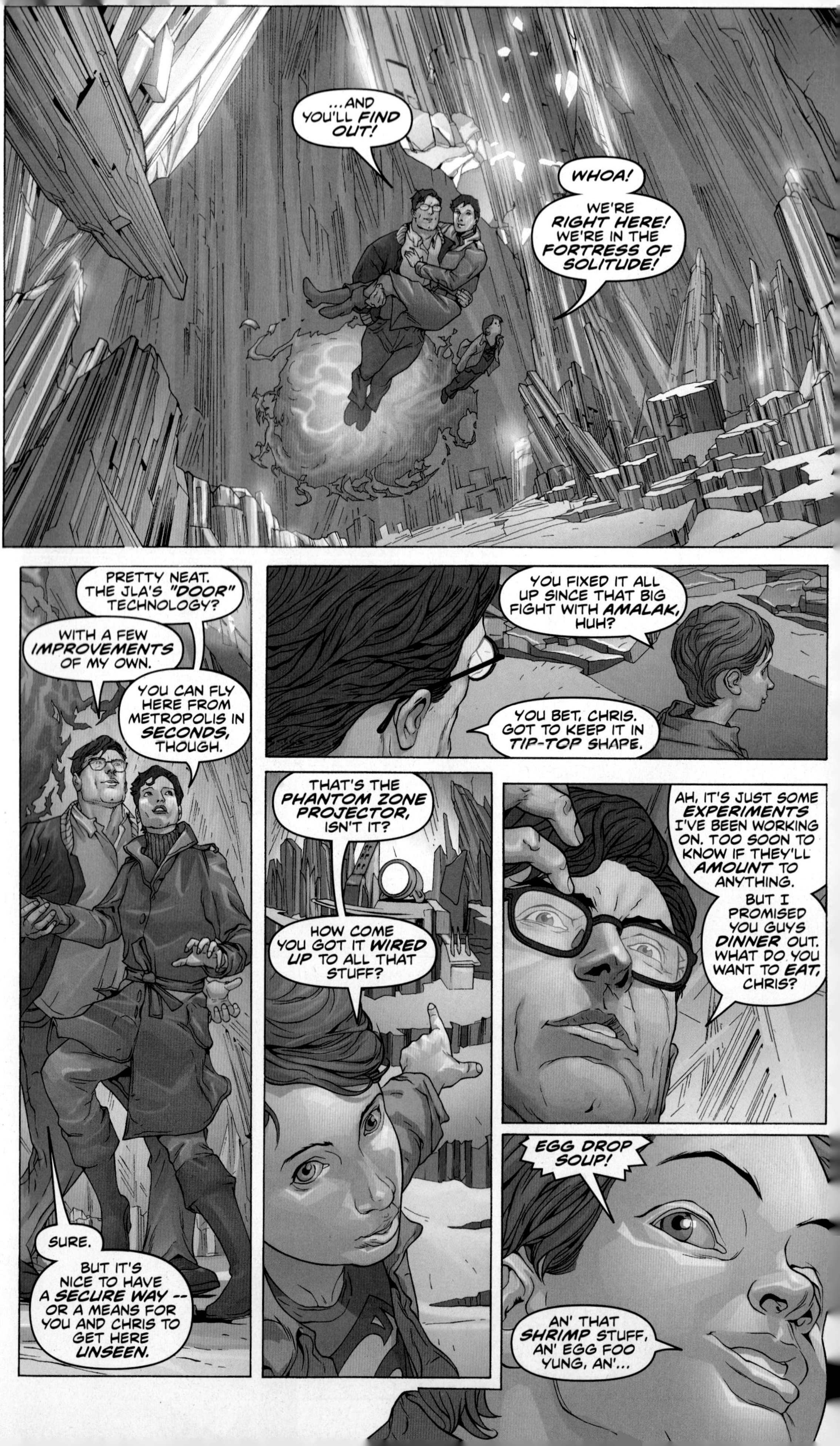
...AND YOU'LL FIND OUT!
WHOA!
WE'RE RIGHT HERE! WE'RE IN THE FORTRESS OF SOLITUDE!
PRETTY NEAT. THE JLA'S "DOOR" TECHNOLOGY?
WITH A FEW IMPROVEMENTS OF MY OWN.
YOU CAN FLY HERE FROM METROPOLIS IN SECONDS, THOUGH.
SURE.
BUT IT'S NICE TO HAVE A SECURE WAY -- OR A MEANS FOR YOU AND CHRIS TO GET HERE UNSEEN.
YOU FIXED IT ALL UP SINCE THAT BIG FIGHT WITH AMALAK, HUH?
YOU BET, CHRIS. GOT TO KEEP IT IN TIP-TOP SHAPE.
THAT'S THE PHANTOM ZONE PROJECTOR, ISN'T IT?
HOW COME YOU GOT IT WIRED UP TO ALL THAT STUFF?
AH, IT'S JUST SOME EXPERIMENTS I'VE BEEN WORKING ON. TOO SOON TO KNOW IF THEY'LL AMOUNT TO ANYTHING.
BUT I PROMISED YOU GUYS DINNER OUT. WHAT DO YOU WANT TO EAT, CHRIS?
EGG DROP SOUP!
AN' THAT SHRIMP STUFF, AN' EGG FOO YUNG, AN'...

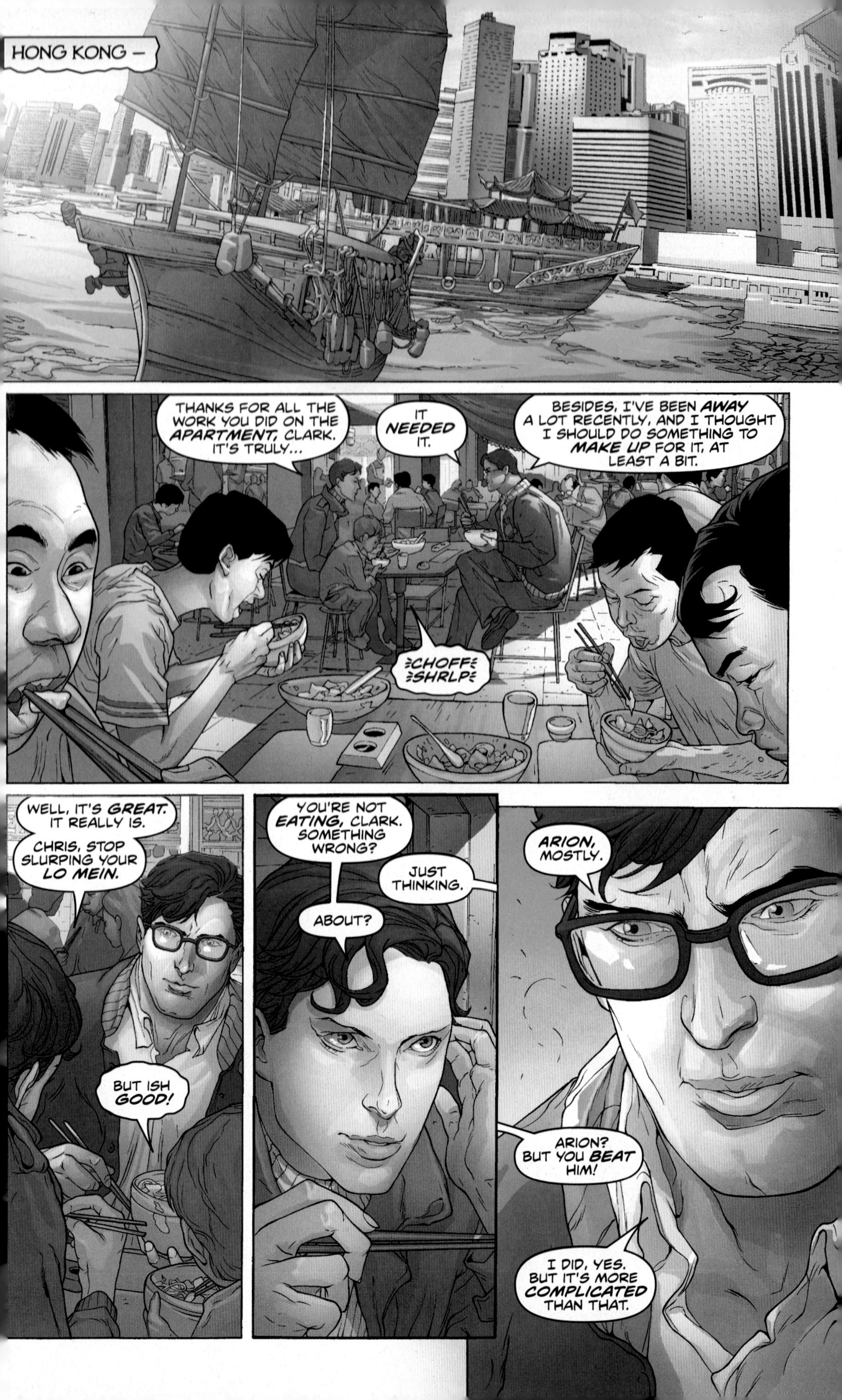

HONG KONG —
THANKS FOR ALL THE WORK YOU DID ON THE APARTMENT, CLARK. IT'S TRULY...
IT NEEDED IT.
BESIDES, I'VE BEEN AWAY A LOT RECENTLY, AND I THOUGHT I SHOULD DO SOMETHING TO MAKE UP FOR IT, AT LEAST A BIT.
CHOFF SHRLP
WELL, IT'S GREAT. IT REALLY IS.
CHRIS, STOP SLURPING YOUR LO MEIN.
BUT ISH GOOD!
YOU'RE NOT EATING, CLARK. SOMETHING WRONG?
JUST THINKING.
ABOUT?
ARION, MOSTLY.
ARION? BUT YOU BEAT HIM!
I DID, YES. BUT IT'S MORE COMPLICATED THAN THAT.

I BEAT HIM, BUT THE *THREAT* HE TALKED ABOUT -- A RISING DARKNESS THAT COULD WIPE AWAY CIVILIZATION, OR *HUMANITY ITSELF* -- IT DIDN'T GO AWAY.

BUT I'VE GOT SOME *IDEAS* ON THAT SCORE...

THE FORTRESS OF SOLITUDE --

Arion's a powerful sorcerer, and even defeated, I've got to take his warnings seriously. If there is a danger, we can fight against it...

...but being defiant isn't enough. We have to be prepared, as well.

Still, I have other things to do...

SERUM COMPOUND 7X-431K. TESTING...

IT WOULD *BOND* WITH THE LEAD IN YOUR SYSTEM. COAT IT, BLOCKING ITS *EFFECT* ON YOU. BUT AS SOON AS YOU CAME OUT OF THE ZONE...

...YOUR INVULNERABILITY WOULD *BREAK DOWN* THE SERUM, RELEASING THE LEAD. YOU'D BE WORSE OFF THAN *BEFORE.*

IT'S... OKAY.

I'M SURE YOU'LL COME U WITH A CURE *SOMEDAY.* I O WISH I COULD L MORE HELP.

WHAT DOES IT *SAY,* SUPERMAN?

NO GOOD. THIS ONE WON'T WORK *EITHER.*

Mon-El. Or at least, that's what I called him when we met, back when I was a teenager.

He's actually Lar Gand, from the planet Daxam — and lead is deadlier to him than Kryptonite is to me.

It'd have killed him by now, if we hadn't put him in the Phantom Zone...

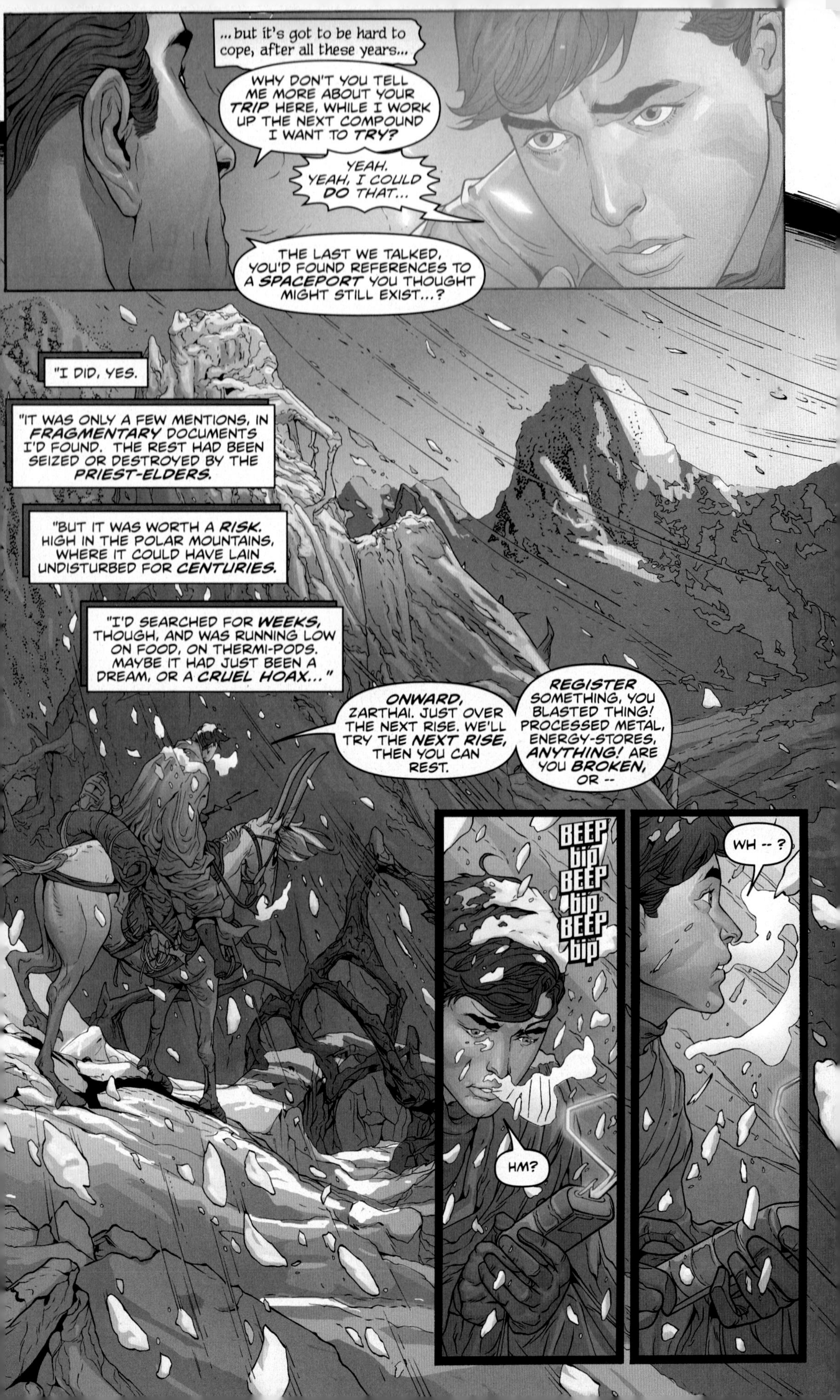
...but it's got to be hard to cope, after all these years...
WHY DON'T YOU TELL ME MORE ABOUT YOUR TRIP HERE, WHILE I WORK UP THE NEXT COMPOUND I WANT TO TRY?
YEAH. YEAH, I COULD DO THAT...
THE LAST WE TALKED, YOU'D FOUND REFERENCES TO A SPACEPORT YOU THOUGHT MIGHT STILL EXIST...?
"I DID, YES.
"IT WAS ONLY A FEW MENTIONS, IN FRAGMENTARY DOCUMENTS I'D FOUND. THE REST HAD BEEN SEIZED OR DESTROYED BY THE PRIEST-ELDERS.
"BUT IT WAS WORTH A RISK. HIGH IN THE POLAR MOUNTAINS, WHERE IT COULD HAVE LAIN UNDISTURBED FOR CENTURIES.
"I'D SEARCHED FOR WEEKS, THOUGH, AND WAS RUNNING LOW ON FOOD, ON THERMI-PODS. MAYBE IT HAD JUST BEEN A DREAM, OR A CRUEL HOAX..."
ONWARD, ZARTHAI. JUST OVER THE NEXT RISE. WE'LL TRY THE NEXT RISE, THEN YOU CAN REST.
REGISTER SOMETHING, YOU BLASTED THING! PROCESSED METAL, ENERGY-STORES, ANYTHING! ARE YOU BROKEN, OR --
BEEP bip BEEP bip BEEP bip
HM?
WH -- ?

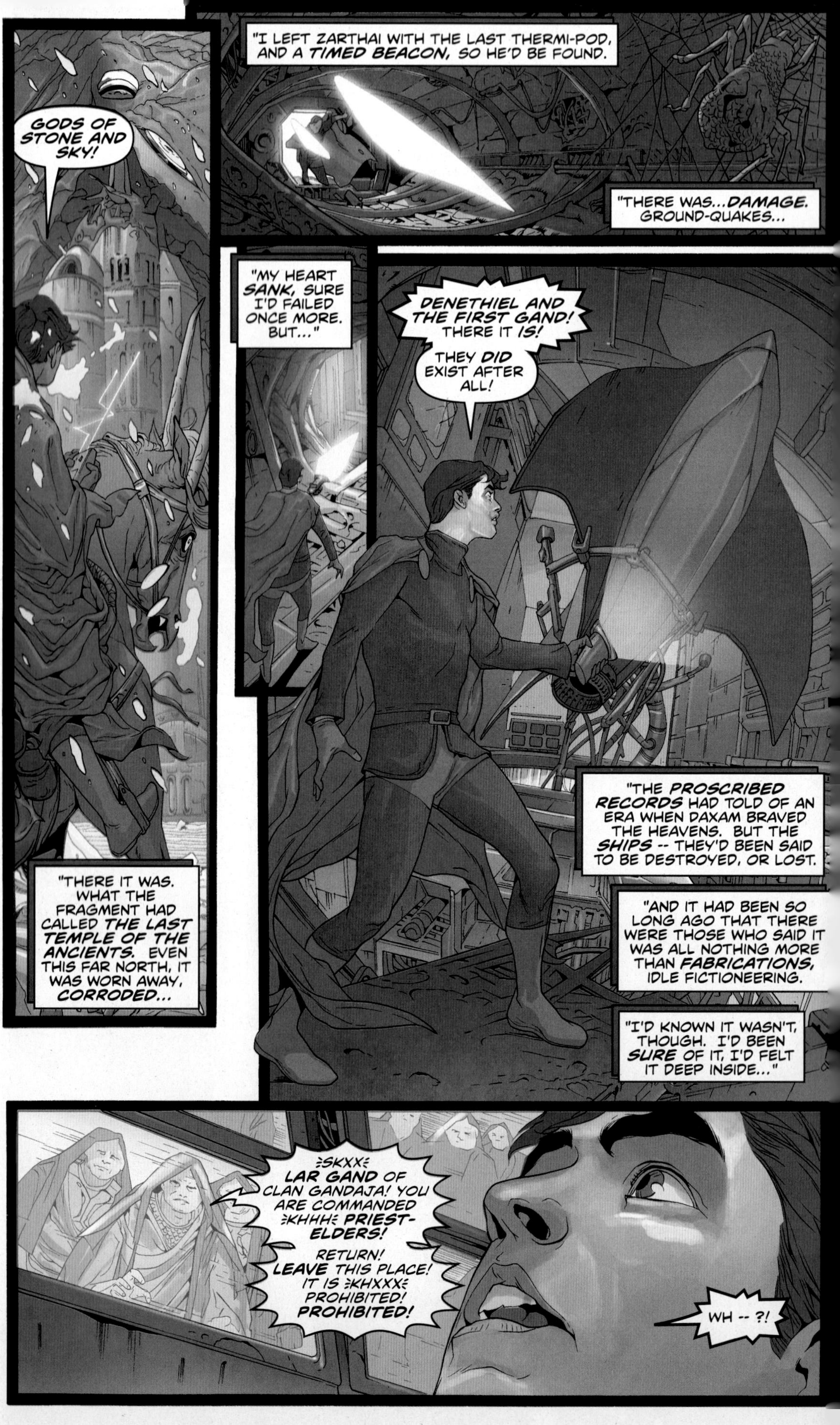
GODS OF STONE AND SKY!
"I LEFT ZARTHAI WITH THE LAST THERMI-POD, AND A TIMED BEACON, SO HE'D BE FOUND.
"THERE WAS...DAMAGE. GROUND-QUAKES...
"THERE IT WAS. WHAT THE FRAGMENT HAD CALLED THE LAST TEMPLE OF THE ANCIENTS. EVEN THIS FAR NORTH, IT WAS WORN AWAY, CORRODED...
"MY HEART SANK, SURE I'D FAILED ONCE MORE. BUT..."
DENETHIEL AND THE FIRST GAND! THERE IT IS!
THEY DID EXIST AFTER ALL!
"THE PROSCRIBED RECORDS HAD TOLD OF AN ERA WHEN DAXAM BRAVED THE HEAVENS. BUT THE SHIPS -- THEY'D BEEN SAID TO BE DESTROYED, OR LOST.
"AND IT HAD BEEN SO LONG AGO THAT THERE WERE THOSE WHO SAID IT WAS ALL NOTHING MORE THAN FABRICATIONS, IDLE FICTIONEERING.
"I'D KNOWN IT WASN'T, THOUGH. I'D BEEN SURE OF IT, I'D FELT IT DEEP INSIDE..."
SKXX LAR GAND OF CLAN GANDAJA! YOU ARE COMMANDED KHHH PRIEST-ELDERS!
RETURN! LEAVE THIS PLACE! IT IS KHXX PROHIBITED! PROHIBITED!
WH -- ?!

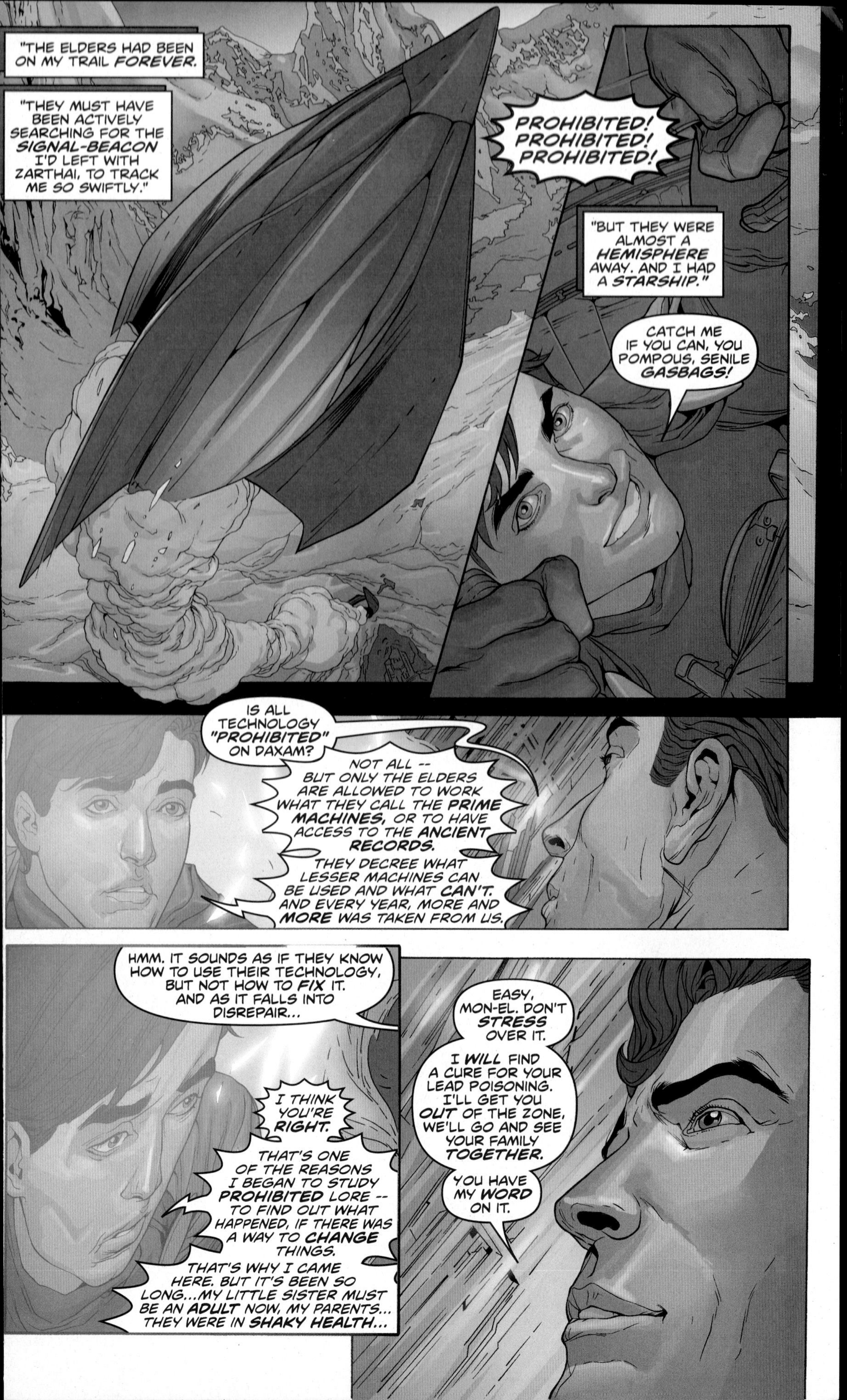
"THE ELDERS HAD BEEN ON MY TRAIL FOREVER.
"THEY MUST HAVE BEEN ACTIVELY SEARCHING FOR THE SIGNAL-BEACON I'D LEFT WITH ZARTHAI, TO TRACK ME SO SWIFTLY."
PROHIBITED! PROHIBITED! PROHIBITED!
"BUT THEY WERE ALMOST A HEMISPHERE AWAY. AND I HAD A STARSHIP."
CATCH ME IF YOU CAN, YOU POMPOUS, SENILE GASBAGS!
IS ALL TECHNOLOGY "PROHIBITED" ON DAXAM?
NOT ALL -- BUT ONLY THE ELDERS ARE ALLOWED TO WORK WHAT THEY CALL THE PRIME MACHINES, OR TO HAVE ACCESS TO THE ANCIENT RECORDS.
THEY DECREE WHAT LESSER MACHINES CAN BE USED AND WHAT CAN'T. AND EVERY YEAR, MORE AND MORE WAS TAKEN FROM US.
HMM. IT SOUNDS AS IF THEY KNOW HOW TO USE THEIR TECHNOLOGY, BUT NOT HOW TO FIX IT. AND AS IT FALLS INTO DISREPAIR...
I THINK YOU'RE RIGHT.
THAT'S ONE OF THE REASONS I BEGAN TO STUDY PROHIBITED LORE -- TO FIND OUT WHAT HAPPENED, IF THERE WAS A WAY TO CHANGE THINGS.
THAT'S WHY I CAME HERE. BUT IT'S BEEN SO LONG...MY LITTLE SISTER MUST BE AN ADULT NOW, MY PARENTS... THEY WERE IN SHAKY HEALTH...
EASY, MON-EL. DON'T STRESS OVER IT.
I WILL FIND A CURE FOR YOUR LEAD POISONING. I'LL GET YOU OUT OF THE ZONE, WE'LL GO AND SEE YOUR FAMILY TOGETHER.
YOU HAVE MY WORD ON IT.

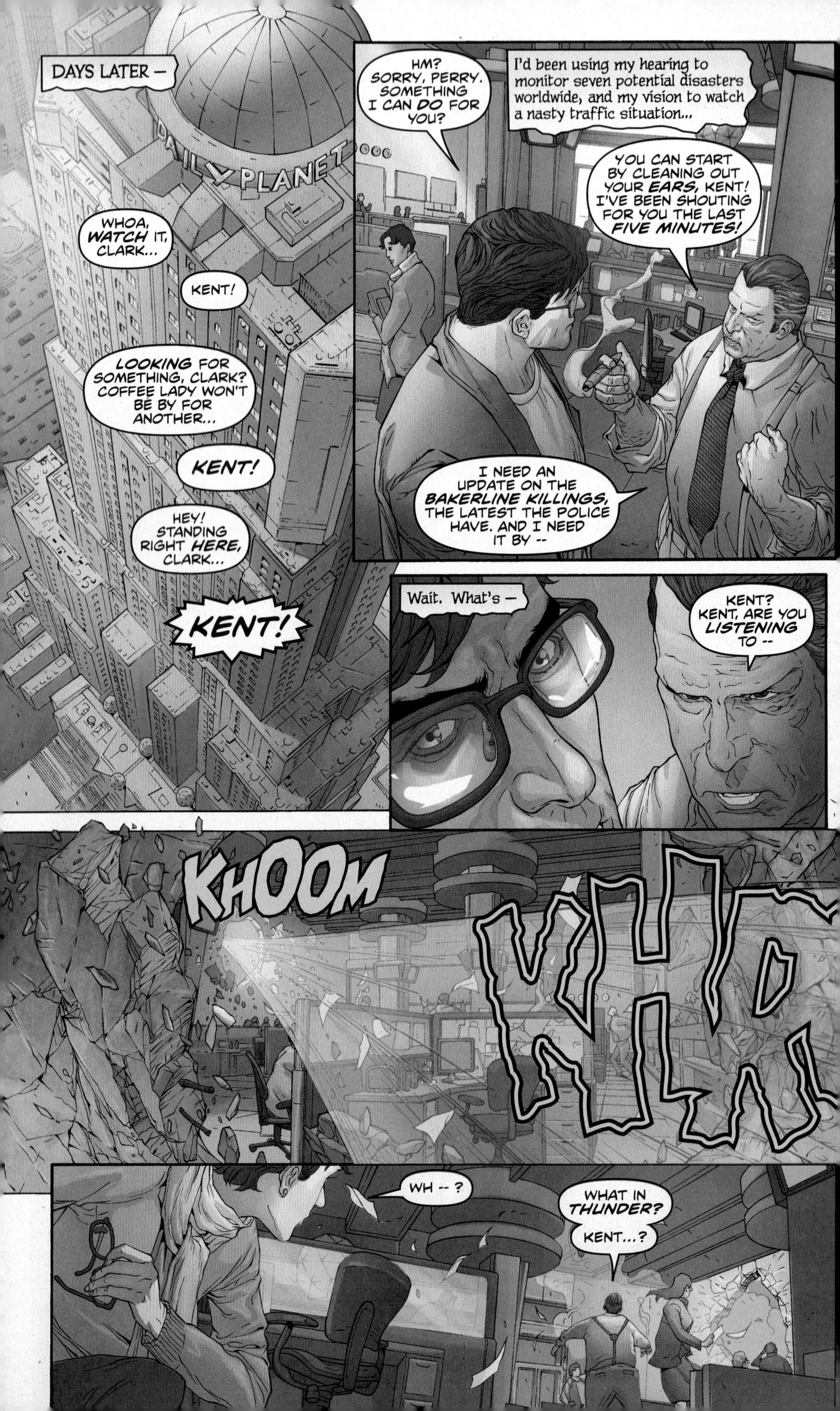
DAYS LATER —
WHOA, WATCH IT, CLARK...
KENT!
LOOKING FOR SOMETHING, CLARK? COFFEE LADY WON'T BE BY FOR ANOTHER...
KENT!
HEY! STANDING RIGHT HERE, CLARK...
KENT!
HM? SORRY, PERRY. SOMETHING I CAN DO FOR YOU?
I'd been using my hearing to monitor seven potential disasters worldwide, and my vision to watch a nasty traffic situation...
YOU CAN START BY CLEANING OUT YOUR EARS, KENT! I'VE BEEN SHOUTING FOR YOU THE LAST FIVE MINUTES!
I NEED AN UPDATE ON THE BAKERLINE KILLINGS, THE LATEST THE POLICE HAVE. AND I NEED IT BY --
Wait. What's —
KENT? KENT, ARE YOU LISTENING TO --
KHOOM
WH -- ?
WHAT IN THUNDER?
KENT...?

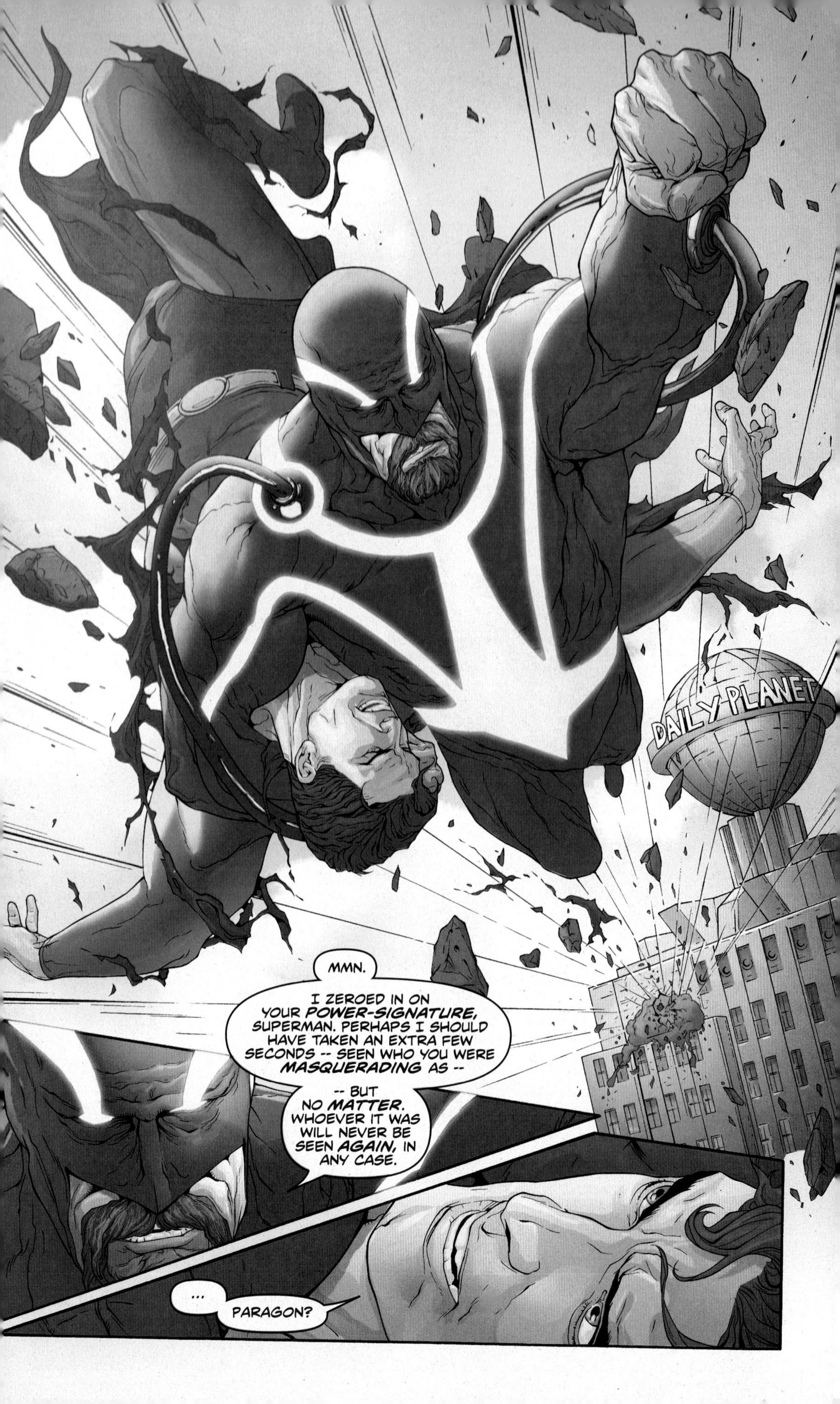

DAILY PLANET
MMN.
I ZEROED IN ON YOUR POWER-SIGNATURE, SUPERMAN. PERHAPS I SHOULD HAVE TAKEN AN EXTRA FEW SECONDS -- SEEN WHO YOU WERE MASQUERADING AS --
-- BUT NO MATTER. WHOEVER IT WAS WILL NEVER BE SEEN AGAIN, IN ANY CASE.
...
PARAGON?

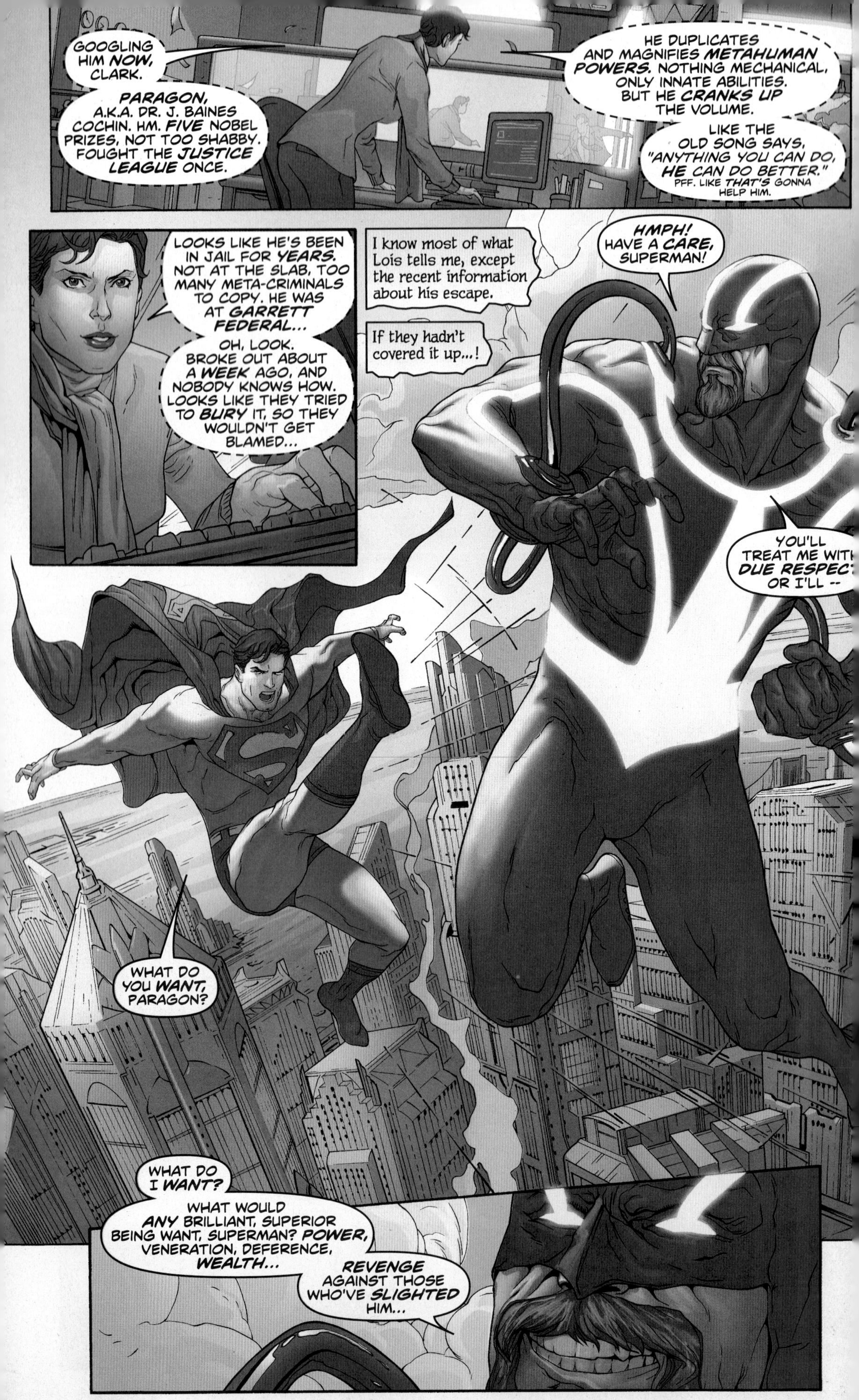
GOOGLING HIM NOW, CLARK.
PARAGON, A.K.A. DR. J. BAINES COCHIN. HM. FIVE NOBEL PRIZES, NOT TOO SHABBY. FOUGHT THE JUSTICE LEAGUE ONCE.
HE DUPLICATES AND MAGNIFIES METAHUMAN POWERS. NOTHING MECHANICAL, ONLY INNATE ABILITIES. BUT HE CRANKS UP THE VOLUME.
LIKE THE OLD SONG SAYS, "ANYTHING YOU CAN DO, HE CAN DO BETTER." PFF. LIKE THAT'S GONNA HELP HIM.
LOOKS LIKE HE'S BEEN IN JAIL FOR YEARS. NOT AT THE SLAB, TOO MANY META-CRIMINALS TO COPY. HE WAS AT GARRETT FEDERAL...
OH, LOOK. BROKE OUT ABOUT A WEEK AGO, AND NOBODY KNOWS HOW. LOOKS LIKE THEY TRIED TO BURY IT, SO THEY WOULDN'T GET BLAMED...
I know most of what Lois tells me, except the recent information about his escape.
If they hadn't covered it up...!
HMPH! HAVE A CARE, SUPERMAN!
YOU'LL TREAT ME WITH DUE RESPECT OR I'LL --
WHAT DO YOU WANT, PARAGON?
WHAT DO I WANT?
WHAT WOULD ANY BRILLIANT, SUPERIOR BEING WANT, SUPERMAN? POWER, VENERATION, DEFERENCE, WEALTH...
REVENGE AGAINST THOSE WHO'VE SLIGHTED HIM...

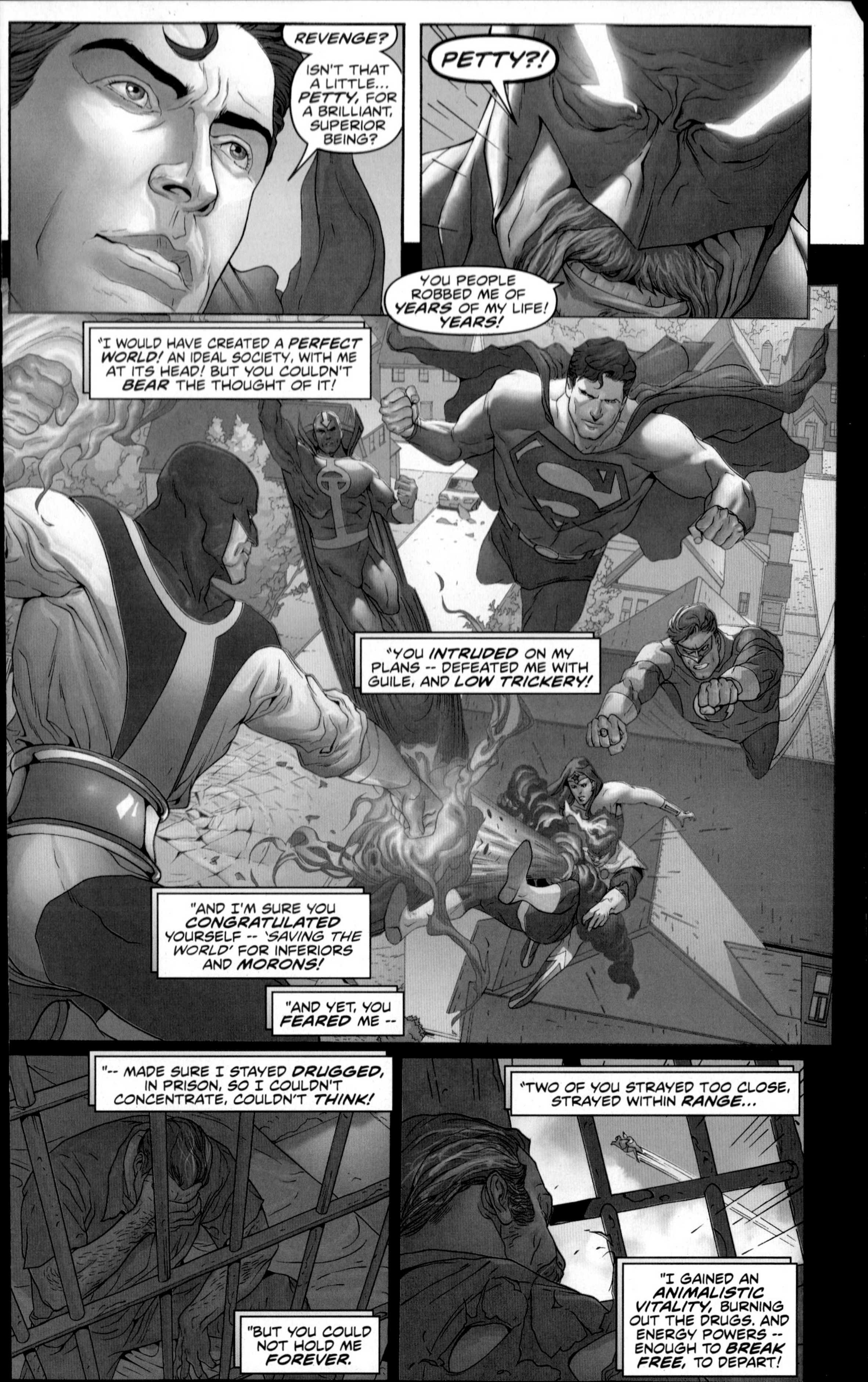
REVENGE?
ISN'T THAT A LITTLE... PETTY, FOR A BRILLIANT, SUPERIOR BEING?
PETTY?!
YOU PEOPLE ROBBED ME OF YEARS OF MY LIFE! YEARS!
"I WOULD HAVE CREATED A PERFECT WORLD! AN IDEAL SOCIETY, WITH ME AT ITS HEAD! BUT YOU COULDN'T BEAR THE THOUGHT OF IT!
"YOU INTRUDED ON MY PLANS -- DEFEATED ME WITH GUILE, AND LOW TRICKERY!
"AND I'M SURE YOU CONGRATULATED YOURSELF -- 'SAVING THE WORLD' FOR INFERIORS AND MORONS!
"AND YET, YOU FEARED ME --
"-- MADE SURE I STAYED DRUGGED, IN PRISON, SO I COULDN'T CONCENTRATE, COULDN'T THINK!
"BUT YOU COULD NOT HOLD ME FOREVER.
"TWO OF YOU STRAYED TOO CLOSE, STRAYED WITHIN RANGE...
"I GAINED AN ANIMALISTIC VITALITY, BURNING OUT THE DRUGS. AND ENERGY POWERS -- ENOUGH TO BREAK FREE, TO DEPART!

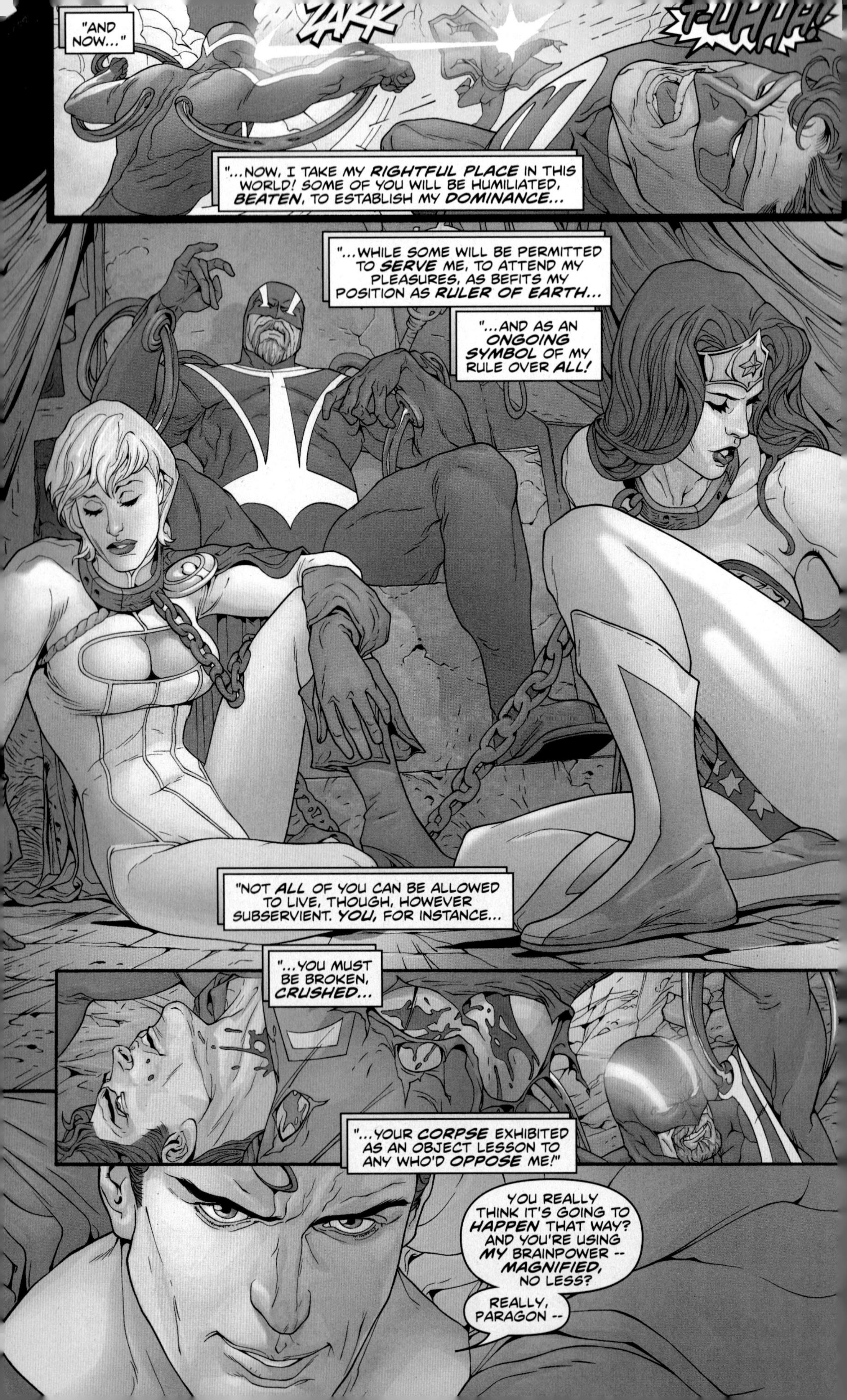
"AND NOW..."
ZAKK
T-UHHH!
"...NOW, I TAKE MY RIGHTFUL PLACE IN THIS WORLD! SOME OF YOU WILL BE HUMILIATED, BEATEN, TO ESTABLISH MY DOMINANCE...
"...WHILE SOME WILL BE PERMITTED TO SERVE ME, TO ATTEND MY PLEASURES, AS BEFITS MY POSITION AS RULER OF EARTH...
"...AND AS AN ONGOING SYMBOL OF MY RULE OVER ALL!
"NOT ALL OF YOU CAN BE ALLOWED TO LIVE, THOUGH, HOWEVER SUBSERVIENT. YOU, FOR INSTANCE...
"...YOU MUST BE BROKEN, CRUSHED...
"...YOUR CORPSE EXHIBITED AS AN OBJECT LESSON TO ANY WHO'D OPPOSE ME!"
YOU REALLY THINK IT'S GOING TO HAPPEN THAT WAY? AND YOU'RE USING MY BRAINPOWER -- MAGNIFIED, NO LESS?
REALLY, PARAGON --

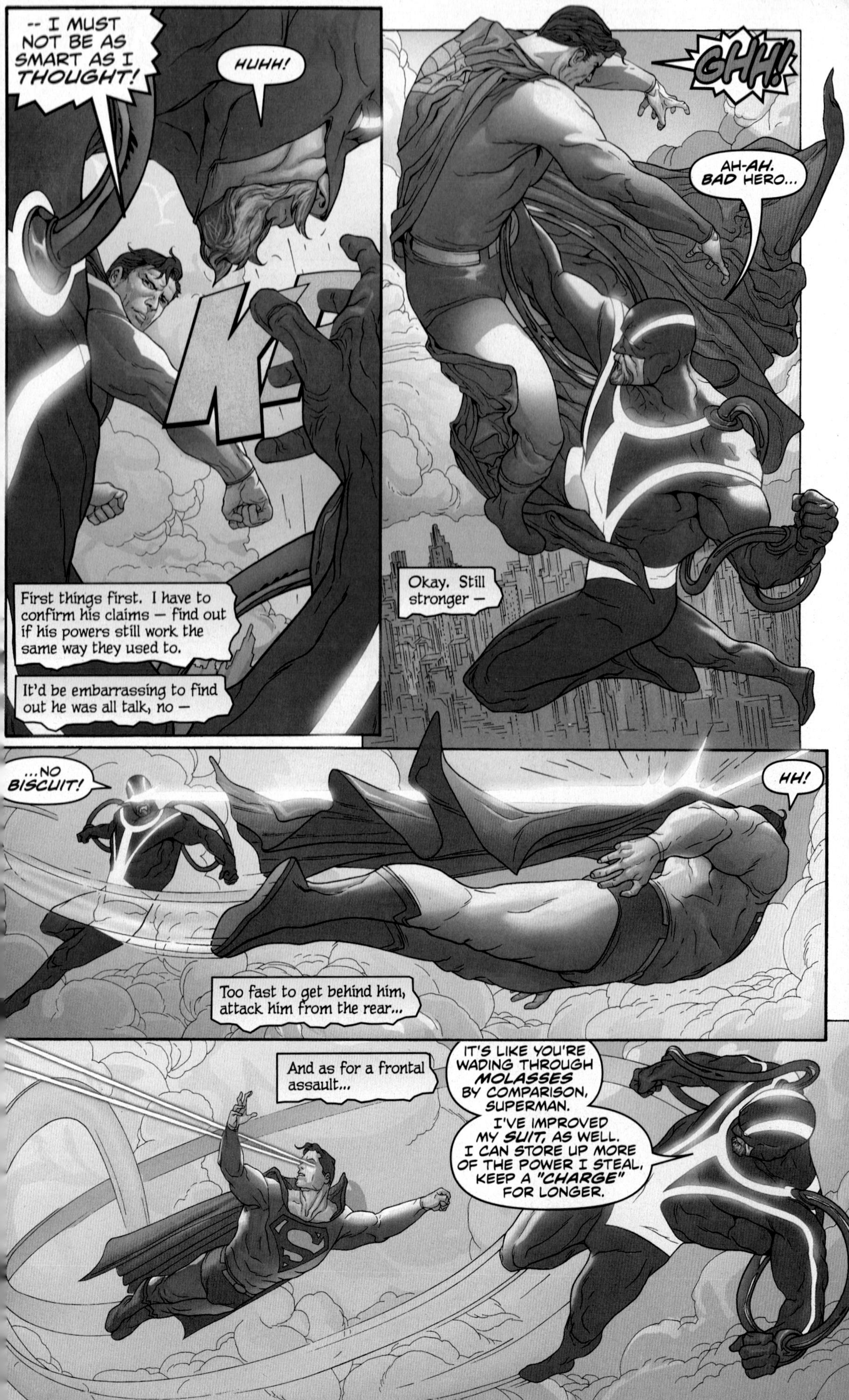
-- I MUST NOT BE AS SMART AS I THOUGHT!
HUHH!
First things first. I have to confirm his claims — find out if his powers still work the same way they used to.
It'd be embarrassing to find out he was all talk, no —
GHH!
AH-AH. BAD HERO...
Okay. Still stronger —
...NO BISCUIT!
HH!
Too fast to get behind him, attack him from the rear...
And as for a frontal assault...
IT'S LIKE YOU'RE WADING THROUGH MOLASSES BY COMPARISON, SUPERMAN.
I'VE IMPROVED MY SUIT, AS WELL. I CAN STORE UP MORE OF THE POWER I STEAL, KEEP A "CHARGE" FOR LONGER.

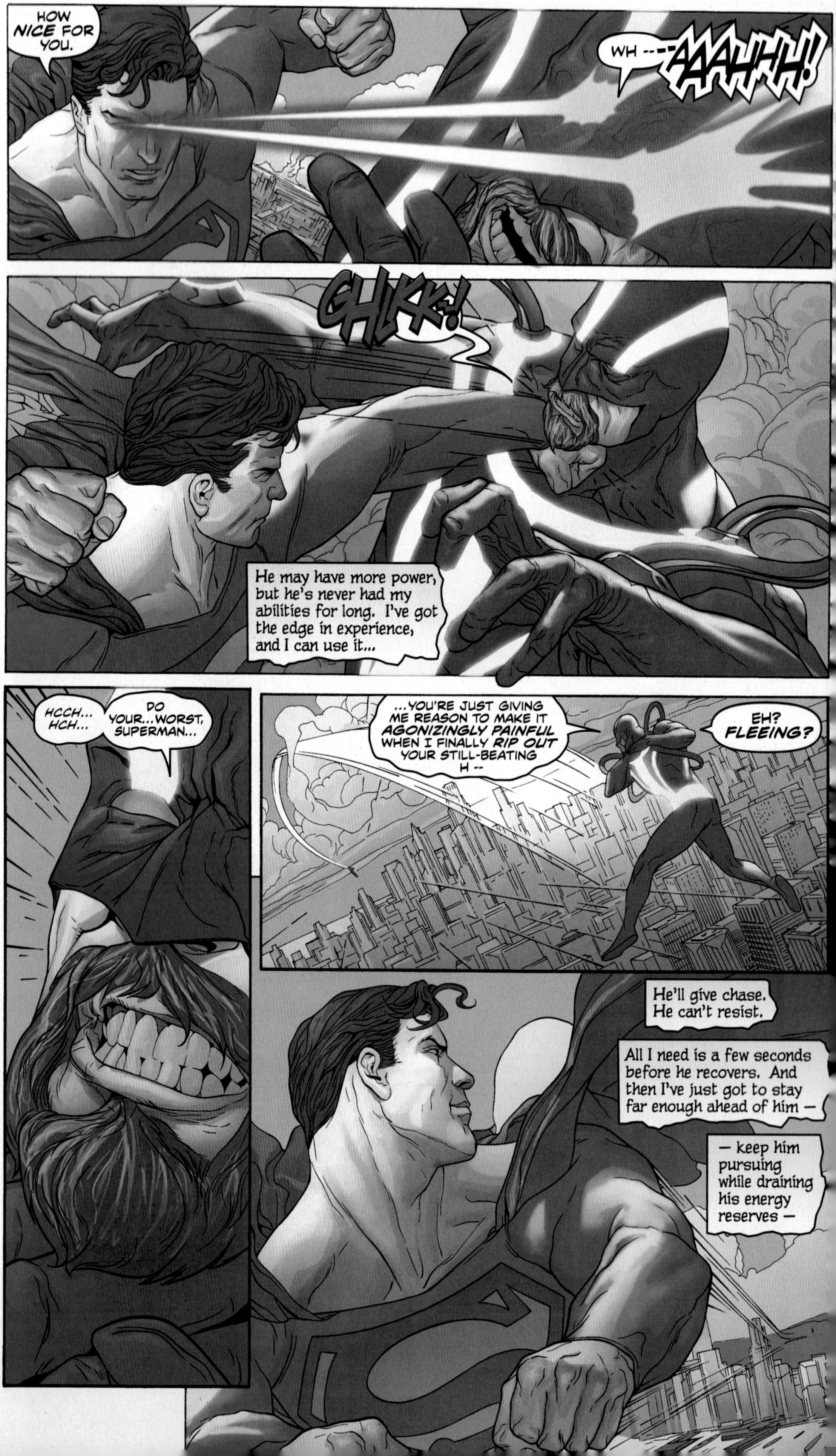
HOW NICE FOR YOU.
WH -- -AAAHHH!
GHKK!
He may have more power, but he's never had my abilities for long. I've got the edge in experience, and I can use it...
HCCH... HCH...
DO YOUR...WORST, SUPERMAN...
...YOU'RE JUST GIVING ME REASON TO MAKE IT AGONIZINGLY PAINFUL WHEN I FINALLY RIP OUT YOUR STILL-BEATING H --
EH? FLEEING?
He'll give chase. He can't resist.
All I need is a few seconds before he recovers. And then I've just got to stay far enough ahead of him —
— keep him pursuing while draining his energy reserves —

SUPERMAN! YOU CAN'T *ESCAPE* ME, YOU COWARDLY --

I'M NOT *TRYING* TO.

TAKE A LOOK AT WHAT I HAVE IN MY *RIGHT HAND*. A GOOD LOOK. USE YOUR X-RAY VISION. ANALYZE THE COMPONENTS WITH MY *STOLEN BRAINPOWER*.

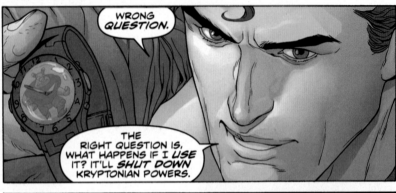

WRONG QUESTION.

THE RIGHT QUESTION IS, WHAT HAPPENS IF I *USE* IT? IT'LL *SHUT DOWN* KRYPTONIAN POWERS.

IT WON'T SHUT *ME* DOWN.

I'M DRAWING MY POWERS FROM *YOU*, NOT FROM SOLAR ENERGY. AS LONG AS *YOU'RE* HERE --

IT'S...A *RED-SUN GENERATOR?* IN A CHILD'S *WATCH?*

WHY WOULD YOU *BUILD* SUCH A --

AND WHAT HAPPENS TO YOU, ALONE IN THE ARCTIC, IF I USE IT ON *MYSELF?*

IF YOU...?

NOT ENOUGH STORED ENERGY TO MAKE IT TO *CIVILIZATION*... WE'D BOTH BE POWERLESS...

I COULD *DIE* BEFORE...

AH.

GO AHEAD, SUPERMAN. *USE* THE WATCH. SHUT DOWN YOUR POWERS, FALL TO YOUR *CERTAIN DEATH*. DON'T WORRY ABOUT *ME*...

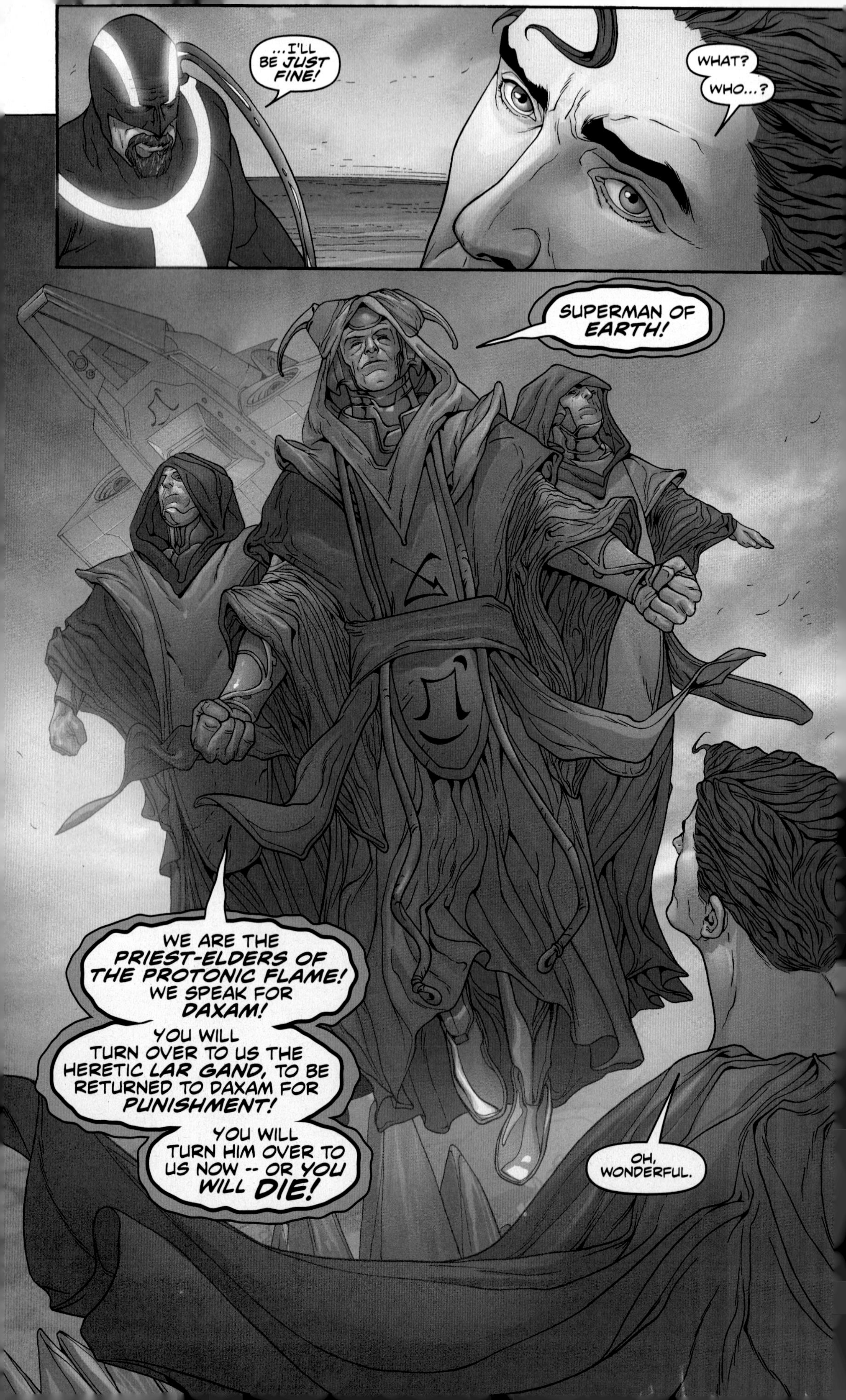
...I'LL BE JUST FINE!
WHAT?
WHO...?
SUPERMAN OF EARTH!
WE ARE THE PRIEST-ELDERS OF THE PROTONIC FLAME! WE SPEAK FOR DAXAM!
YOU WILL TURN OVER TO US THE HERETIC LAR GAND, TO BE RETURNED TO DAXAM FOR PUNISHMENT!
YOU WILL TURN HIM OVER TO US NOW -- OR YOU WILL DIE!
OH, WONDERFUL.

COVER ART BY ALEX ROSS

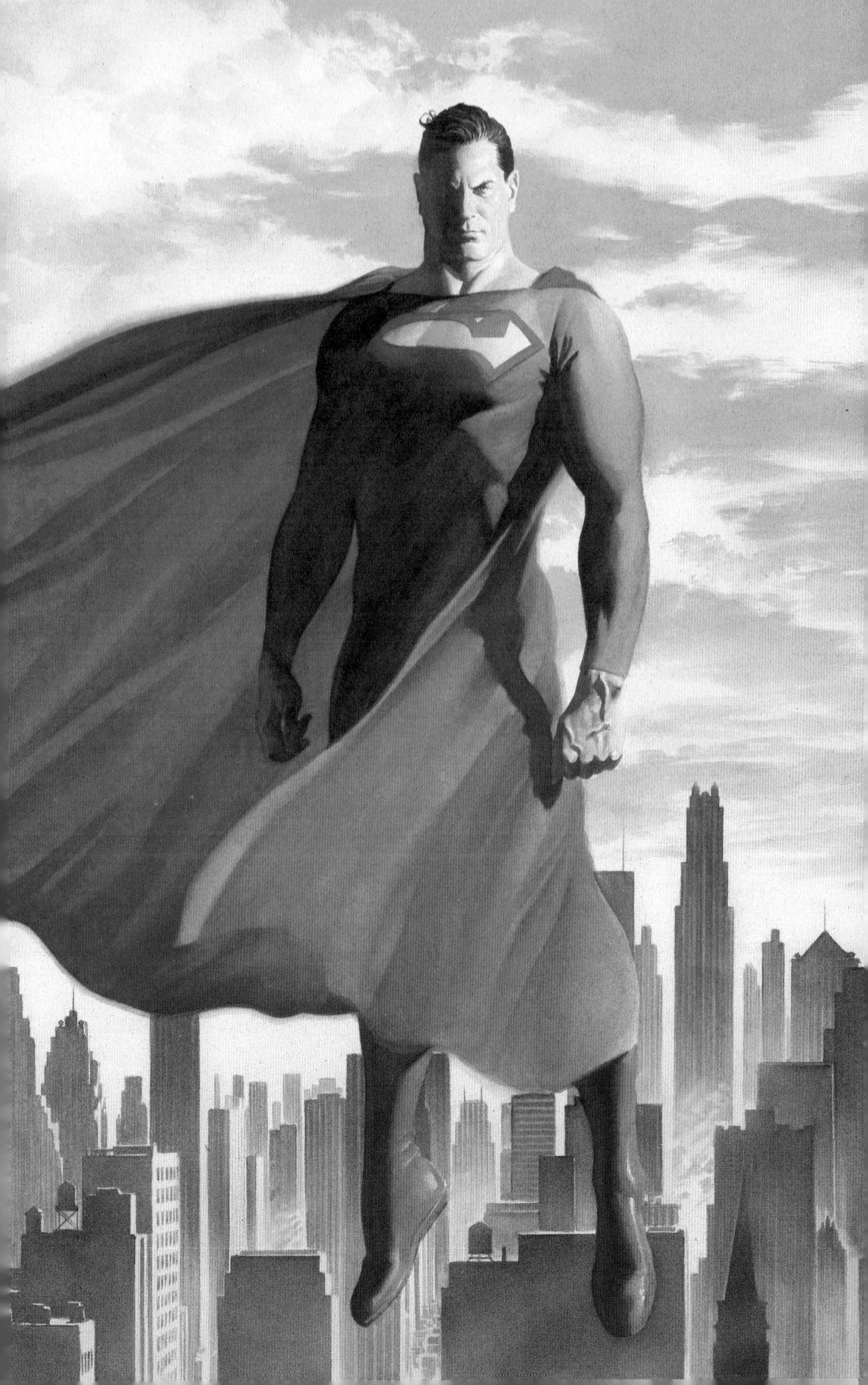

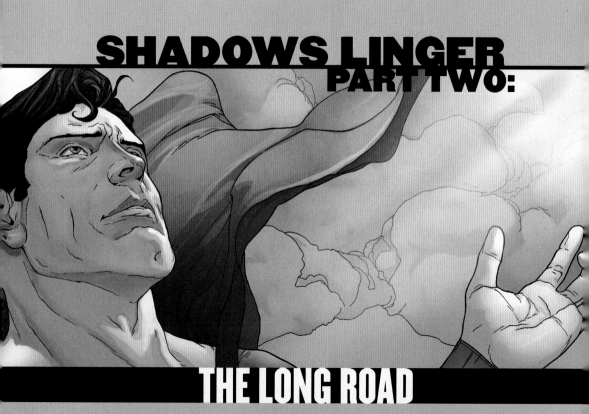

SHADOWS LINGER
PART TWO:

THE LONG ROAD

ART BY **RENATO GUEDES** & **JOSÉ WILSON MAGALHÁES** (PAGES 103-122, 133-140)
AND **JORGÉ CORREA JR.** (PAGES 123-132) COLORS BY **DAVID CURIEL**

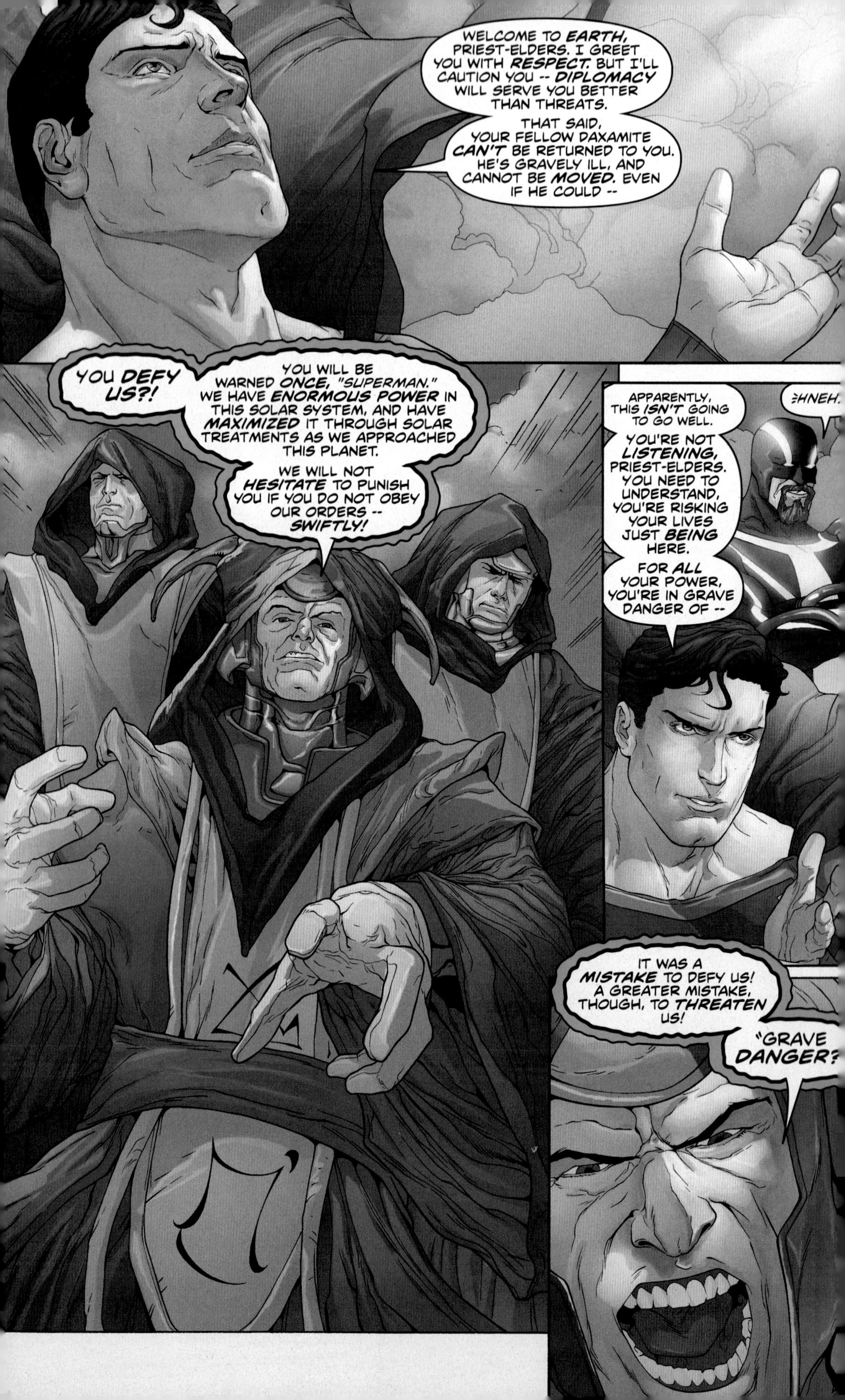
WELCOME TO EARTH, PRIEST-ELDERS. I GREET YOU WITH RESPECT. BUT I'LL CAUTION YOU -- DIPLOMACY WILL SERVE YOU BETTER THAN THREATS.
THAT SAID, YOUR FELLOW DAXAMITE CAN'T BE RETURNED TO YOU. HE'S GRAVELY ILL, AND CANNOT BE MOVED. EVEN IF HE COULD --
YOU DEFY US?!
YOU WILL BE WARNED ONCE, "SUPERMAN." WE HAVE ENORMOUS POWER IN THIS SOLAR SYSTEM, AND HAVE MAXIMIZED IT THROUGH SOLAR TREATMENTS AS WE APPROACHED THIS PLANET.
WE WILL NOT HESITATE TO PUNISH YOU IF YOU DO NOT OBEY OUR ORDERS -- SWIFTLY!
APPARENTLY, THIS ISN'T GOING TO GO WELL.
YOU'RE NOT LISTENING, PRIEST-ELDERS. YOU NEED TO UNDERSTAND, YOU'RE RISKING YOUR LIVES JUST BEING HERE.
FOR ALL YOUR POWER, YOU'RE IN GRAVE DANGER OF --
IT WAS A MISTAKE TO DEFY US! A GREATER MISTAKE, THOUGH, TO THREATEN US!
"GRAVE DANGER?

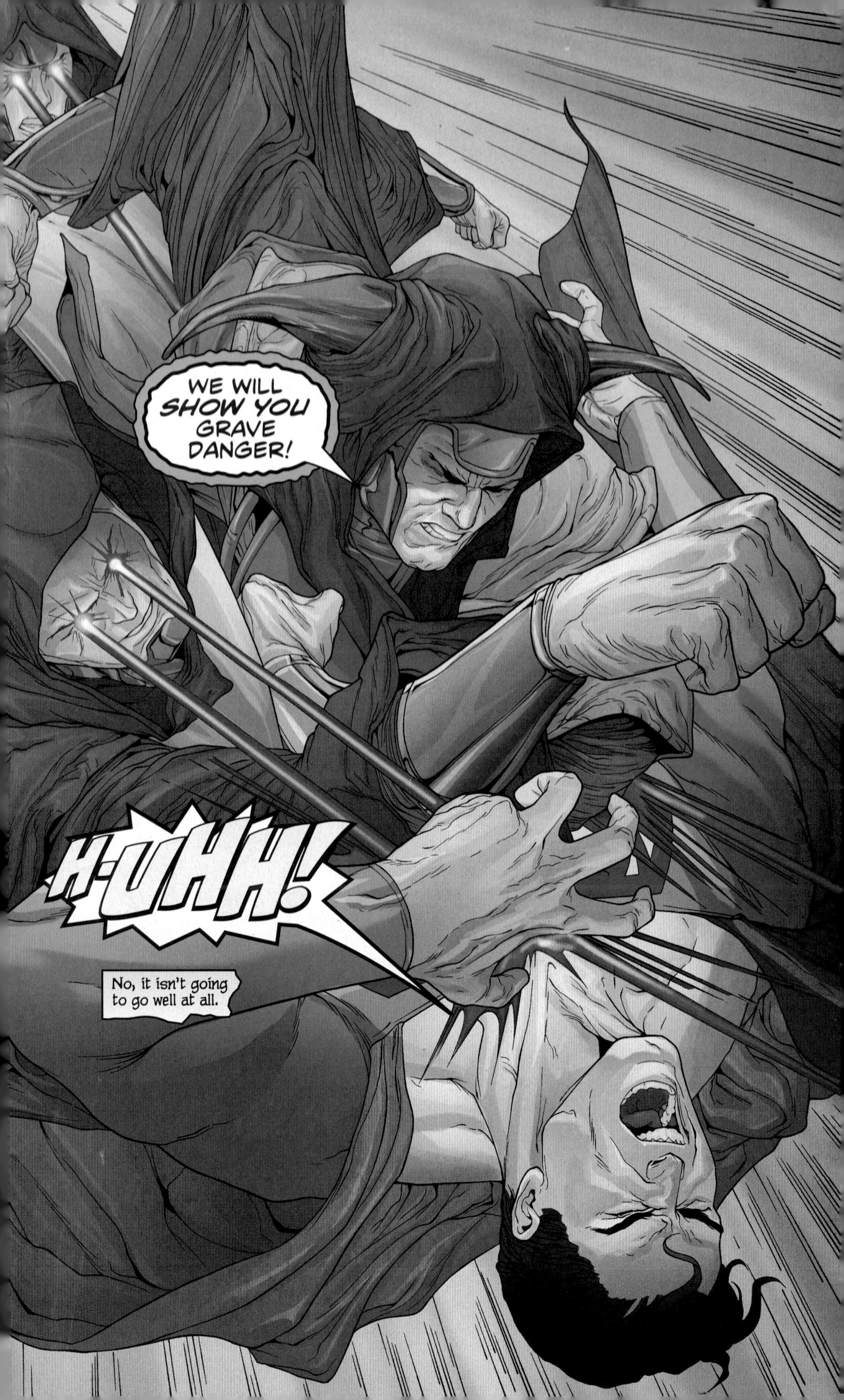
WE WILL SHOW YOU GRAVE DANGER!
H-UHH!
No, it isn't going to go well at all.

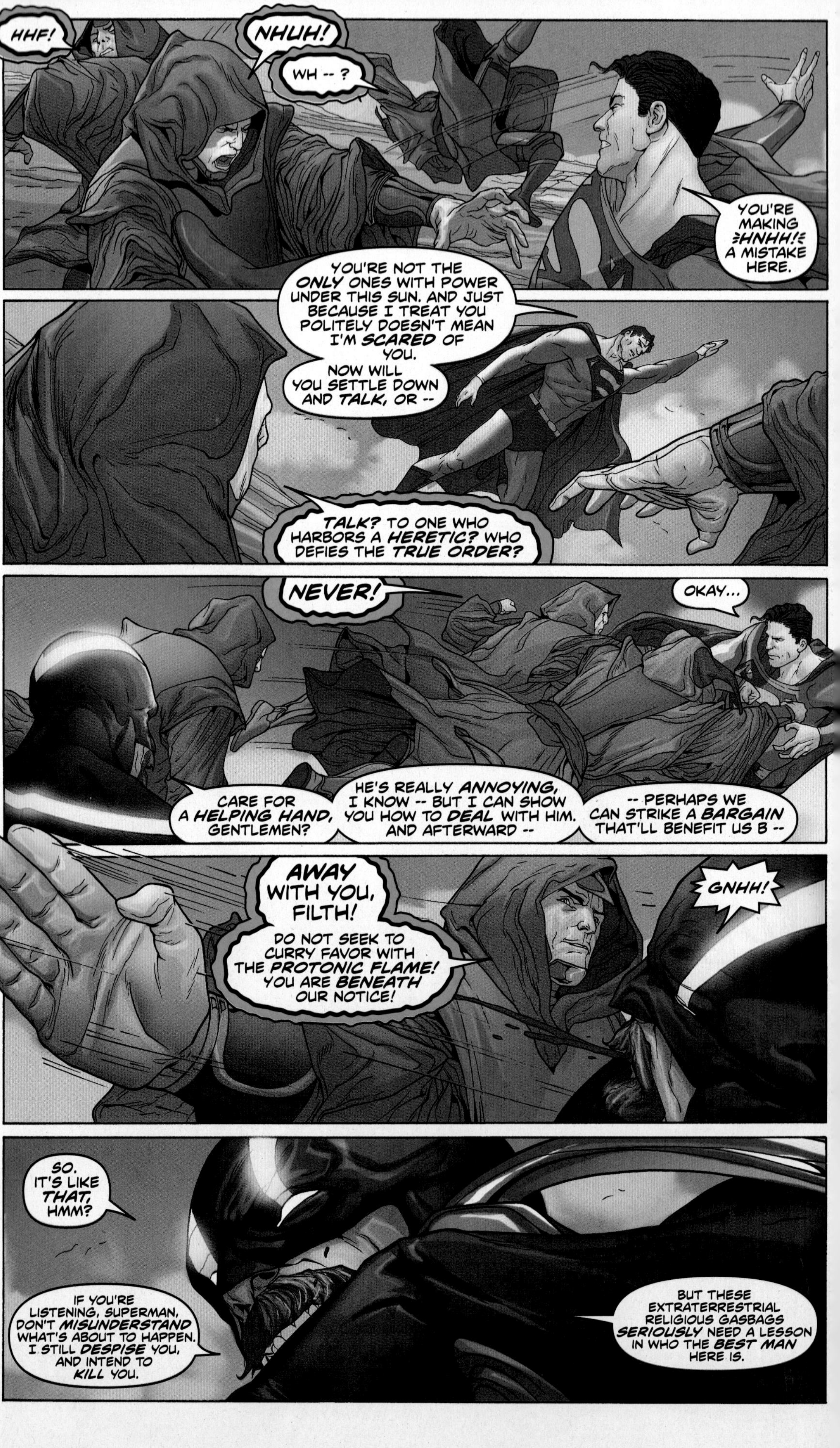
HHF!
NHUH!
WH -- ?
YOU'RE MAKING HNHH! A MISTAKE HERE.
YOU'RE NOT THE ONLY ONES WITH POWER UNDER THIS SUN. AND JUST BECAUSE I TREAT YOU POLITELY DOESN'T MEAN I'M SCARED OF YOU.
NOW WILL YOU SETTLE DOWN AND TALK, OR --
TALK? TO ONE WHO HARBORS A HERETIC? WHO DEFIES THE TRUE ORDER?
NEVER!
OKAY...
CARE FOR A HELPING HAND, GENTLEMEN?
HE'S REALLY ANNOYING, I KNOW -- BUT I CAN SHOW YOU HOW TO DEAL WITH HIM. AND AFTERWARD --
-- PERHAPS WE CAN STRIKE A BARGAIN THAT'LL BENEFIT US B --
AWAY WITH YOU, FILTH!
DO NOT SEEK TO CURRY FAVOR WITH THE PROTONIC FLAME! YOU ARE BENEATH OUR NOTICE!
GNHH!
SO. IT'S LIKE THAT, HMM?
IF YOU'RE LISTENING, SUPERMAN, DON'T MISUNDERSTAND WHAT'S ABOUT TO HAPPEN. I STILL DESPISE YOU, AND INTEND TO KILL YOU.
BUT THESE EXTRATERRESTRIAL RELIGIOUS GASBAGS SERIOUSLY NEED A LESSON IN WHO THE BEST MAN HERE IS.

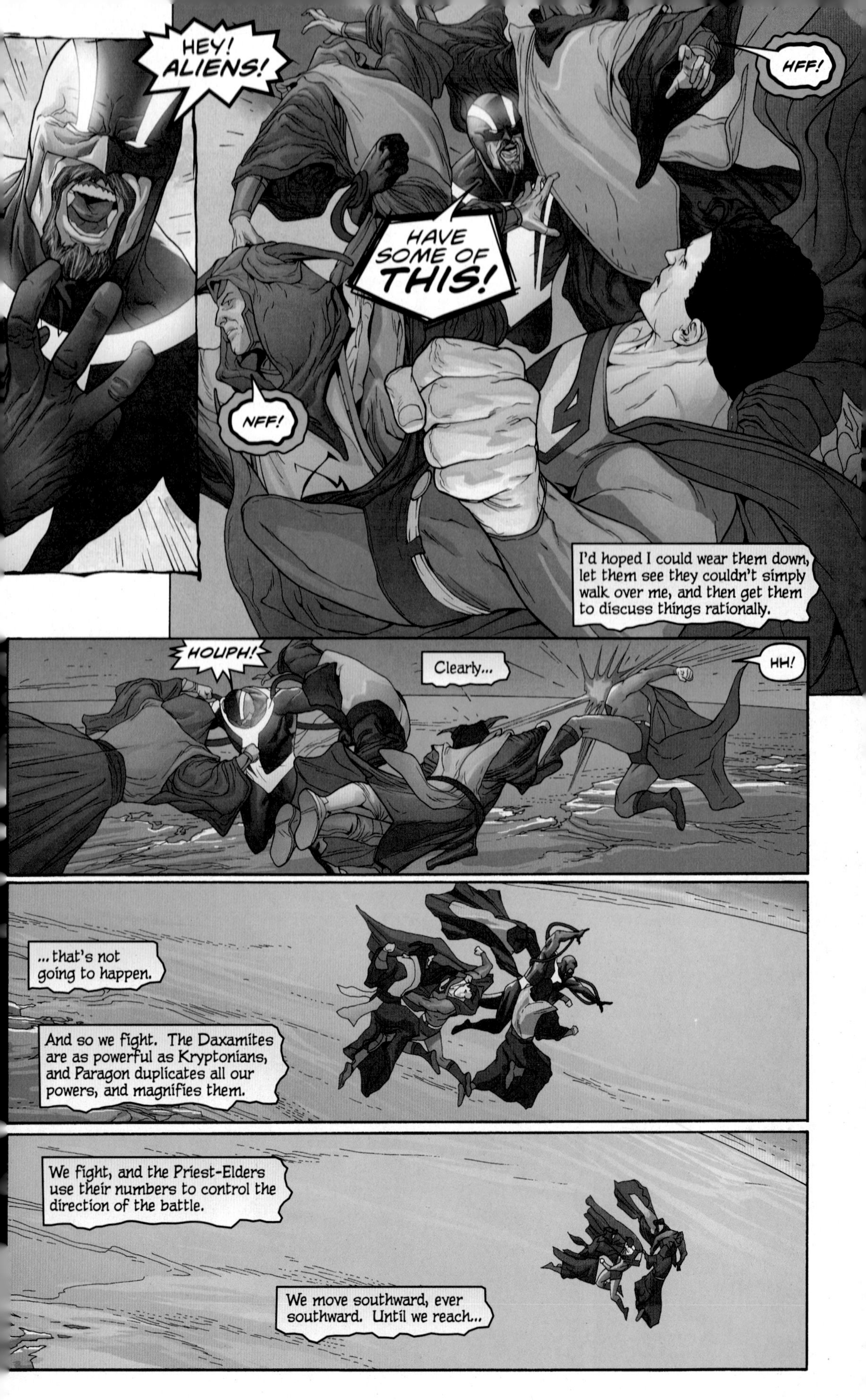
HEY! ALIENS!
HFF!
HAVE SOME OF THIS!
NFF!
I'd hoped I could wear them down, let them see they couldn't simply walk over me, and then get them to discuss things rationally.
HOUPH!
Clearly...
HH!
...that's not going to happen.
And so we fight. The Daxamites are as powerful as Kryptonians, and Paragon duplicates all our powers, and magnifies them.
We fight, and the Priest-Elders use their numbers to control the direction of the battle.
We move southward, ever southward. Until we reach...

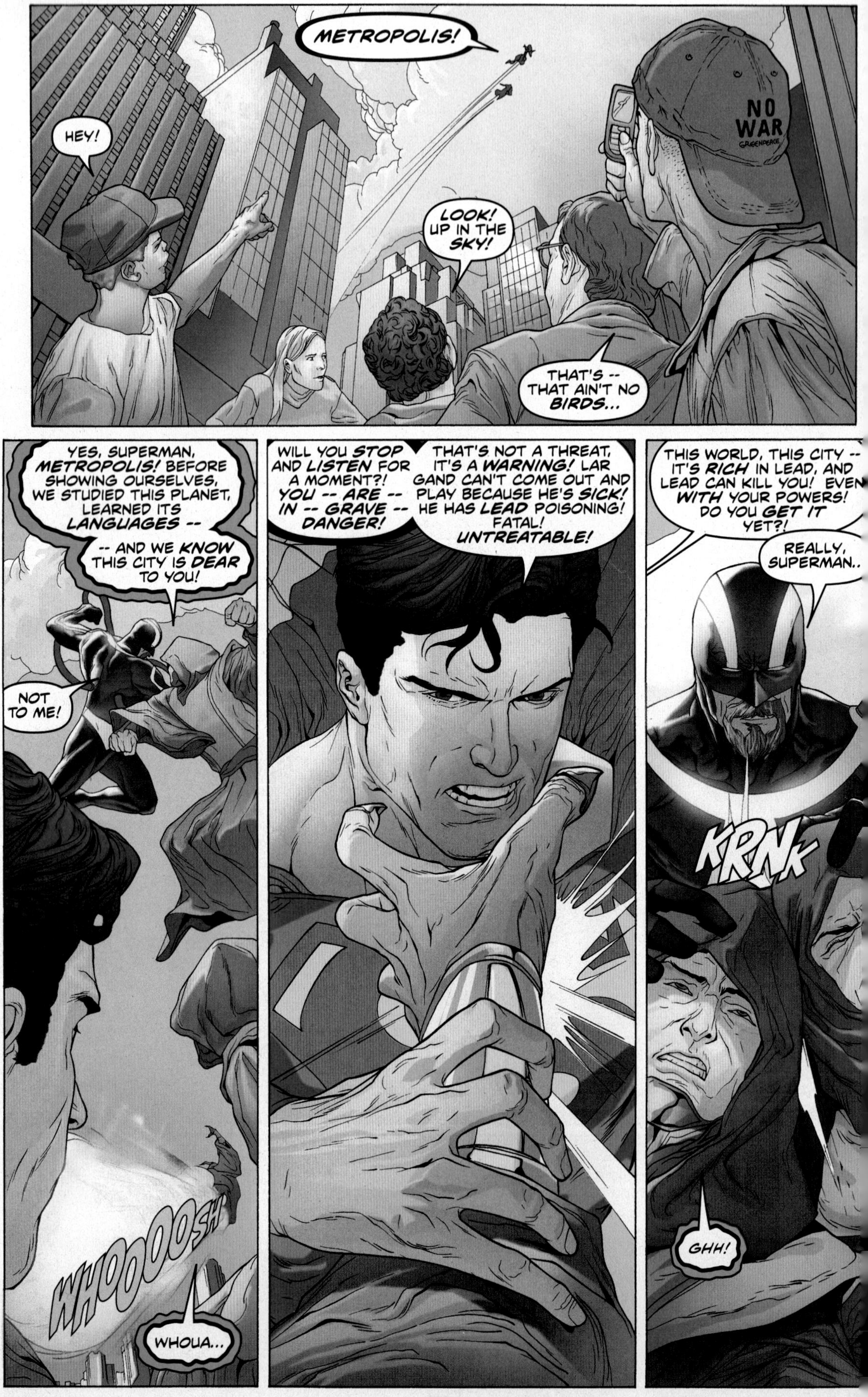
METROPOLIS!
HEY!
LOOK! UP IN THE SKY!
NO WAR GREENPEACE
THAT'S -- THAT AIN'T NO BIRDS...
YES, SUPERMAN, METROPOLIS! BEFORE SHOWING OURSELVES, WE STUDIED THIS PLANET, LEARNED ITS LANGUAGES --
-- AND WE KNOW THIS CITY IS DEAR TO YOU!
NOT TO ME!
WHOOOOSH
WHOUA...
WILL YOU STOP AND LISTEN FOR A MOMENT?! YOU -- ARE -- IN -- GRAVE -- DANGER!
THAT'S NOT A THREAT, IT'S A WARNING! LAR GAND CAN'T COME OUT AND PLAY BECAUSE HE'S SICK! HE HAS LEAD POISONING! FATAL! UNTREATABLE!
THIS WORLD, THIS CITY -- IT'S RICH IN LEAD, AND LEAD CAN KILL YOU! EVEN WITH YOUR POWERS! DO YOU GET IT YET?!
REALLY, SUPERMAN..
KRNK
GHH!

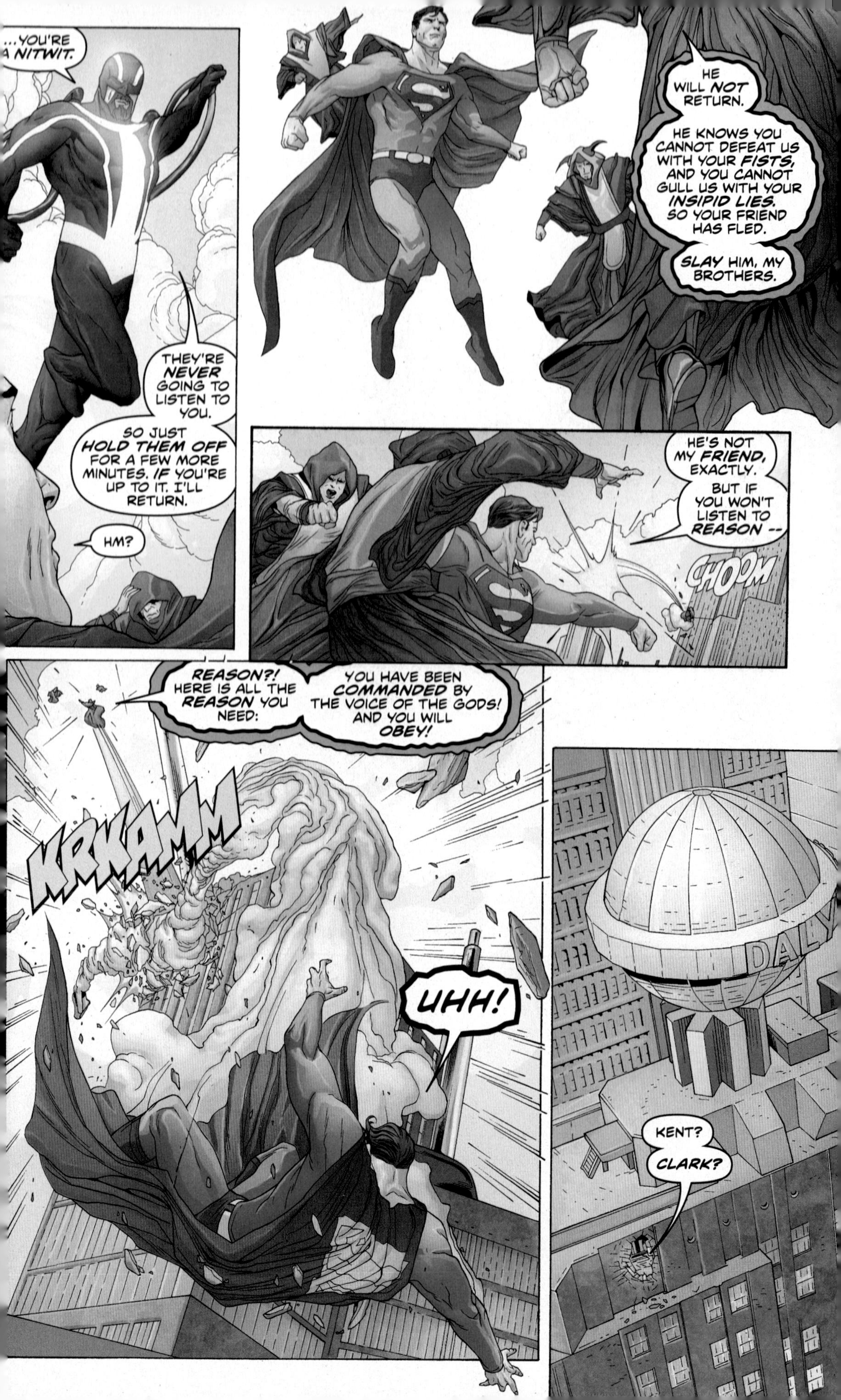
...YOU'RE A NITWIT.
THEY'RE NEVER GOING TO LISTEN TO YOU.
SO JUST HOLD THEM OFF FOR A FEW MORE MINUTES. IF YOU'RE UP TO IT. I'LL RETURN.
HM?
HE WILL NOT RETURN.
HE KNOWS YOU CANNOT DEFEAT US WITH YOUR FISTS, AND YOU CANNOT GULL US WITH YOUR INSIPID LIES. SO YOUR FRIEND HAS FLED.
SLAY HIM, MY BROTHERS.
HE'S NOT MY FRIEND, EXACTLY.
BUT IF YOU WON'T LISTEN TO REASON --
CHOOM
REASON?! HERE IS ALL THE REASON YOU NEED:
YOU HAVE BEEN COMMANDED BY THE VOICE OF THE GODS! AND YOU WILL OBEY!
KRKAMM
UHH!
DAI
KENT?
CLARK?

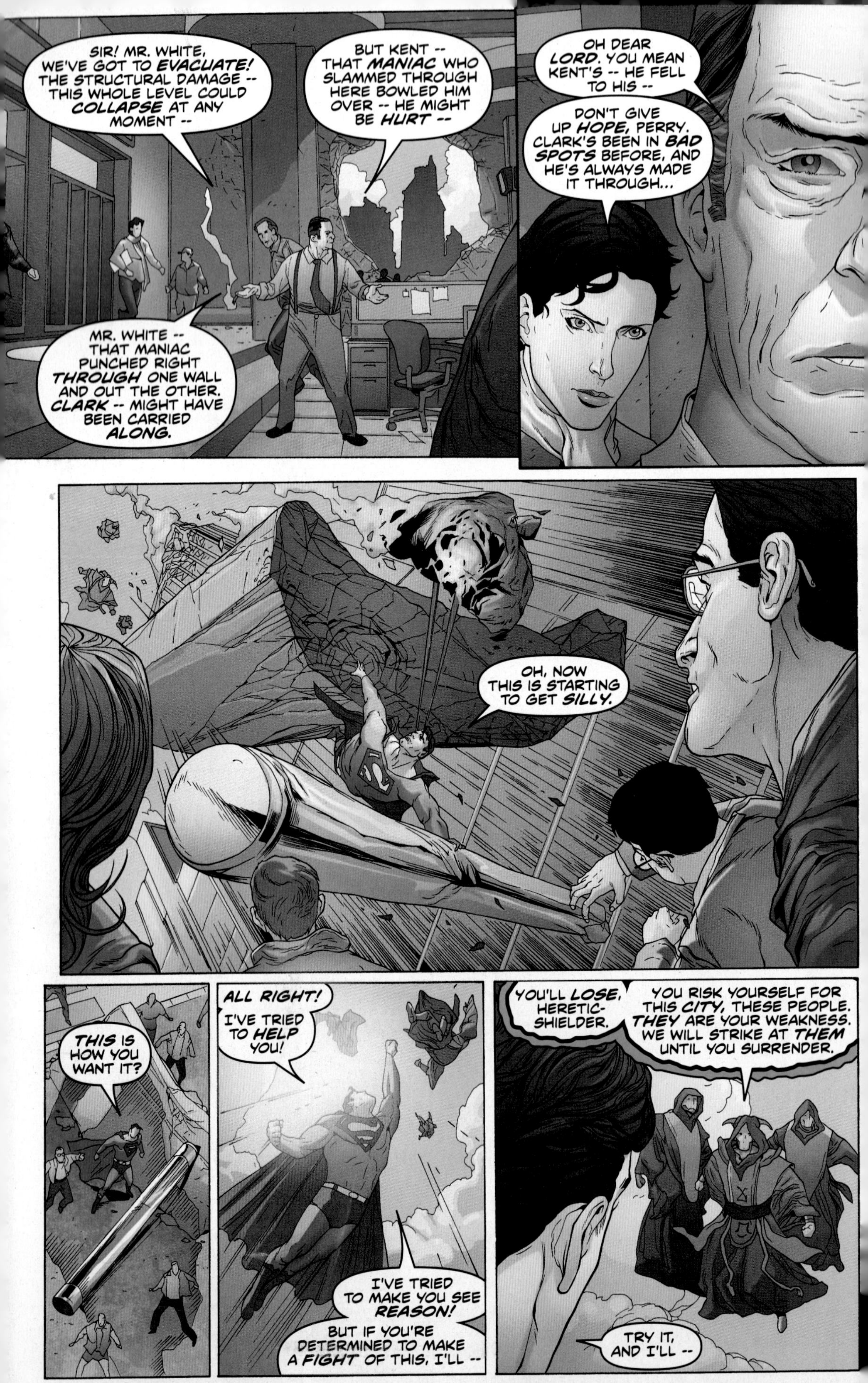
SIR! MR. WHITE, WE'VE GOT TO EVACUATE! THE STRUCTURAL DAMAGE -- THIS WHOLE LEVEL COULD COLLAPSE AT ANY MOMENT --
BUT KENT -- THAT MANIAC WHO SLAMMED THROUGH HERE BOWLED HIM OVER -- HE MIGHT BE HURT --
MR. WHITE -- THAT MANIAC PUNCHED RIGHT THROUGH ONE WALL AND OUT THE OTHER. CLARK -- MIGHT HAVE BEEN CARRIED ALONG.
OH DEAR LORD. YOU MEAN KENT'S -- HE FELL TO HIS --
DON'T GIVE UP HOPE, PERRY. CLARK'S BEEN IN BAD SPOTS BEFORE, AND HE'S ALWAYS MADE IT THROUGH...
OH, NOW THIS IS STARTING TO GET SILLY.
THIS IS HOW YOU WANT IT?
ALL RIGHT!
I'VE TRIED TO HELP YOU!
I'VE TRIED TO MAKE YOU SEE REASON!
BUT IF YOU'RE DETERMINED TO MAKE A FIGHT OF THIS, I'LL --
YOU'LL LOSE, HERETIC-SHIELDER.
YOU RISK YOURSELF FOR THIS CITY, THESE PEOPLE. THEY ARE YOUR WEAKNESS. WE WILL STRIKE AT THEM UNTIL YOU SURRENDER.
TRY IT, AND I'LL --

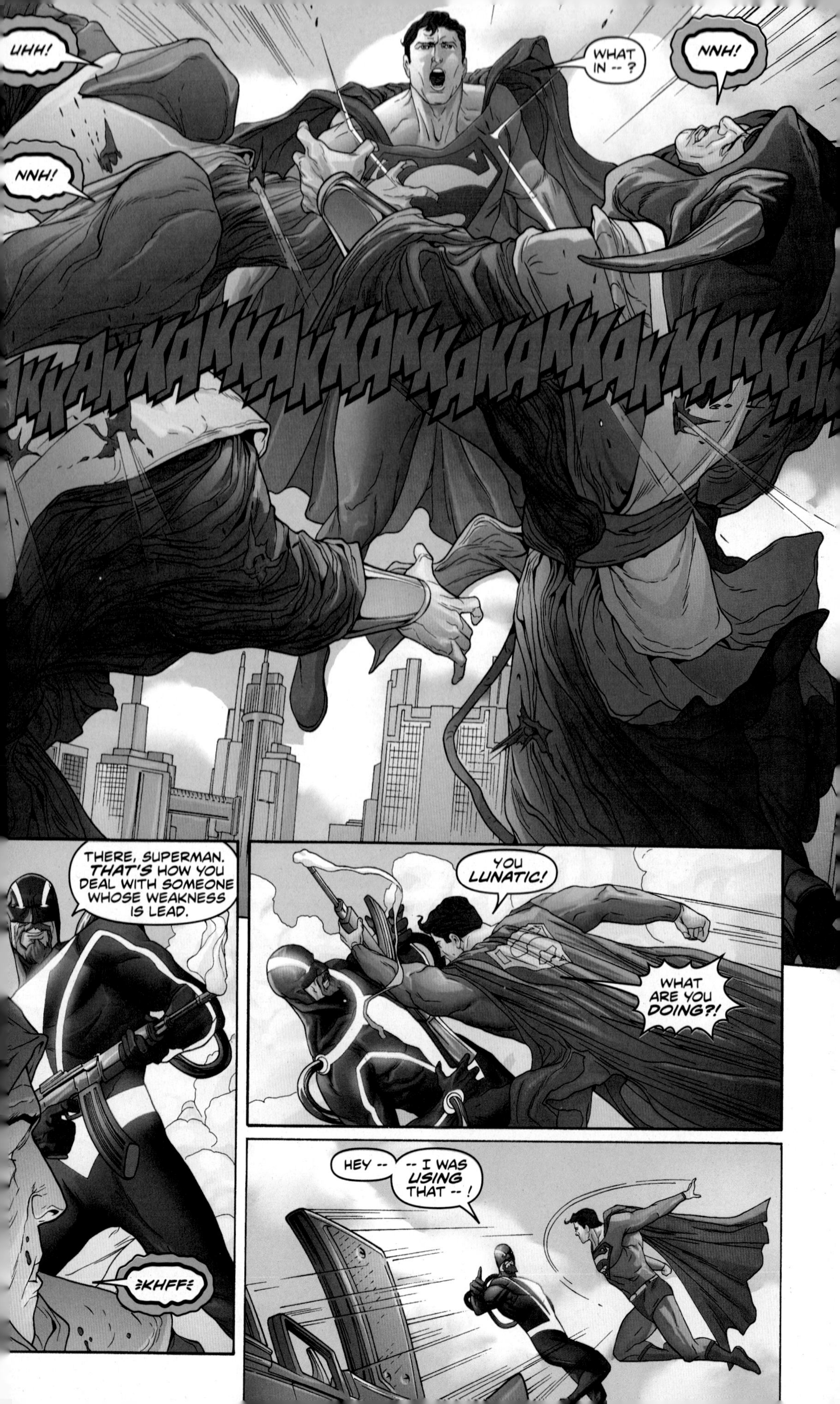
UHH!
WHAT IN -- ?
NNH!
NNH!
KAKKAKKAKKAKKAKKAKKAKKAKKAK
THERE, SUPERMAN. THAT'S HOW YOU DEAL WITH SOMEONE WHOSE WEAKNESS IS LEAD.
YOU LUNATIC!
WHAT ARE YOU DOING?!
KHFF
HEY --
-- I WAS USING THAT -- !

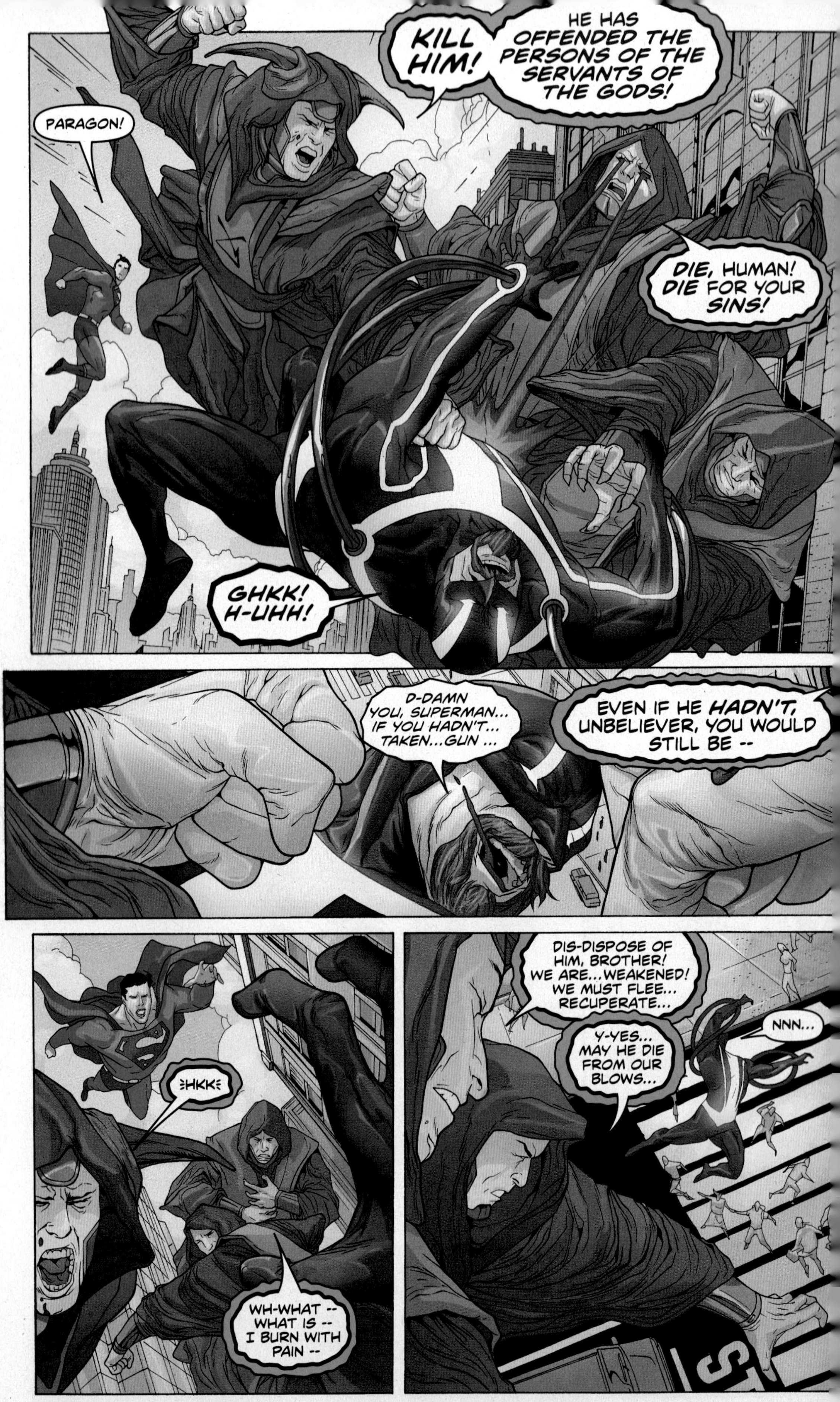
PARAGON!
KILL HIM!
HE HAS OFFENDED THE PERSONS OF THE SERVANTS OF THE GODS!
DIE, HUMAN! DIE FOR YOUR SINS!
GHKK! H-UHH!
D-DAMN YOU, SUPERMAN... IF YOU HADN'T... TAKEN...GUN ...
EVEN IF HE HADN'T, UNBELIEVER, YOU WOULD STILL BE --
HKK
WH-WHAT -- WHAT IS -- I BURN WITH PAIN --
DIS-DISPOSE OF HIM, BROTHER! WE ARE...WEAKENED! WE MUST FLEE... RECUPERATE...
Y-YES... MAY HE DIE FROM OUR BLOWS...
NNN...

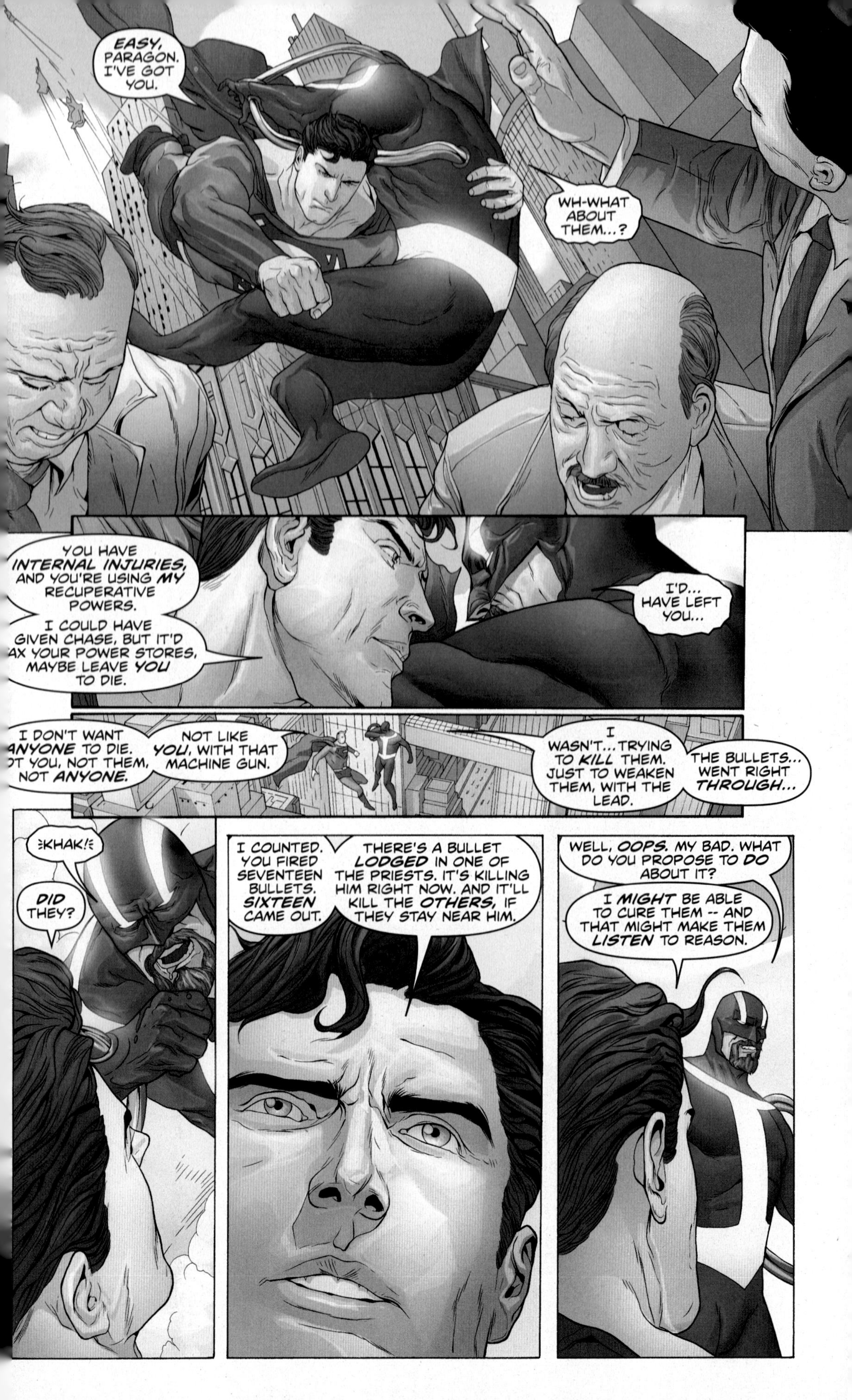
EASY, PARAGON. I'VE GOT YOU.
WH-WHAT ABOUT THEM...?
YOU HAVE INTERNAL INJURIES, AND YOU'RE USING MY RECUPERATIVE POWERS.
I COULD HAVE GIVEN CHASE, BUT IT'D AX YOUR POWER STORES, MAYBE LEAVE YOU TO DIE.
I'D... HAVE LEFT YOU...
I DON'T WANT ANYONE TO DIE. OT YOU, NOT THEM, NOT ANYONE.
NOT LIKE YOU, WITH THAT MACHINE GUN.
I WASN'T... TRYING TO KILL THEM. JUST TO WEAKEN THEM, WITH THE LEAD.
THE BULLETS... WENT RIGHT THROUGH...
KHAK!
DID THEY?
I COUNTED. YOU FIRED SEVENTEEN BULLETS. SIXTEEN CAME OUT.
THERE'S A BULLET LODGED IN ONE OF THE PRIESTS. IT'S KILLING HIM RIGHT NOW. AND IT'LL KILL THE OTHERS, IF THEY STAY NEAR HIM.
WELL, OOPS. MY BAD. WHAT DO YOU PROPOSE TO DO ABOUT IT?
I MIGHT BE ABLE TO CURE THEM -- AND THAT MIGHT MAKE THEM LISTEN TO REASON.

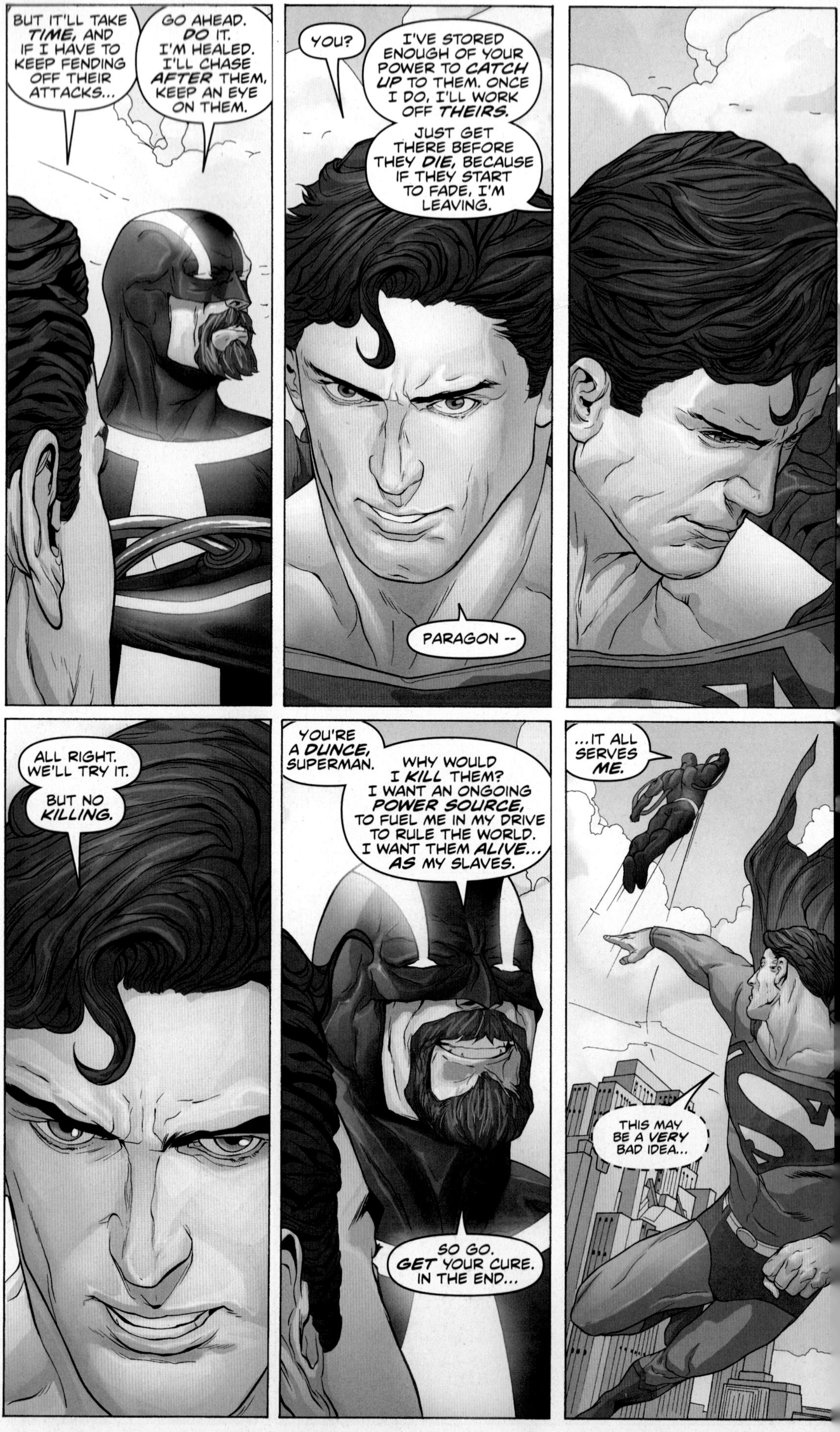
BUT IT'LL TAKE TIME, AND IF I HAVE TO KEEP FENDING OFF THEIR ATTACKS...
GO AHEAD. DO IT. I'M HEALED. I'LL CHASE AFTER THEM, KEEP AN EYE ON THEM.
YOU?
I'VE STORED ENOUGH OF YOUR POWER TO CATCH UP TO THEM. ONCE I DO, I'LL WORK OFF THEIRS.
JUST GET THERE BEFORE THEY DIE, BECAUSE IF THEY START TO FADE, I'M LEAVING.
PARAGON --
ALL RIGHT. WE'LL TRY IT.
BUT NO KILLING.
YOU'RE A DUNCE, SUPERMAN.
WHY WOULD I KILL THEM? I WANT AN ONGOING POWER SOURCE, TO FUEL ME IN MY DRIVE TO RULE THE WORLD. I WANT THEM ALIVE... AS MY SLAVES.
SO GO. GET YOUR CURE. IN THE END...
...IT ALL SERVES ME.
THIS MAY BE A VERY BAD IDEA...

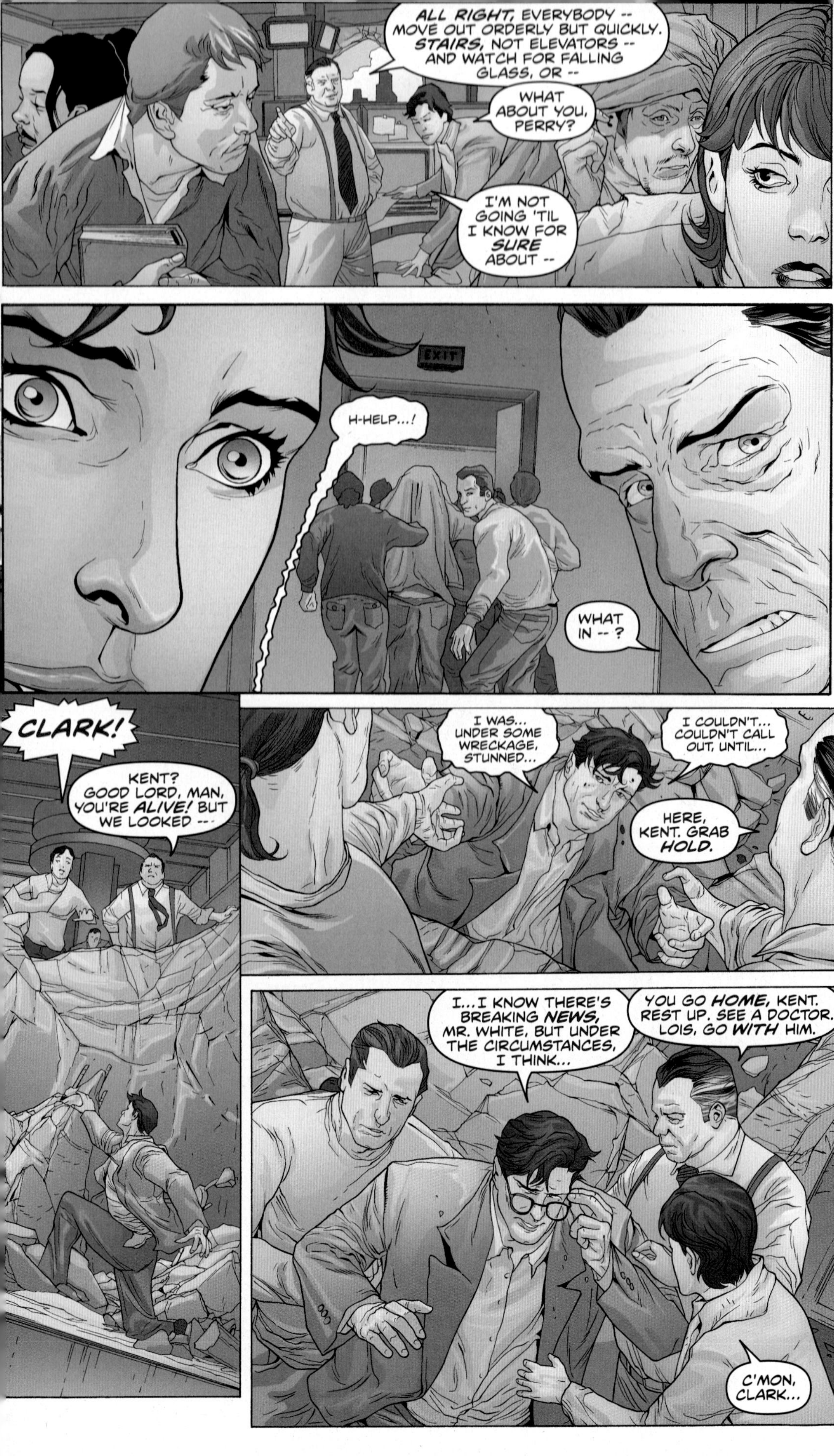
ALL RIGHT, EVERYBODY -- MOVE OUT ORDERLY BUT QUICKLY. STAIRS, NOT ELEVATORS -- AND WATCH FOR FALLING GLASS, OR --
WHAT ABOUT YOU, PERRY?
I'M NOT GOING 'TIL I KNOW FOR SURE ABOUT --
EXIT
H-HELP...!
WHAT IN -- ?
CLARK!
KENT? GOOD LORD, MAN, YOU'RE ALIVE! BUT WE LOOKED ---
I WAS... UNDER SOME WRECKAGE, STUNNED...
I COULDN'T... COULDN'T CALL OUT, UNTIL...
HERE, KENT. GRAB HOLD.
I...I KNOW THERE'S BREAKING NEWS, MR. WHITE, BUT UNDER THE CIRCUMSTANCES, I THINK...
YOU GO HOME, KENT. REST UP. SEE A DOCTOR. LOIS, GO WITH HIM.
C'MON, CLARK...

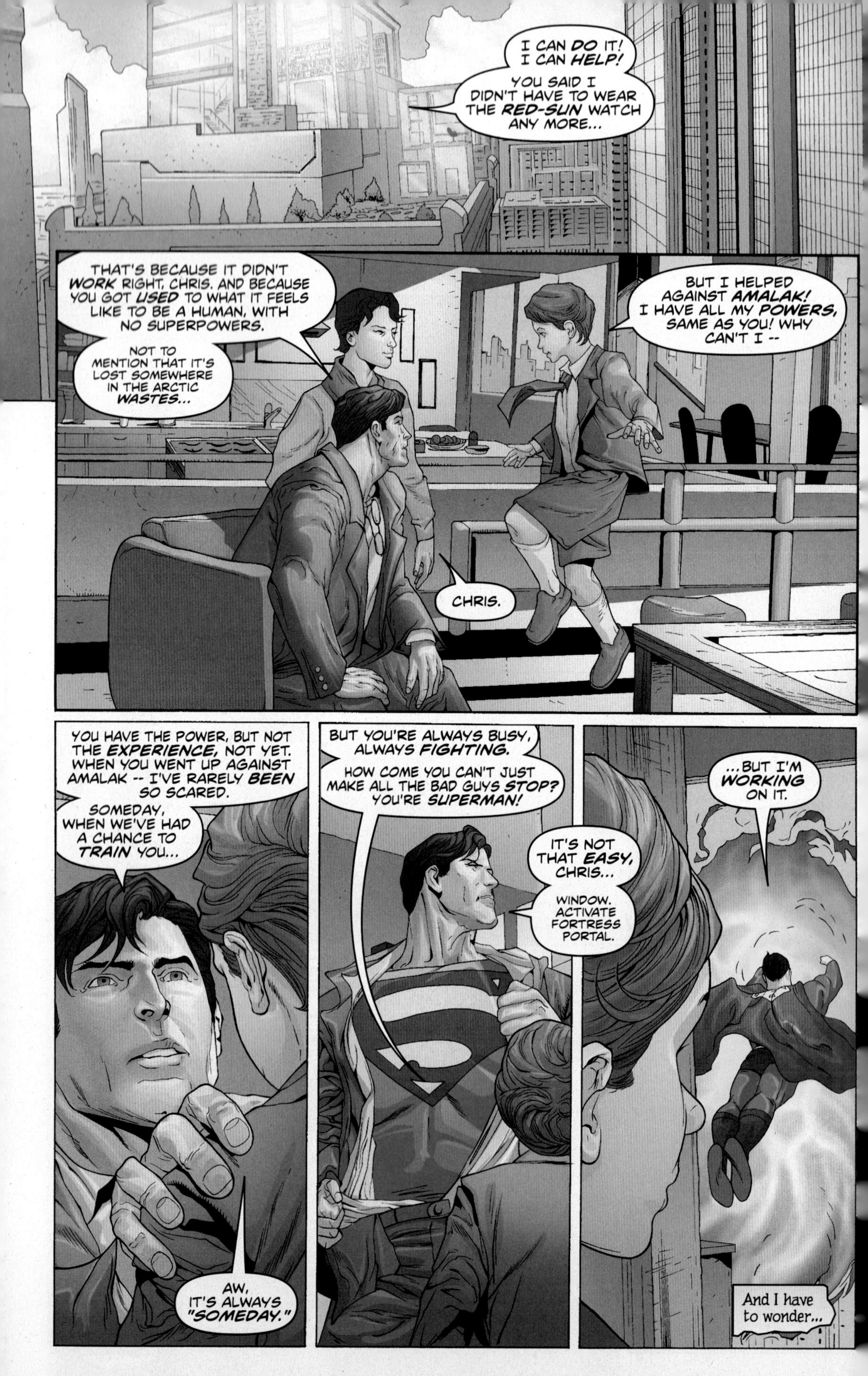
I CAN DO IT! I CAN HELP!
YOU SAID I DIDN'T HAVE TO WEAR THE RED-SUN WATCH ANY MORE...
THAT'S BECAUSE IT DIDN'T WORK RIGHT, CHRIS. AND BECAUSE YOU GOT USED TO WHAT IT FEELS LIKE TO BE A HUMAN, WITH NO SUPERPOWERS.
NOT TO MENTION THAT IT'S LOST SOMEWHERE IN THE ARCTIC WASTES...
BUT I HELPED AGAINST AMALAK! I HAVE ALL MY POWERS, SAME AS YOU! WHY CAN'T I --
CHRIS.
YOU HAVE THE POWER, BUT NOT THE EXPERIENCE, NOT YET. WHEN YOU WENT UP AGAINST AMALAK -- I'VE RARELY BEEN SO SCARED.
SOMEDAY, WHEN WE'VE HAD A CHANCE TO TRAIN YOU...
AW, IT'S ALWAYS "SOMEDAY."
BUT YOU'RE ALWAYS BUSY, ALWAYS FIGHTING.
HOW COME YOU CAN'T JUST MAKE ALL THE BAD GUYS STOP? YOU'RE SUPERMAN!
IT'S NOT THAT EASY, CHRIS...
WINDOW. ACTIVATE FORTRESS PORTAL.
...BUT I'M WORKING ON IT.
And I have to wonder...

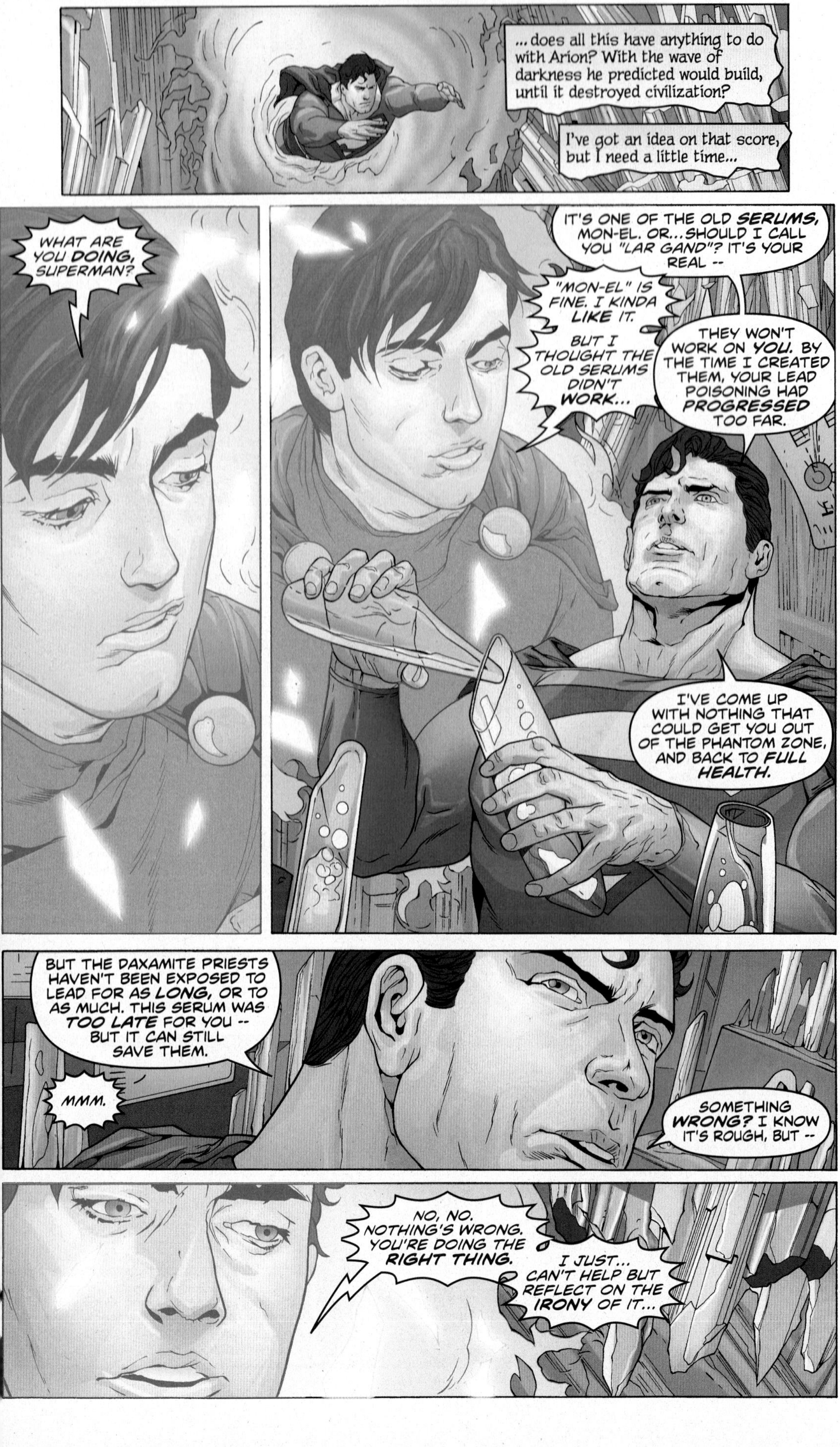
... does all this have anything to do with Arion? With the wave of darkness he predicted would build, until it destroyed civilization?
I've got an idea on that score, but I need a little time...
WHAT ARE YOU DOING, SUPERMAN?
IT'S ONE OF THE OLD SERUMS, MON-EL. OR...SHOULD I CALL YOU "LAR GAND"? IT'S YOUR REAL --
"MON-EL" IS FINE. I KINDA LIKE IT.
BUT I THOUGHT THE OLD SERUMS DIDN'T WORK...
THEY WON'T WORK ON YOU. BY THE TIME I CREATED THEM, YOUR LEAD POISONING HAD PROGRESSED TOO FAR.
I'VE COME UP WITH NOTHING THAT COULD GET YOU OUT OF THE PHANTOM ZONE, AND BACK TO FULL HEALTH.
BUT THE DAXAMITE PRIESTS HAVEN'T BEEN EXPOSED TO LEAD FOR AS LONG, OR TO AS MUCH. THIS SERUM WAS TOO LATE FOR YOU -- BUT IT CAN STILL SAVE THEM.
MMM.
SOMETHING WRONG? I KNOW IT'S ROUGH, BUT --
NO, NO. NOTHING'S WRONG. YOU'RE DOING THE RIGHT THING.
I JUST... CAN'T HELP BUT REFLECT ON THE IRONY OF IT...

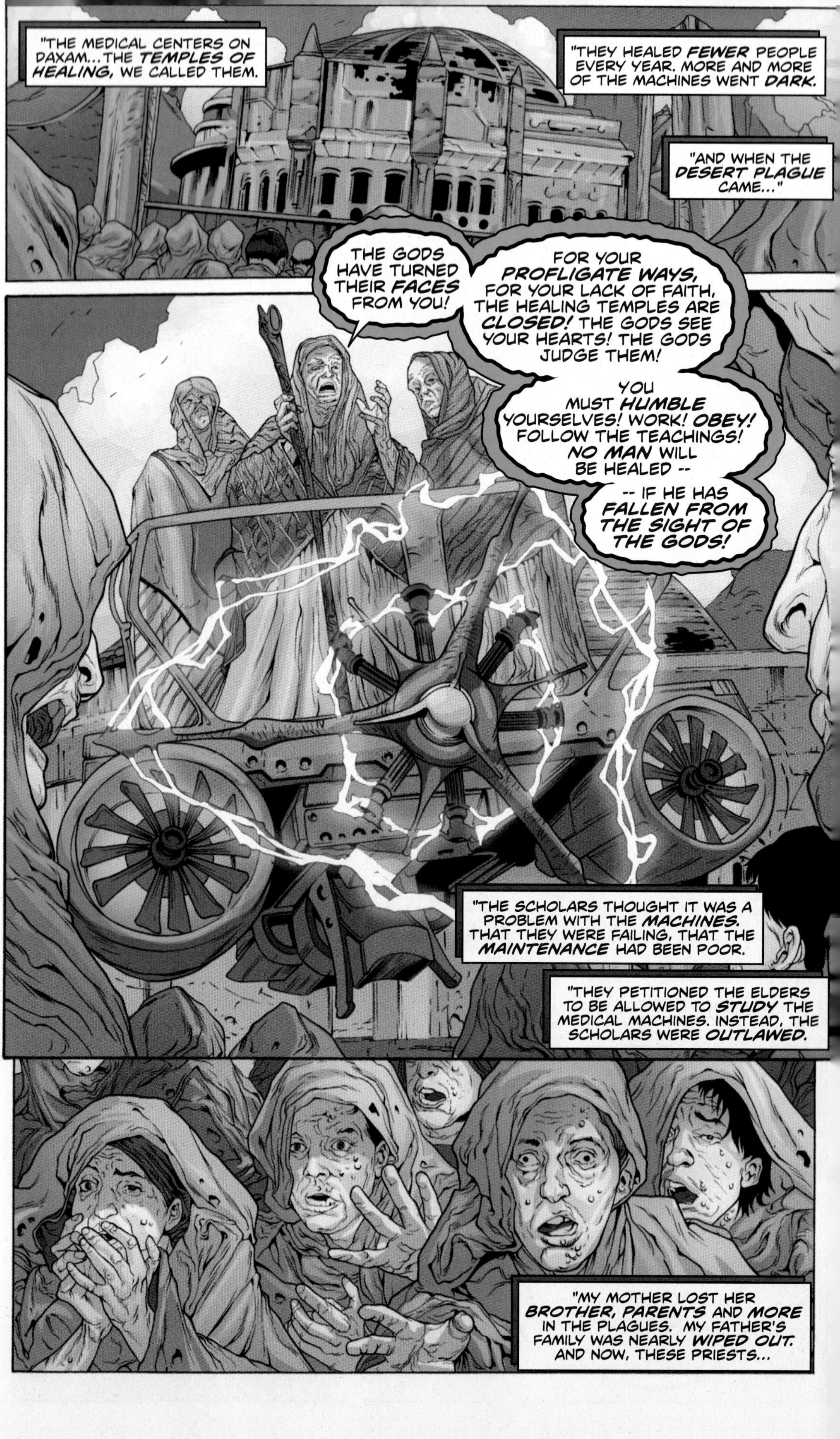
"THE MEDICAL CENTERS ON DAXAM... THE TEMPLES OF HEALING, WE CALLED THEM.
"THEY HEALED FEWER PEOPLE EVERY YEAR. MORE AND MORE OF THE MACHINES WENT DARK.
"AND WHEN THE DESERT PLAGUE CAME..."
THE GODS HAVE TURNED THEIR FACES FROM YOU!
FOR YOUR PROFLIGATE WAYS, FOR YOUR LACK OF FAITH, THE HEALING TEMPLES ARE CLOSED! THE GODS SEE YOUR HEARTS! THE GODS JUDGE THEM!
YOU MUST HUMBLE YOURSELVES! WORK! OBEY! FOLLOW THE TEACHINGS! NO MAN WILL BE HEALED --
-- IF HE HAS FALLEN FROM THE SIGHT OF THE GODS!
"THE SCHOLARS THOUGHT IT WAS A PROBLEM WITH THE MACHINES. THAT THEY WERE FAILING, THAT THE MAINTENANCE HAD BEEN POOR.
"THEY PETITIONED THE ELDERS TO BE ALLOWED TO STUDY THE MEDICAL MACHINES. INSTEAD, THE SCHOLARS WERE OUTLAWED.
"MY MOTHER LOST HER BROTHER, PARENTS AND MORE IN THE PLAGUES. MY FATHER'S FAMILY WAS NEARLY WIPED OUT. AND NOW, THESE PRIESTS...

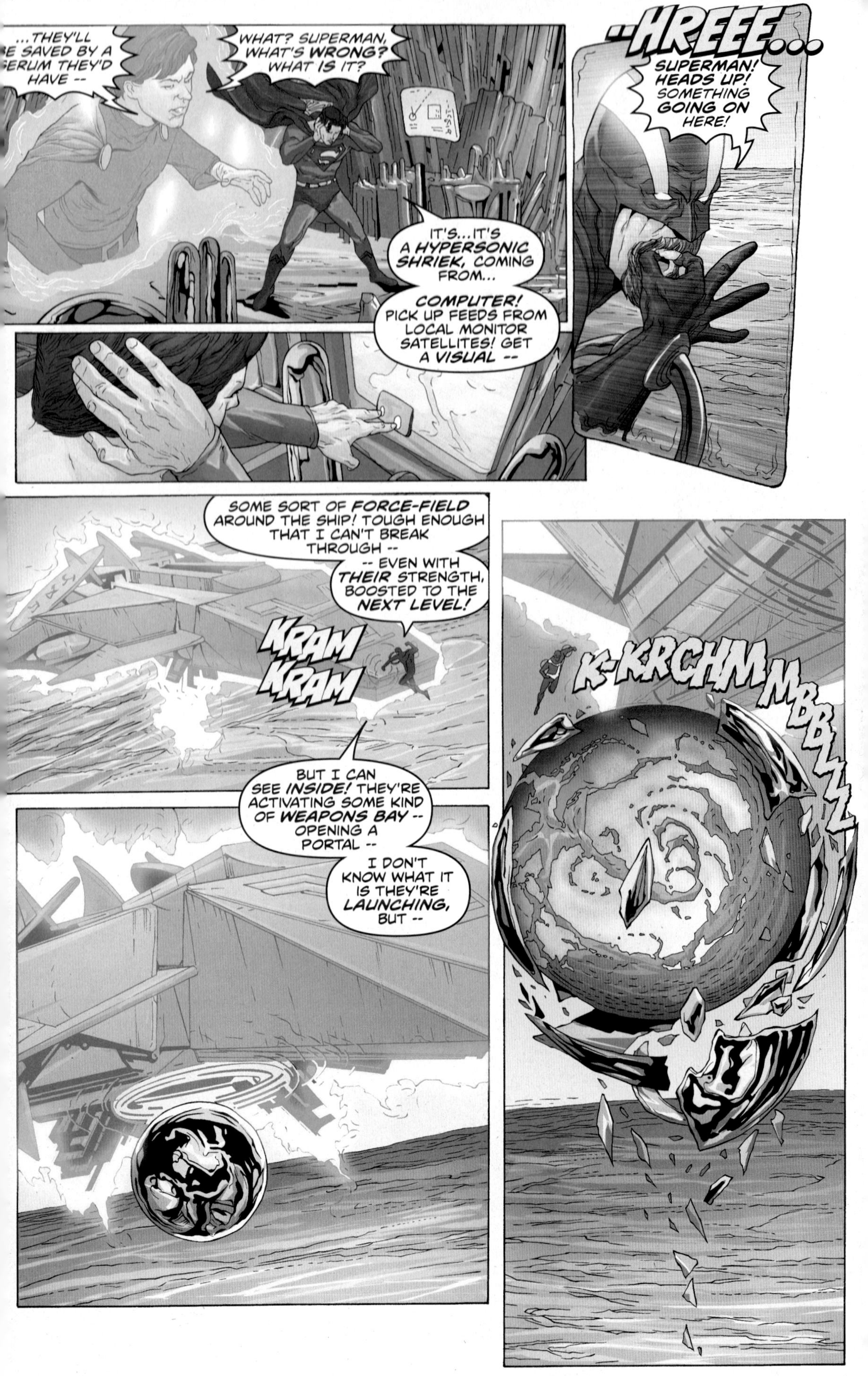
...THEY'LL BE SAVED BY A SERUM THEY'D HAVE --
WHAT? SUPERMAN, WHAT'S WRONG? WHAT IS IT?
IT'S...IT'S A HYPERSONIC SHRIEK, COMING FROM...
COMPUTER! PICK UP FEEDS FROM LOCAL MONITOR SATELLITES! GET A VISUAL --
..HREEE...
SUPERMAN! HEADS UP! SOMETHING GOING ON HERE!
SOME SORT OF FORCE-FIELD AROUND THE SHIP! TOUGH ENOUGH THAT I CAN'T BREAK THROUGH --
-- EVEN WITH THEIR STRENGTH, BOOSTED TO THE NEXT LEVEL!
KRAM KRAM
BUT I CAN SEE INSIDE! THEY'RE ACTIVATING SOME KIND OF WEAPONS BAY -- OPENING A PORTAL --
I DON'T KNOW WHAT IT IS THEY'RE LAUNCHING, BUT --
K-KRCHMMBBLLL

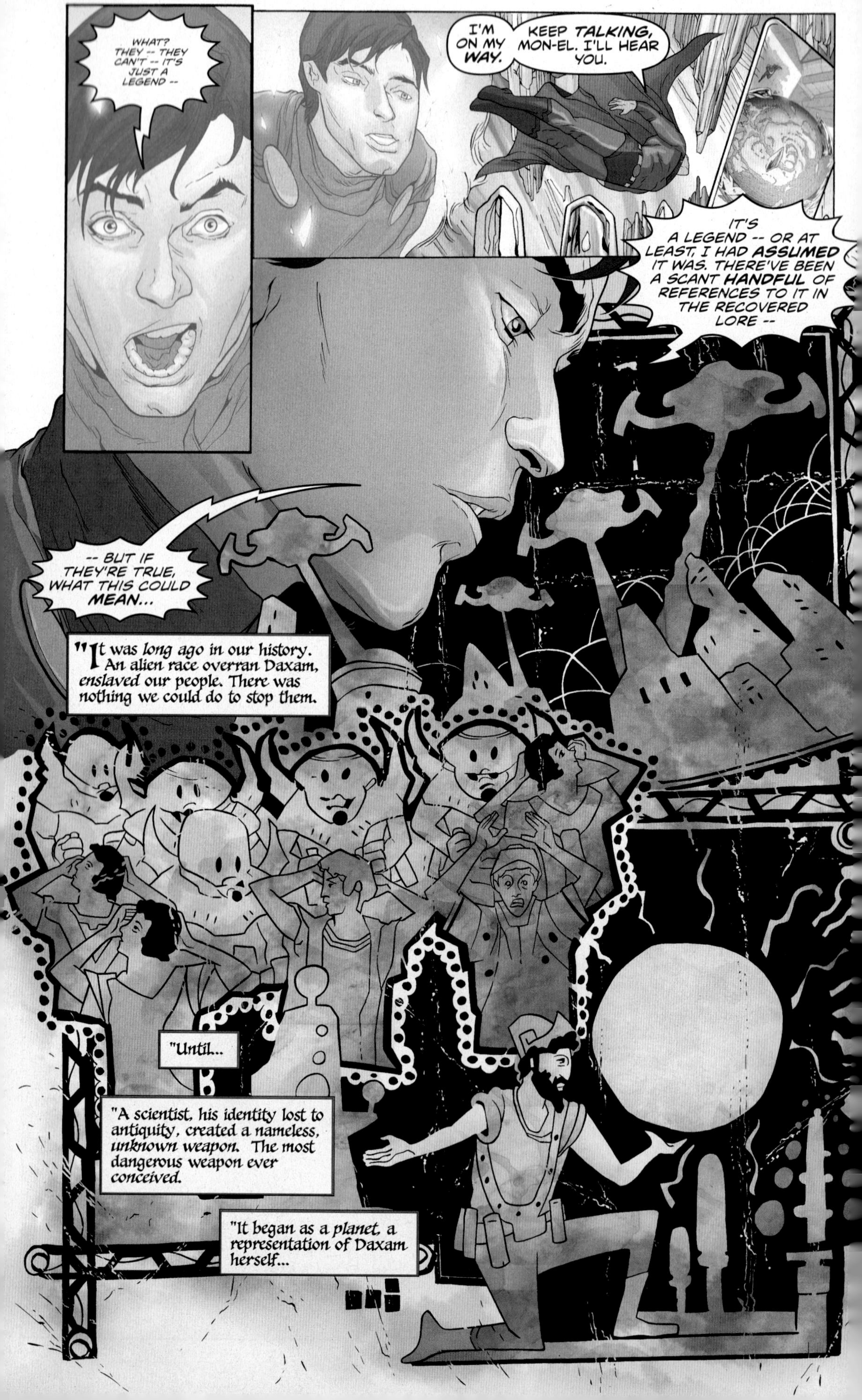
WHAT? THEY -- THEY CAN'T -- IT'S JUST A LEGEND --
I'M ON MY **WAY.**
KEEP **TALKING,** MON-EL. I'LL HEAR YOU.
IT'S A LEGEND -- OR AT LEAST, I HAD **ASSUMED** IT WAS. THERE'VE BEEN A SCANT **HANDFUL** OF REFERENCES TO IT IN THE RECOVERED LORE --
-- BUT IF THEY'RE TRUE, WHAT THIS COULD **MEAN...**
"It was *long ago* in our history. An alien race overran Daxam, enslaved our people. There was nothing we could do to stop them.
"Until...
"A scientist, his identity lost to antiquity, created a nameless, *unknown* weapon. The most dangerous weapon ever conceived.
"It began as a *planet,* a representation of Daxam herself...

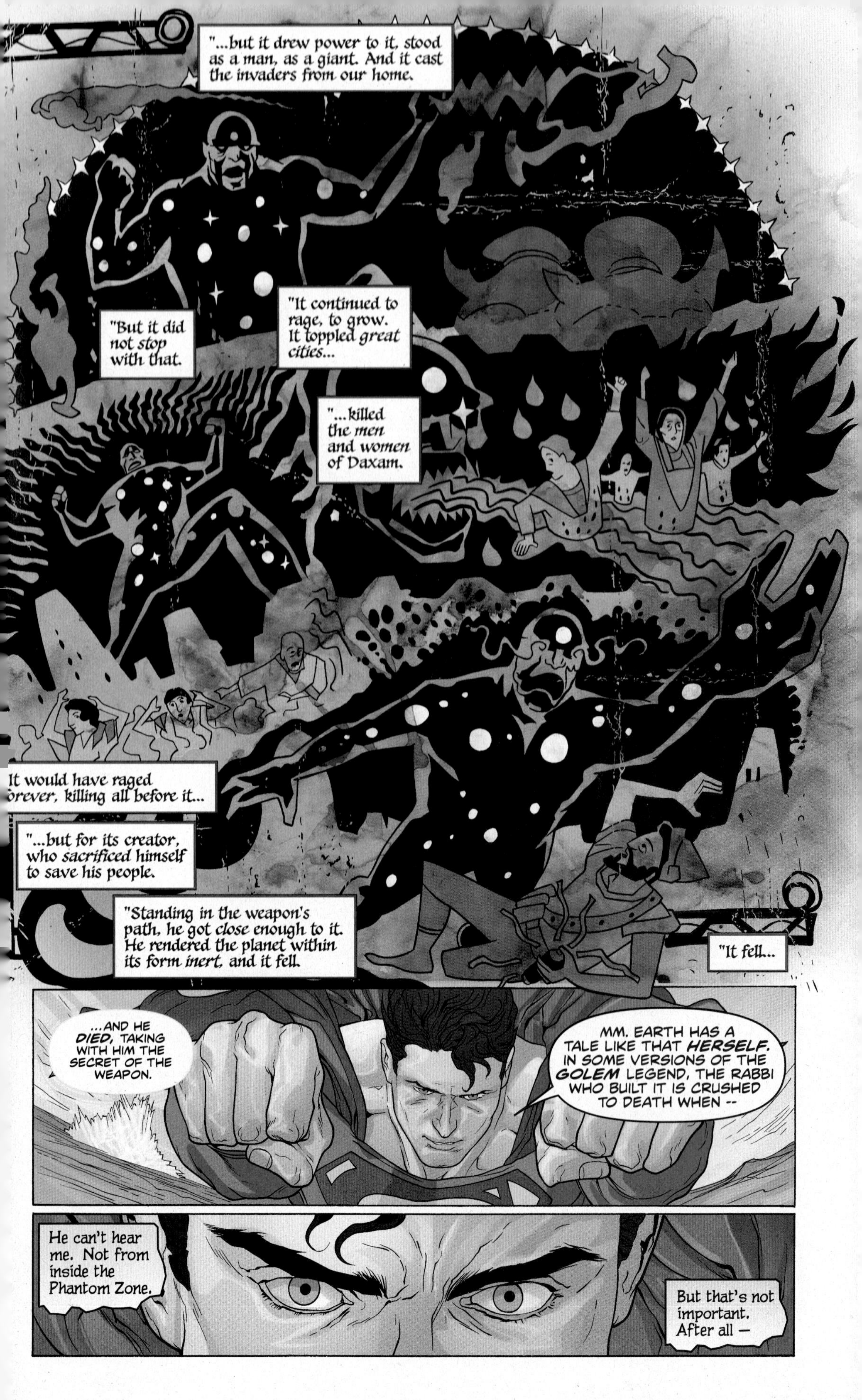
"...but it drew power to it, stood as a man, as a giant. And it cast the invaders from our home.
"But it did not *stop* with that.
"It continued to rage, to grow. It toppled *great* cities...
"...killed the *men* and *women* of Daxam.
It would have raged *forever*, killing all before it...
"...but for its creator, who *sacrificed* himself to save his people.
"Standing in the weapon's path, he got *close* enough to it. He rendered the planet within its form *inert*, and it fell.
"It fell...
...AND HE *DIED*, TAKING WITH HIM THE SECRET OF THE WEAPON.
MM. EARTH HAS A TALE LIKE THAT *HERSELF.* IN SOME VERSIONS OF THE *GOLEM* LEGEND, THE RABBI WHO BUILT IT IS CRUSHED TO DEATH WHEN --
He can't hear me. Not from inside the Phantom Zone.
But that's not important. After all —

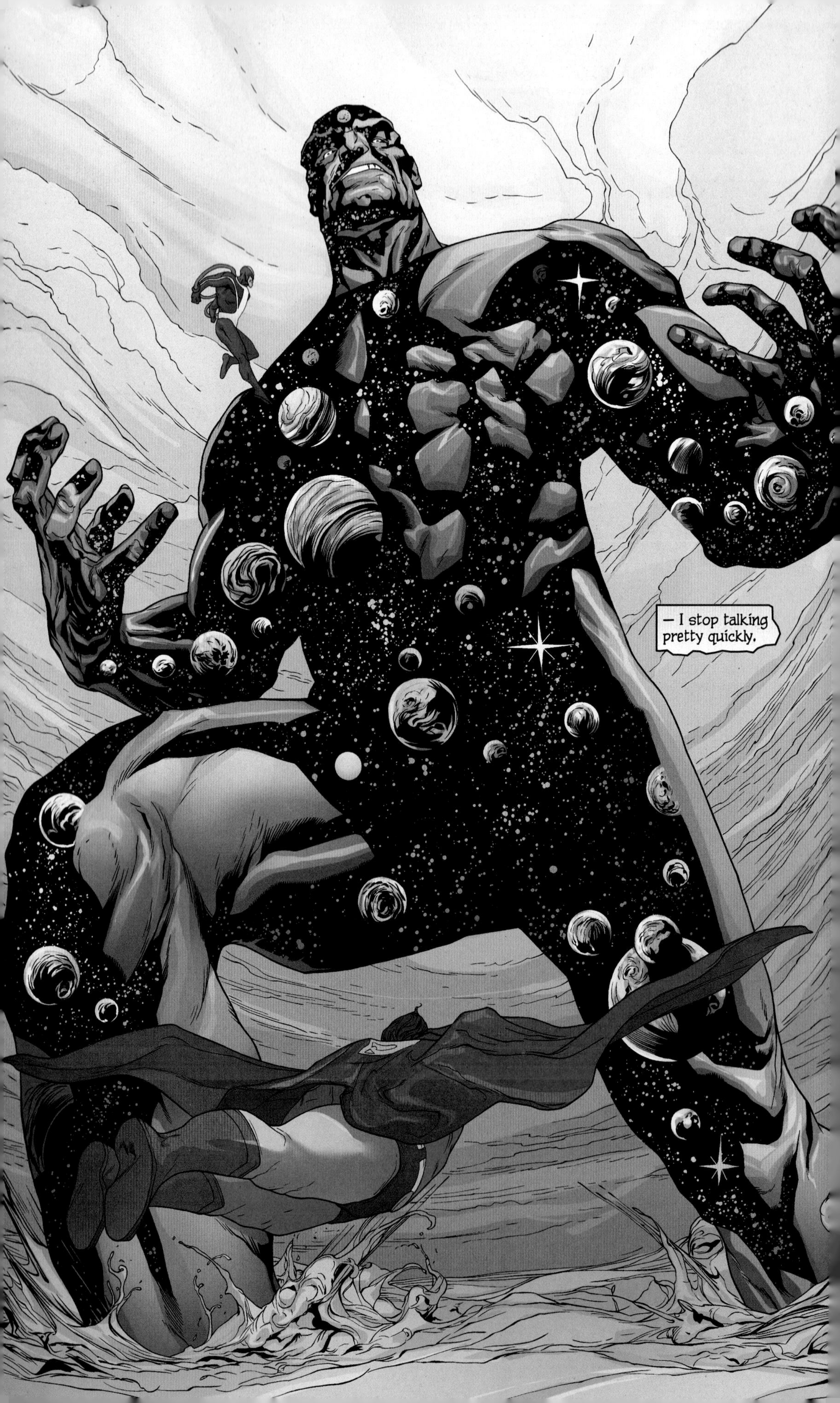
– I stop talking
pretty quickly.

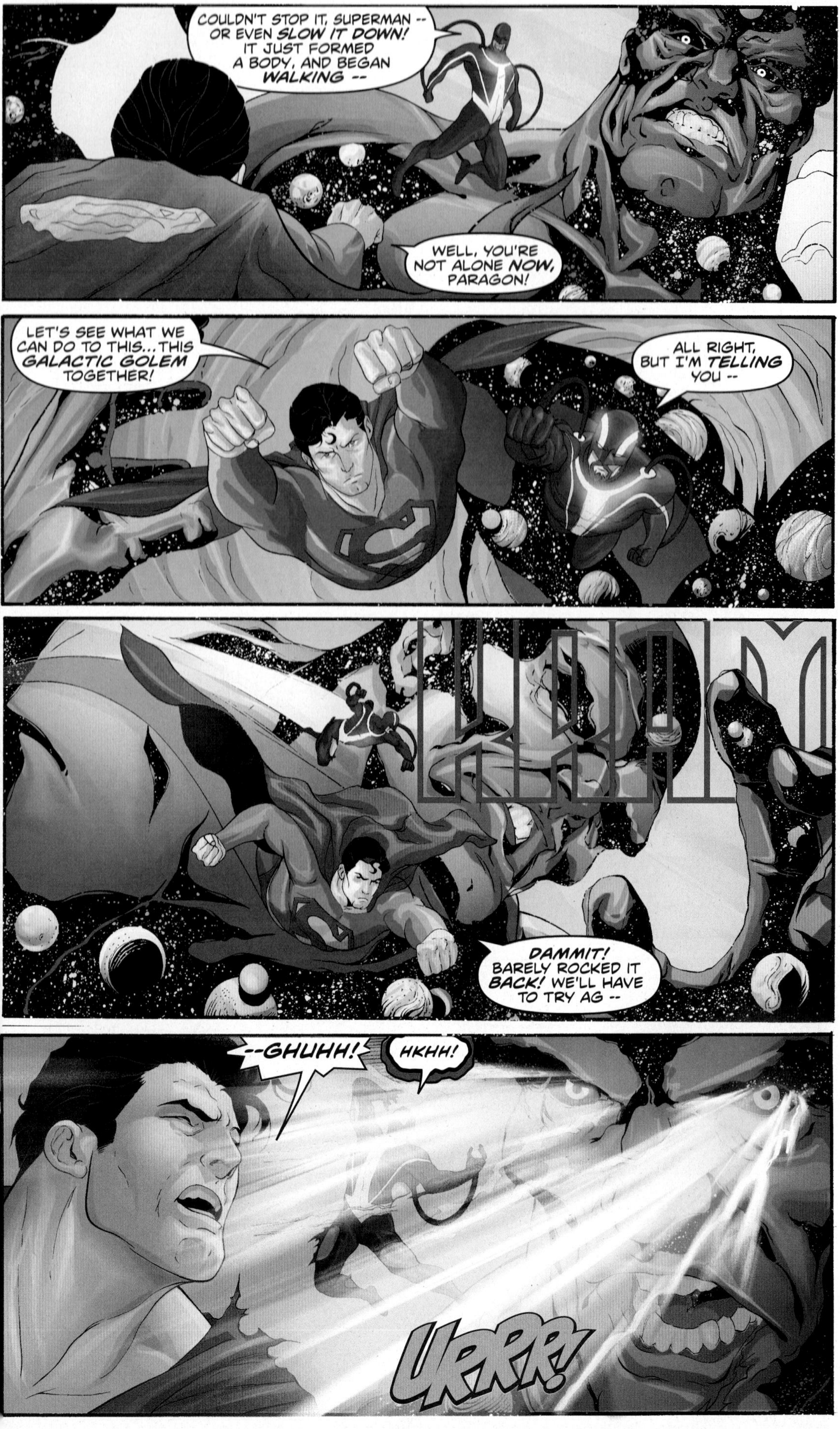
COULDN'T STOP IT, SUPERMAN -- OR EVEN SLOW IT DOWN! IT JUST FORMED A BODY, AND BEGAN WALKING --
WELL, YOU'RE NOT ALONE NOW, PARAGON!
LET'S SEE WHAT WE CAN DO TO THIS...THIS GALACTIC GOLEM TOGETHER!
ALL RIGHT, BUT I'M TELLING YOU --
KRAM
DAMMIT! BARELY ROCKED IT BACK! WE'LL HAVE TO TRY AG --
--GHUHH!
HKHH!
URRR!

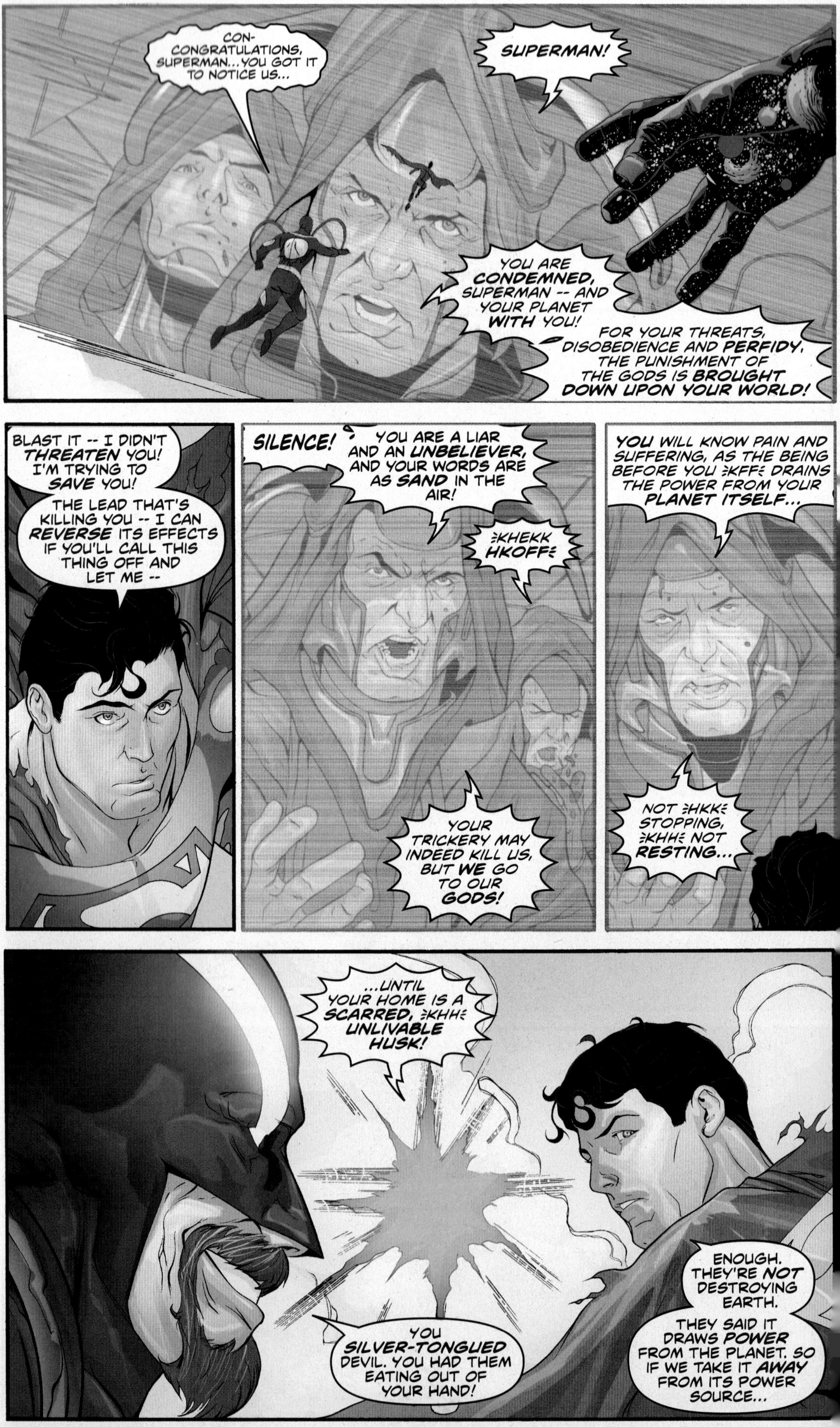
CON-CONGRATULATIONS, SUPERMAN... YOU GOT IT TO NOTICE US...
SUPERMAN!
YOU ARE CONDEMNED, SUPERMAN -- AND YOUR PLANET WITH YOU!
FOR YOUR THREATS, DISOBEDIENCE AND PERFIDY, THE PUNISHMENT OF THE GODS IS BROUGHT DOWN UPON YOUR WORLD!
BLAST IT -- I DIDN'T THREATEN YOU! I'M TRYING TO SAVE YOU!
THE LEAD THAT'S KILLING YOU -- I CAN REVERSE ITS EFFECTS IF YOU'LL CALL THIS THING OFF AND LET ME --
SILENCE!
YOU ARE A LIAR AND AN UNBELIEVER, AND YOUR WORDS ARE AS SAND IN THE AIR!
KHEKK HKOFF
YOUR TRICKERY MAY INDEED KILL US, BUT WE GO TO OUR GODS!
YOU WILL KNOW PAIN AND SUFFERING, AS THE BEING BEFORE YOU KFF DRAINS THE POWER FROM YOUR PLANET ITSELF...
NOT HKK STOPPING, KHH NOT RESTING...
...UNTIL YOUR HOME IS A SCARRED, KHH UNLIVABLE HUSK!
YOU SILVER-TONGUED DEVIL. YOU HAD THEM EATING OUT OF YOUR HAND!
ENOUGH. THEY'RE NOT DESTROYING EARTH.
THEY SAID IT DRAWS POWER FROM THE PLANET. SO IF WE TAKE IT AWAY FROM ITS POWER SOURCE...

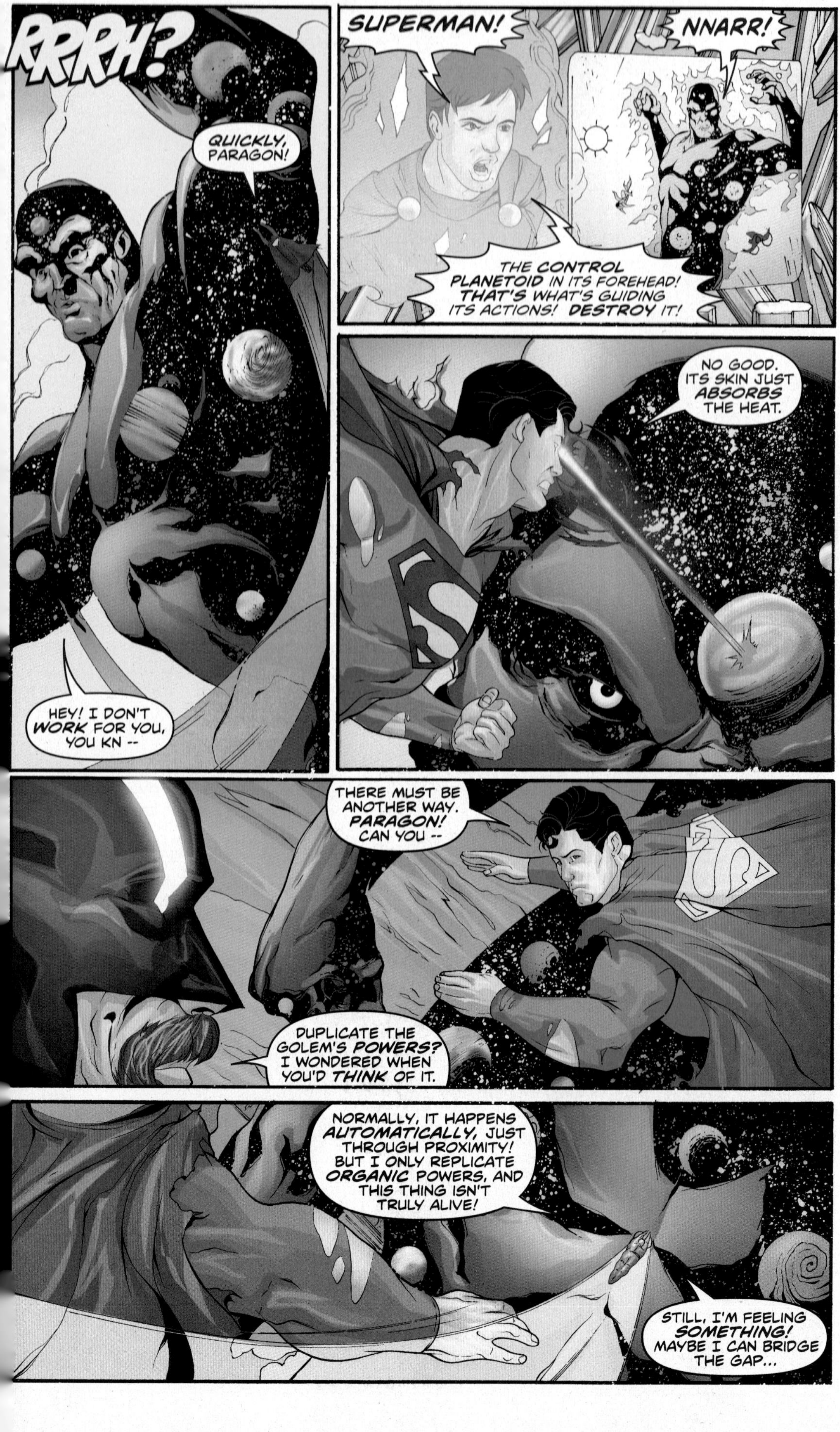
RRRH?
QUICKLY, PARAGON!
HEY! I DON'T WORK FOR YOU, YOU KN --
SUPERMAN!
NNARR!
THE CONTROL PLANETOID IN ITS FOREHEAD! THAT'S WHAT'S GUIDING ITS ACTIONS! DESTROY IT!
NO GOOD. ITS SKIN JUST ABSORBS THE HEAT.
THERE MUST BE ANOTHER WAY. PARAGON! CAN YOU --
DUPLICATE THE GOLEM'S POWERS? I WONDERED WHEN YOU'D THINK OF IT.
NORMALLY, IT HAPPENS AUTOMATICALLY, JUST THROUGH PROXIMITY! BUT I ONLY REPLICATE ORGANIC POWERS, AND THIS THING ISN'T TRULY ALIVE!
STILL, I'M FEELING SOMETHING! MAYBE I CAN BRIDGE THE GAP...

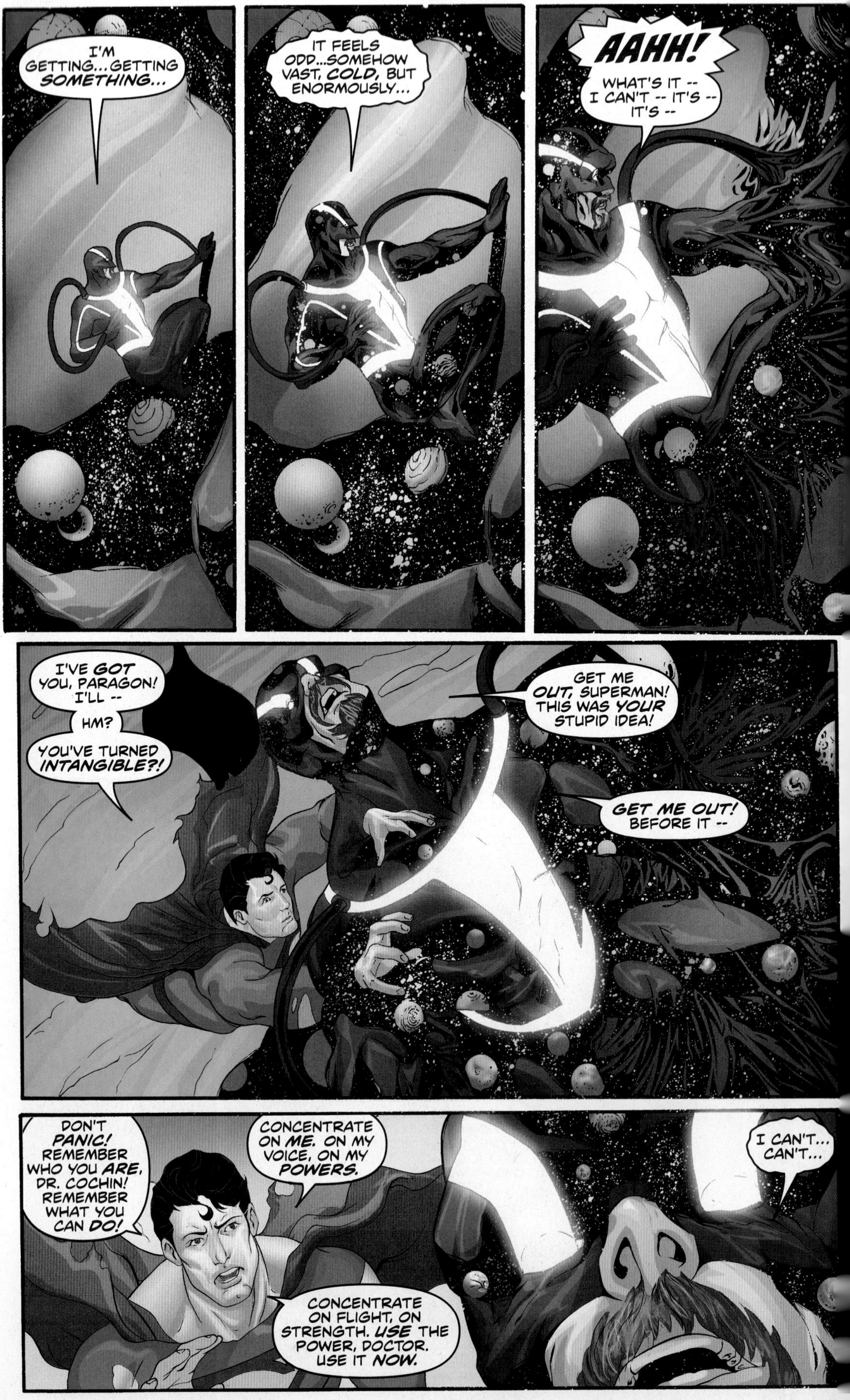
I'M GETTING... GETTING SOMETHING...
IT FEELS ODD...SOMEHOW VAST, COLD, BUT ENORMOUSLY...
AAHH!
WHAT'S IT -- I CAN'T -- IT'S -- IT'S --
I'VE GOT YOU, PARAGON! I'LL --
HM?
YOU'VE TURNED INTANGIBLE?!
GET ME OUT, SUPERMAN! THIS WAS YOUR STUPID IDEA!
GET ME OUT! BEFORE IT --
DON'T PANIC! REMEMBER WHO YOU ARE, DR. COCHIN! REMEMBER WHAT YOU CAN DO!
CONCENTRATE ON ME. ON MY VOICE, ON MY POWERS.
CONCENTRATE ON FLIGHT, ON STRENGTH. USE THE POWER, DOCTOR. USE IT NOW.
I CAN'T... CAN'T...

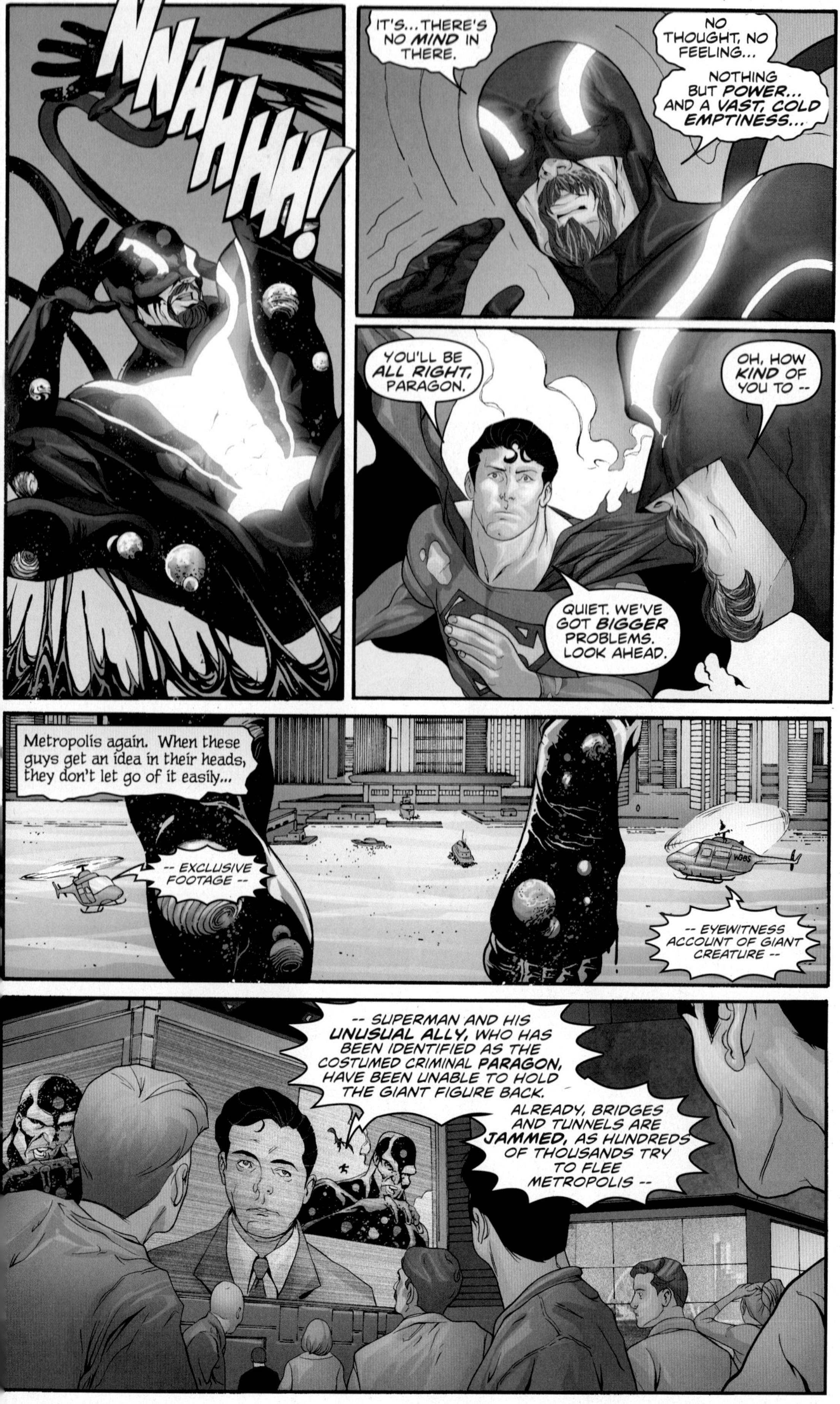
NNAHHHH!
IT'S... THERE'S NO MIND IN THERE.
NO THOUGHT, NO FEELING...
NOTHING BUT POWER... AND A VAST, COLD EMPTINESS...
YOU'LL BE ALL RIGHT, PARAGON.
OH, HOW KIND OF YOU TO --
QUIET. WE'VE GOT BIGGER PROBLEMS. LOOK AHEAD.
Metropolis again. When these guys get an idea in their heads, they don't let go of it easily...
-- EXCLUSIVE FOOTAGE --
-- EYEWITNESS ACCOUNT OF GIANT CREATURE --
-- SUPERMAN AND HIS UNUSUAL ALLY, WHO HAS BEEN IDENTIFIED AS THE COSTUMED CRIMINAL PARAGON, HAVE BEEN UNABLE TO HOLD THE GIANT FIGURE BACK.
ALREADY, BRIDGES AND TUNNELS ARE JAMMED, AS HUNDREDS OF THOUSANDS TRY TO FLEE METROPOLIS --

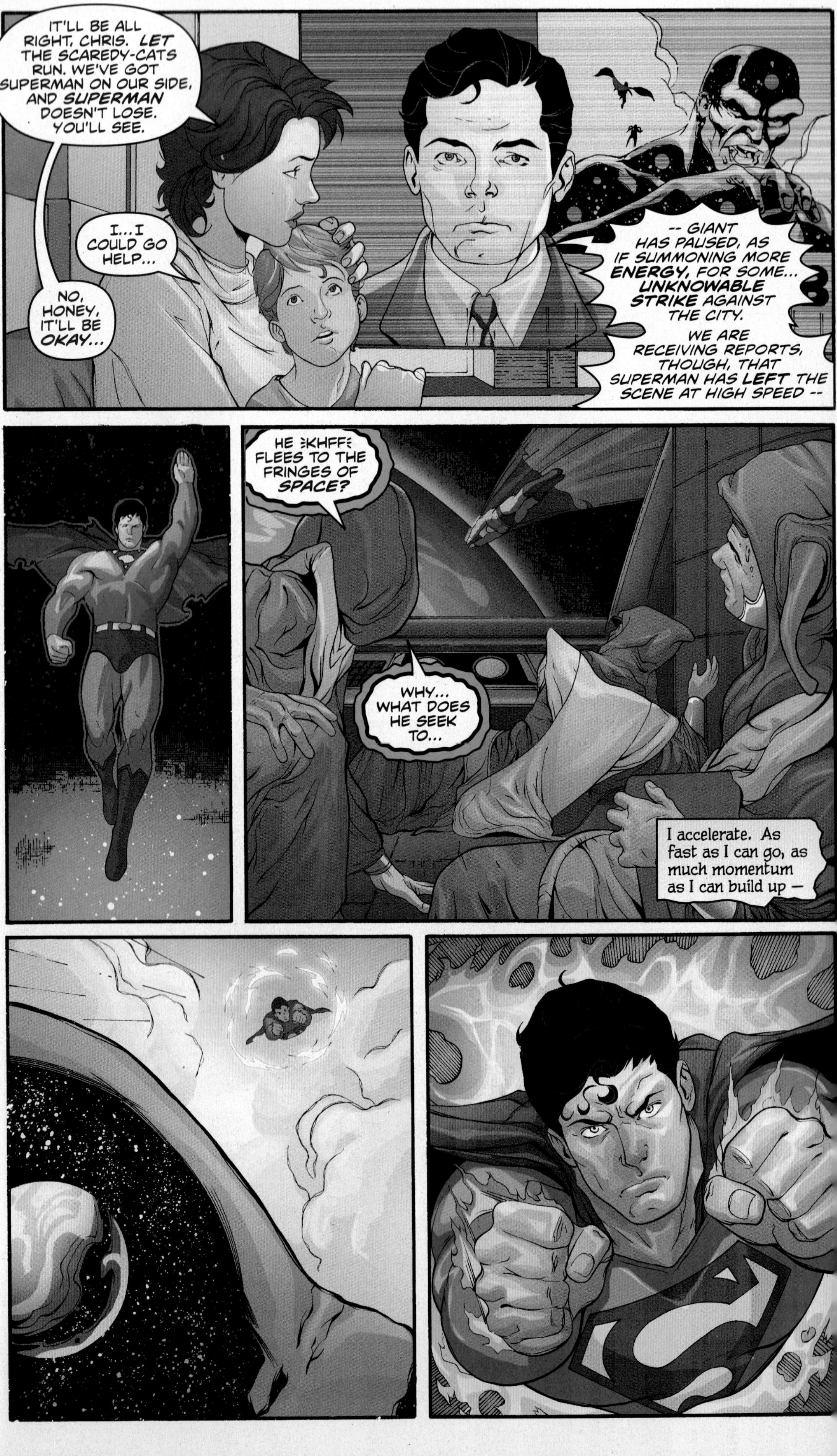
IT'LL BE ALL RIGHT, CHRIS. LET THE SCAREDY-CATS RUN. WE'VE GOT SUPERMAN ON OUR SIDE, AND SUPERMAN DOESN'T LOSE. YOU'LL SEE.
I... I COULD GO HELP...
NO, HONEY, IT'LL BE OKAY...
-- GIANT HAS PAUSED, AS IF SUMMONING MORE ENERGY, FOR SOME... UNKNOWABLE STRIKE AGAINST THE CITY.
WE ARE RECEIVING REPORTS, THOUGH, THAT SUPERMAN HAS LEFT THE SCENE AT HIGH SPEED --
HE KHFF FLEES TO THE FRINGES OF SPACE?
WHY... WHAT DOES HE SEEK TO...
I accelerate. As fast as I can go, as much momentum as I can build up —

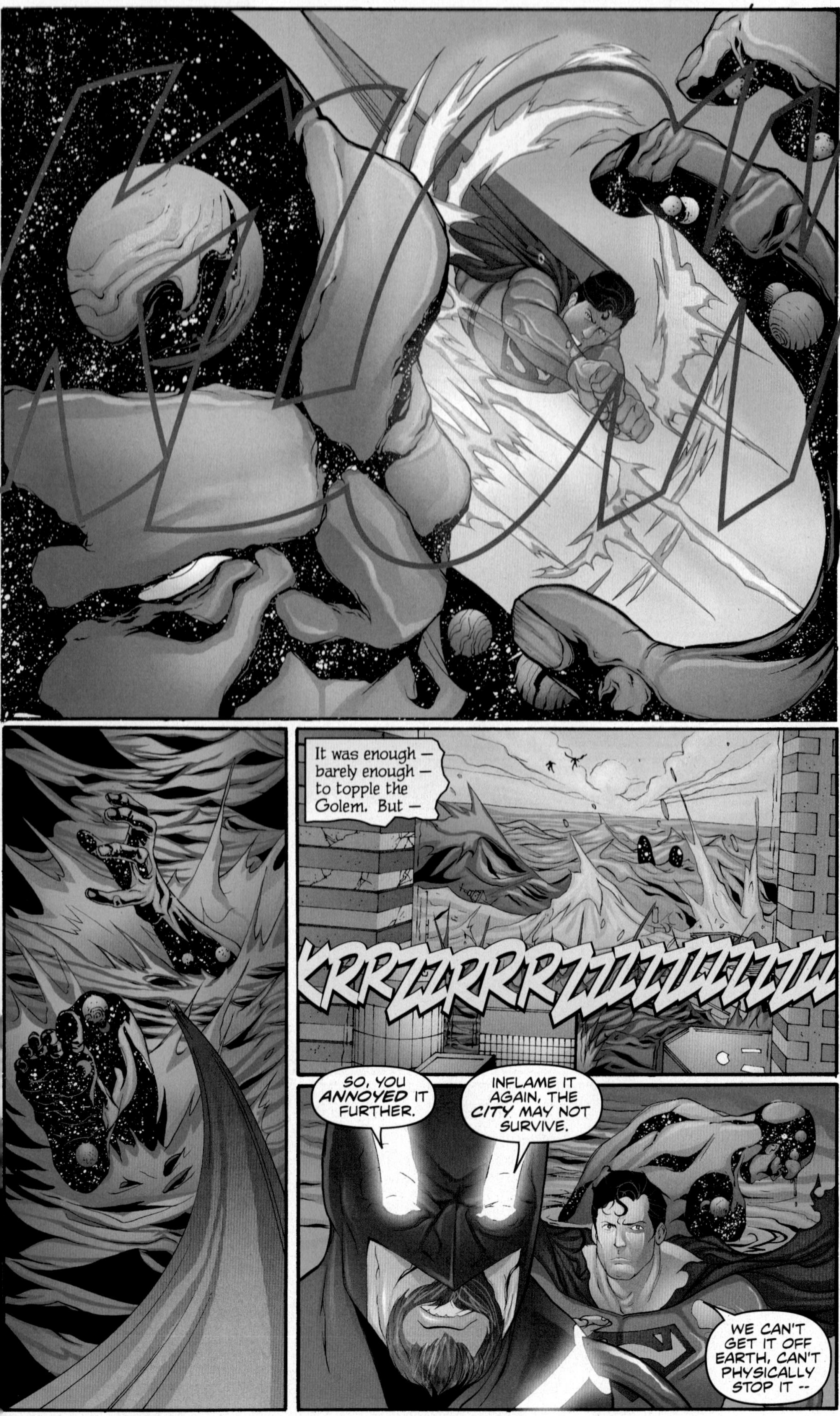
It was enough — barely enough — to topple the Golem. But —
KRRZZRRRRZZZZZZZZZZZ
SO, YOU ANNOYED IT FURTHER.
INFLAME IT AGAIN, THE CITY MAY NOT SURVIVE.
WE CAN'T GET IT OFF EARTH, CAN'T PHYSICALLY STOP IT --

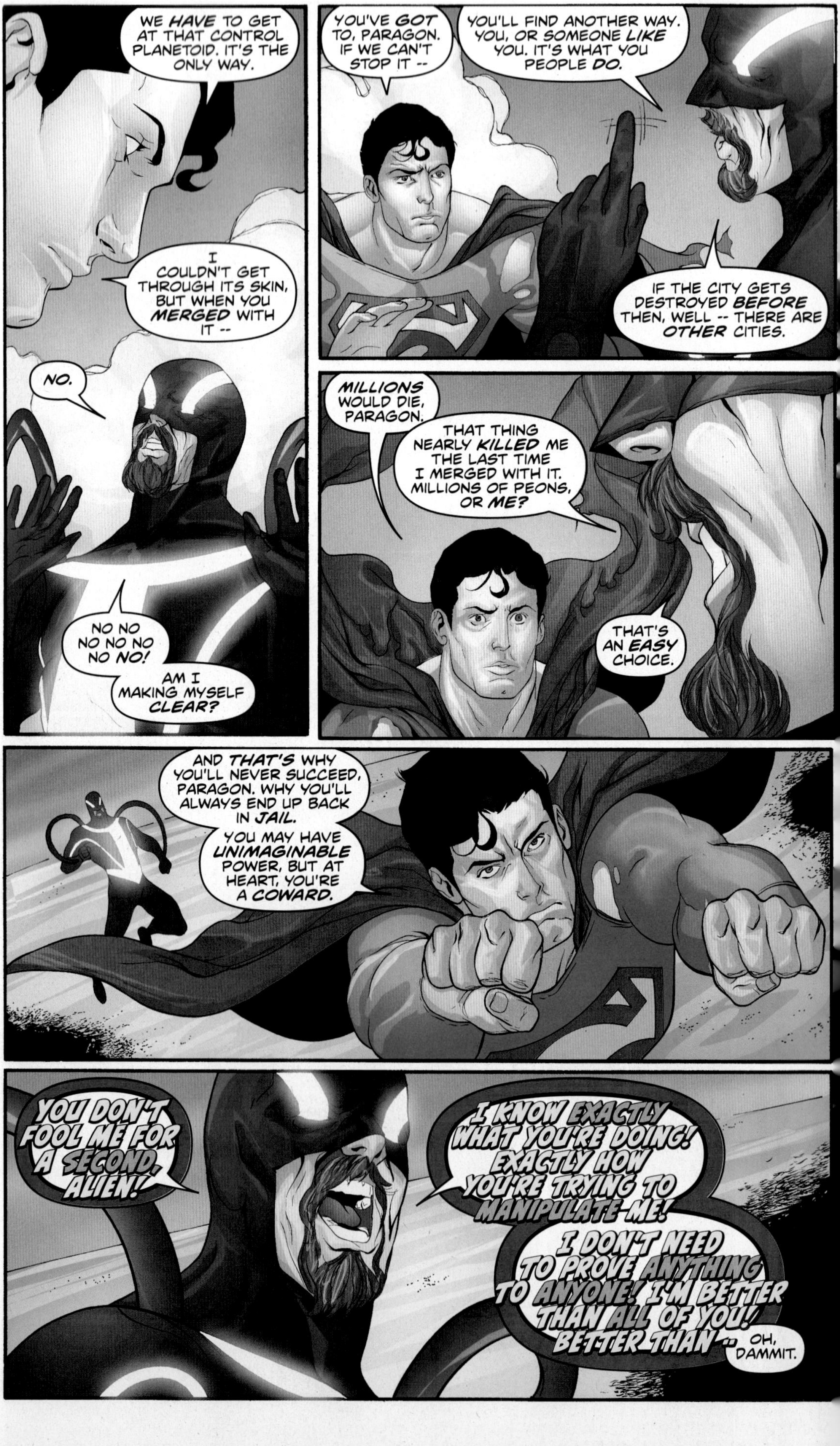

WE HAVE TO GET AT THAT CONTROL PLANETOID. IT'S THE ONLY WAY.
I COULDN'T GET THROUGH ITS SKIN, BUT WHEN YOU MERGED WITH IT --
NO.
NO NO NO NO NO NO NO!
AM I MAKING MYSELF CLEAR?
YOU'VE GOT TO, PARAGON. IF WE CAN'T STOP IT --
YOU'LL FIND ANOTHER WAY. YOU, OR SOMEONE LIKE YOU. IT'S WHAT YOU PEOPLE DO.
IF THE CITY GETS DESTROYED BEFORE THEN, WELL -- THERE ARE OTHER CITIES.
MILLIONS WOULD DIE, PARAGON.
THAT THING NEARLY KILLED ME THE LAST TIME I MERGED WITH IT. MILLIONS OF PEONS, OR ME?
THAT'S AN EASY CHOICE.
AND THAT'S WHY YOU'LL NEVER SUCCEED, PARAGON. WHY YOU'LL ALWAYS END UP BACK IN JAIL.
YOU MAY HAVE UNIMAGINABLE POWER, BUT AT HEART, YOU'RE A COWARD.
YOU DON'T FOOL ME FOR A SECOND, ALIEN!
I KNOW EXACTLY WHAT YOU'RE DOING! EXACTLY HOW YOU'RE TRYING TO MANIPULATE ME!
I DON'T NEED TO PROVE ANYTHING TO ANYONE! I'M BETTER THAN ALL OF YOU! BETTER THAN --
OH, DAMMIT.

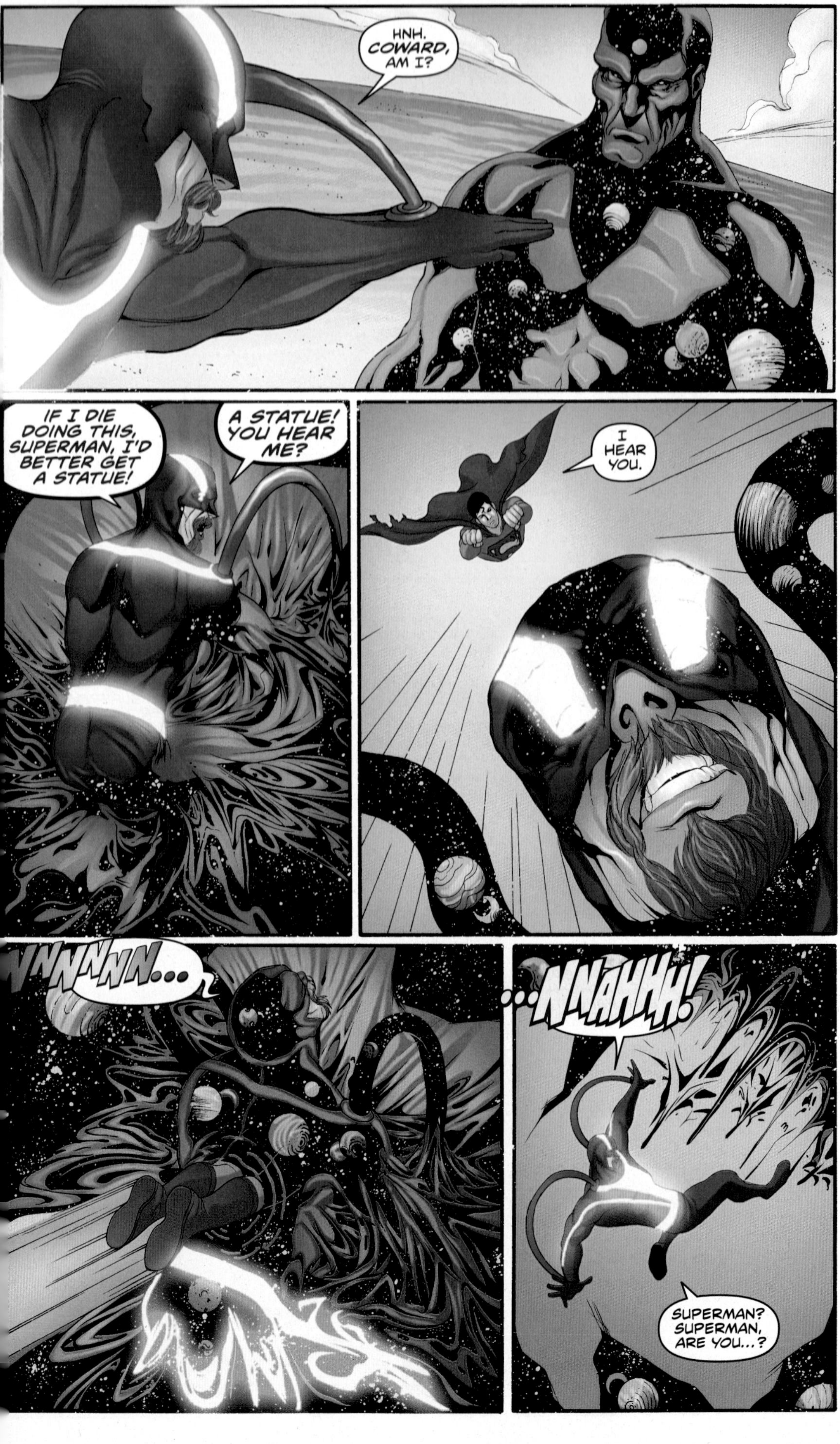
HNH. COWARD, AM I?
IF I DIE DOING THIS, SUPERMAN, I'D BETTER GET A STATUE!
A STATUE! YOU HEAR ME?
I HEAR YOU.
NNNNNN...
...NNAHHH!
SUPERMAN? SUPERMAN, ARE YOU...?

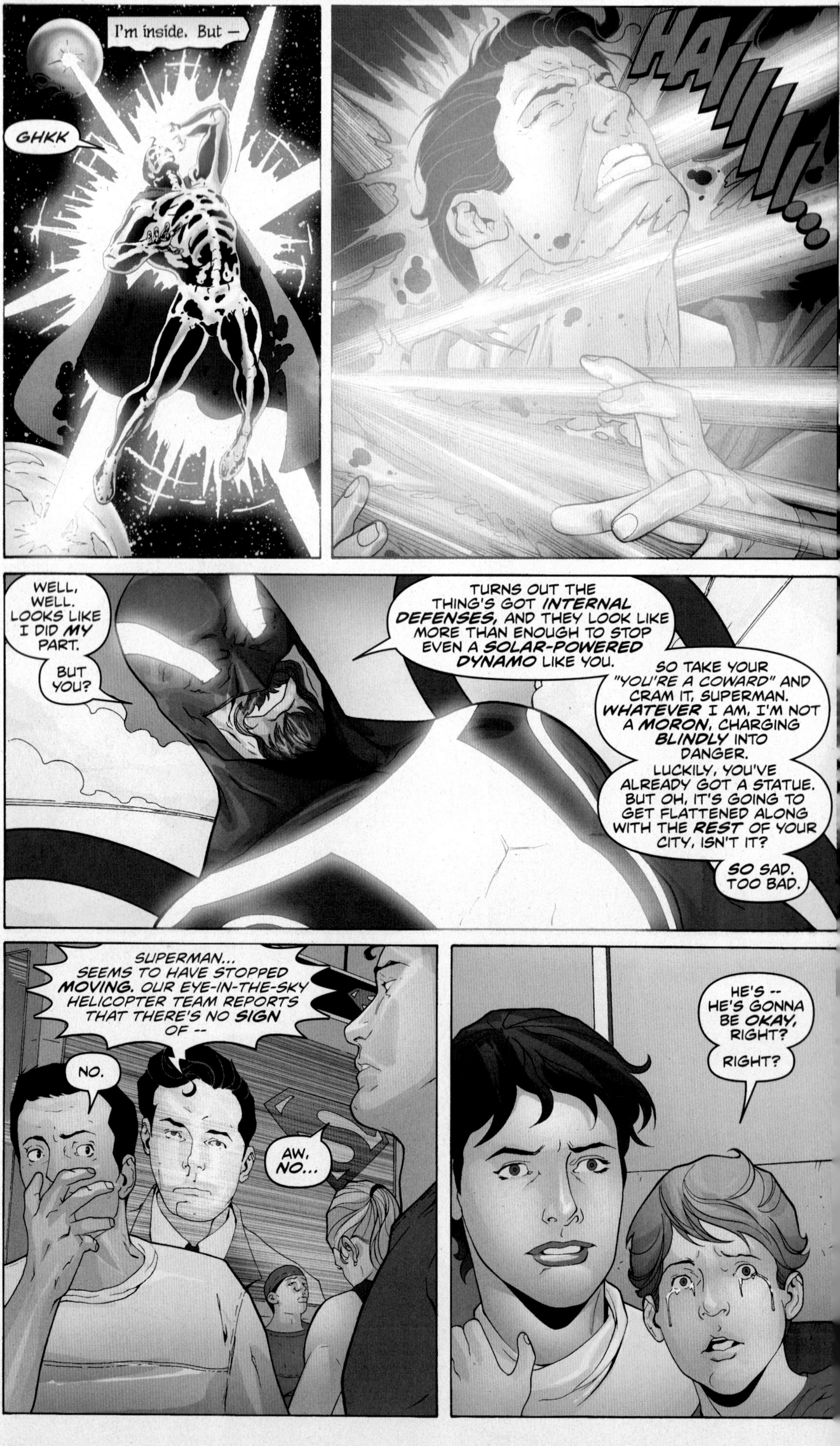
I'm inside. But —
GHKK
HAAIIIII...
WELL, WELL. LOOKS LIKE I DID MY PART.
BUT YOU?
TURNS OUT THE THING'S GOT INTERNAL DEFENSES, AND THEY LOOK LIKE MORE THAN ENOUGH TO STOP EVEN A SOLAR-POWERED DYNAMO LIKE YOU.
SO TAKE YOUR "YOU'RE A COWARD" AND CRAM IT, SUPERMAN. WHATEVER I AM, I'M NOT A MORON, CHARGING BLINDLY INTO DANGER.
LUCKILY, YOU'VE ALREADY GOT A STATUE. BUT OH, IT'S GOING TO GET FLATTENED ALONG WITH THE REST OF YOUR CITY, ISN'T IT?
SO SAD. TOO BAD.
SUPERMAN... SEEMS TO HAVE STOPPED MOVING. OUR EYE-IN-THE-SKY HELICOPTER TEAM REPORTS THAT THERE'S NO SIGN OF --
NO.
AW, NO...
HE'S -- HE'S GONNA BE OKAY, RIGHT?
RIGHT?

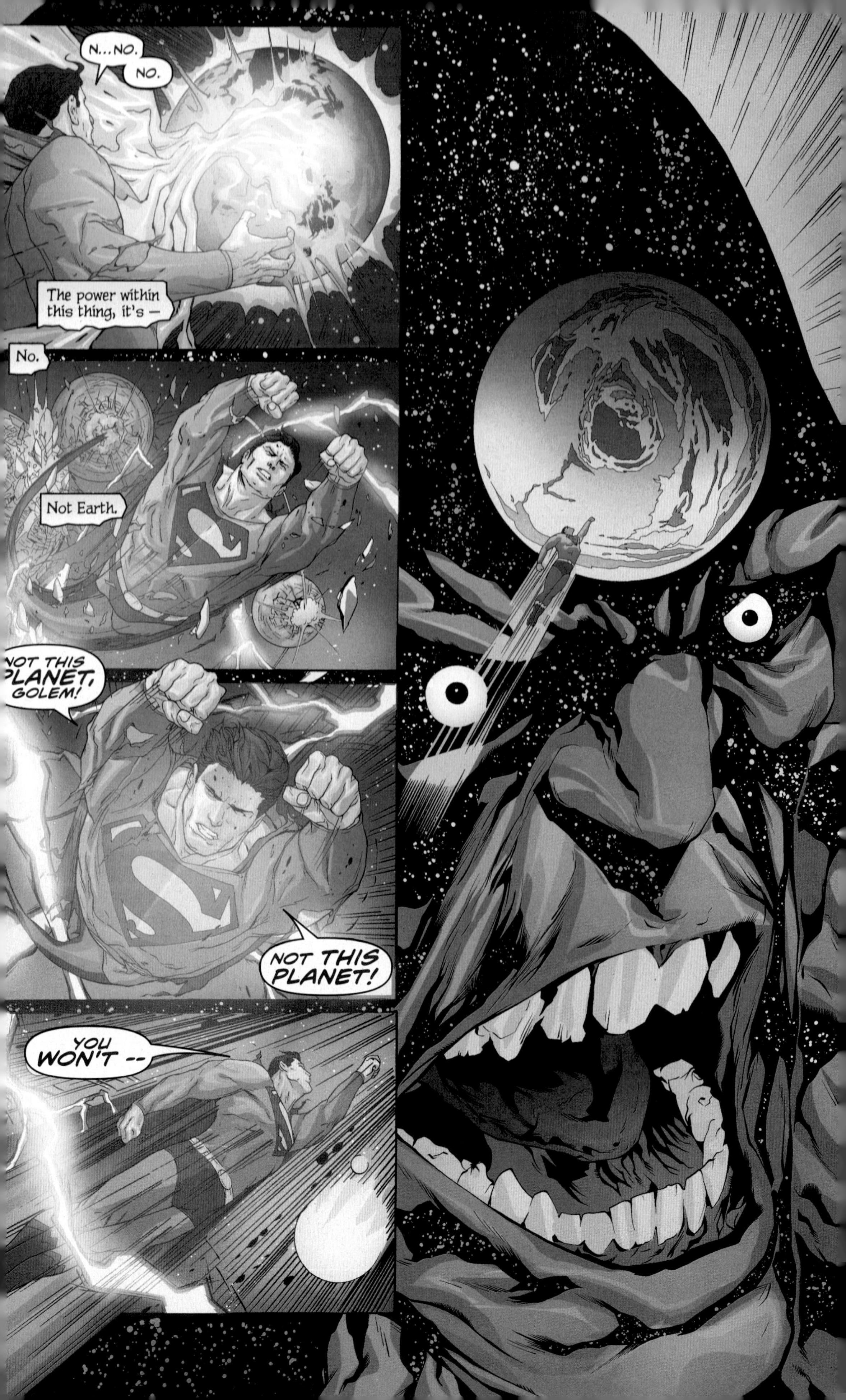
N...NO.
NO.
The power within this thing, it's —
No.
Not Earth.
NOT THIS PLANET, GOLEM!
NOT THIS PLANET!
YOU WON'T --

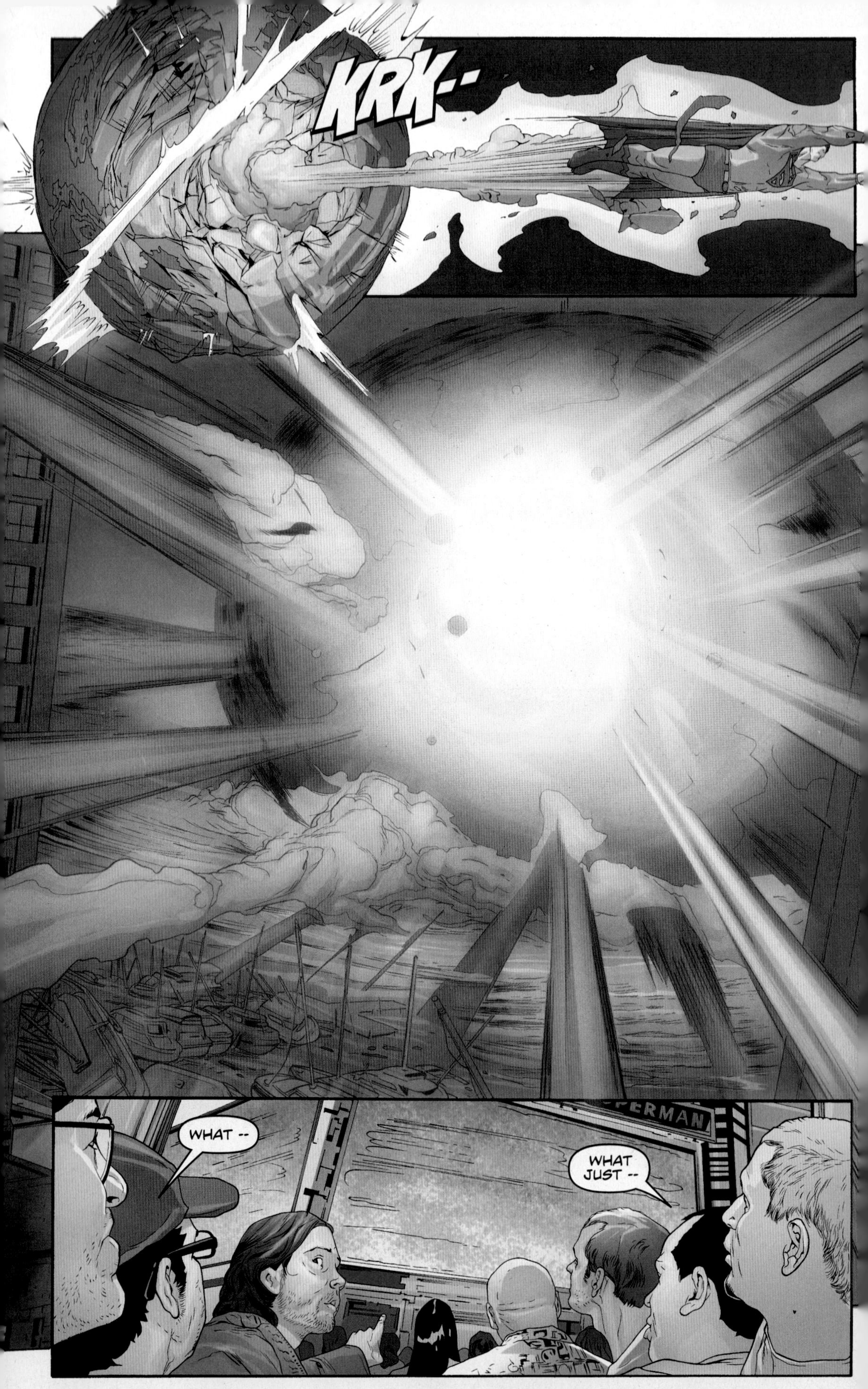
KRK--
WHAT --
WHAT JUST --

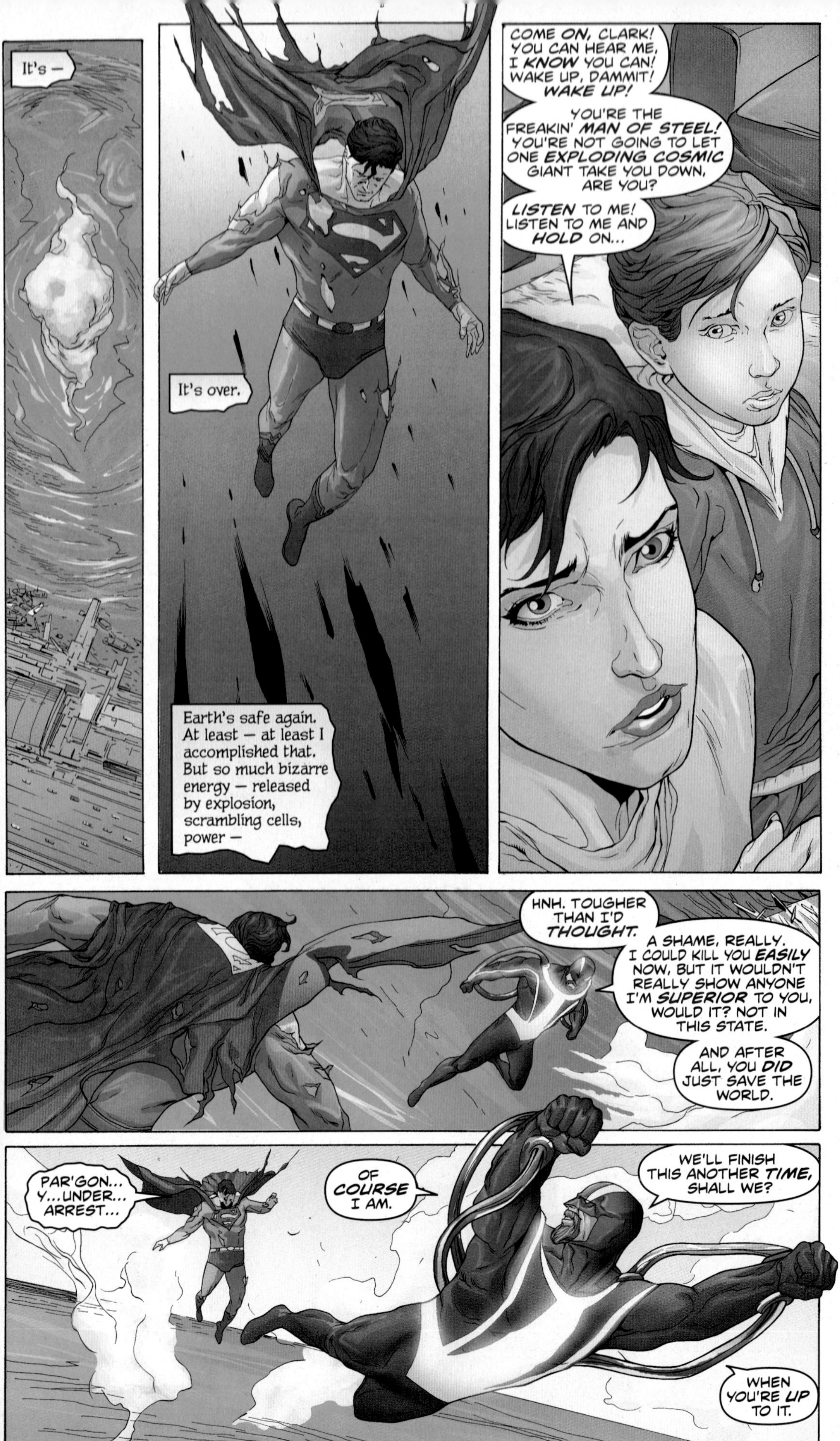
It's —
It's over.
Earth's safe again. At least — at least I accomplished that. But so much bizarre energy — released by explosion, scrambling cells, power —
COME ON, CLARK! YOU CAN HEAR ME, I KNOW YOU CAN! WAKE UP, DAMMIT! WAKE UP!
YOU'RE THE FREAKIN' MAN OF STEEL! YOU'RE NOT GOING TO LET ONE EXPLODING COSMIC GIANT TAKE YOU DOWN, ARE YOU?
LISTEN TO ME! LISTEN TO ME AND HOLD ON...
HNH. TOUGHER THAN I'D THOUGHT.
A SHAME, REALLY. I COULD KILL YOU EASILY NOW, BUT IT WOULDN'T REALLY SHOW ANYONE I'M SUPERIOR TO YOU, WOULD IT? NOT IN THIS STATE.
AND AFTER ALL, YOU DID JUST SAVE THE WORLD.
PAR'GON... Y...UNDER... ARREST...
OF COURSE I AM.
WE'LL FINISH THIS ANOTHER TIME, SHALL WE?
WHEN YOU'RE UP TO IT.

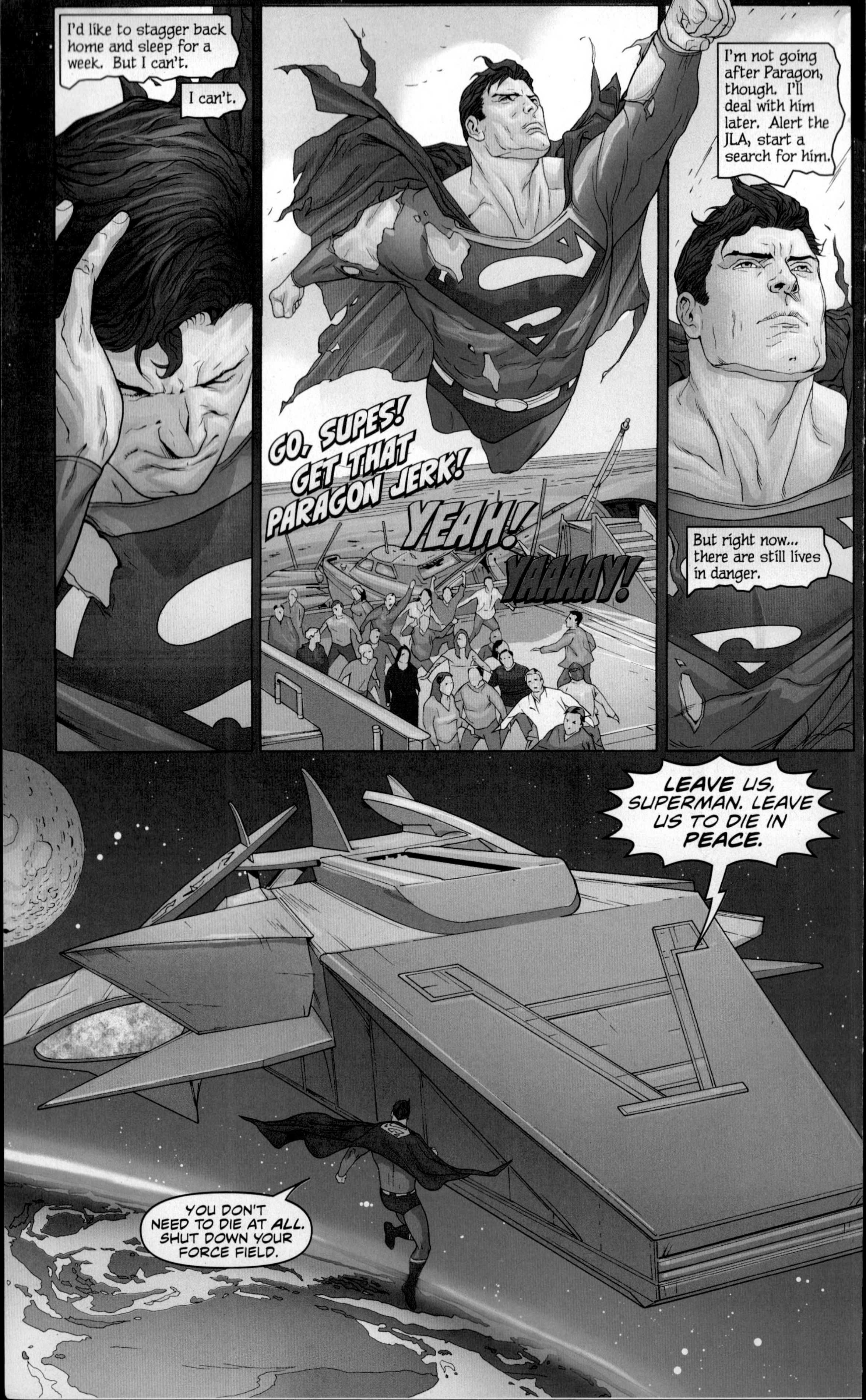

I'd like to stagger back home and sleep for a week. But I can't.
I can't.
GO, SUPES! GET THAT PARAGON JERK!
YEAH!
YAAAAY!
I'm not going after Paragon, though. I'll deal with him later. Alert the JLA, start a search for him.
But right now... there are still lives in danger.
LEAVE US, SUPERMAN. LEAVE US TO DIE IN PEACE.
YOU DON'T NEED TO DIE AT ALL. SHUT DOWN YOUR FORCE FIELD.

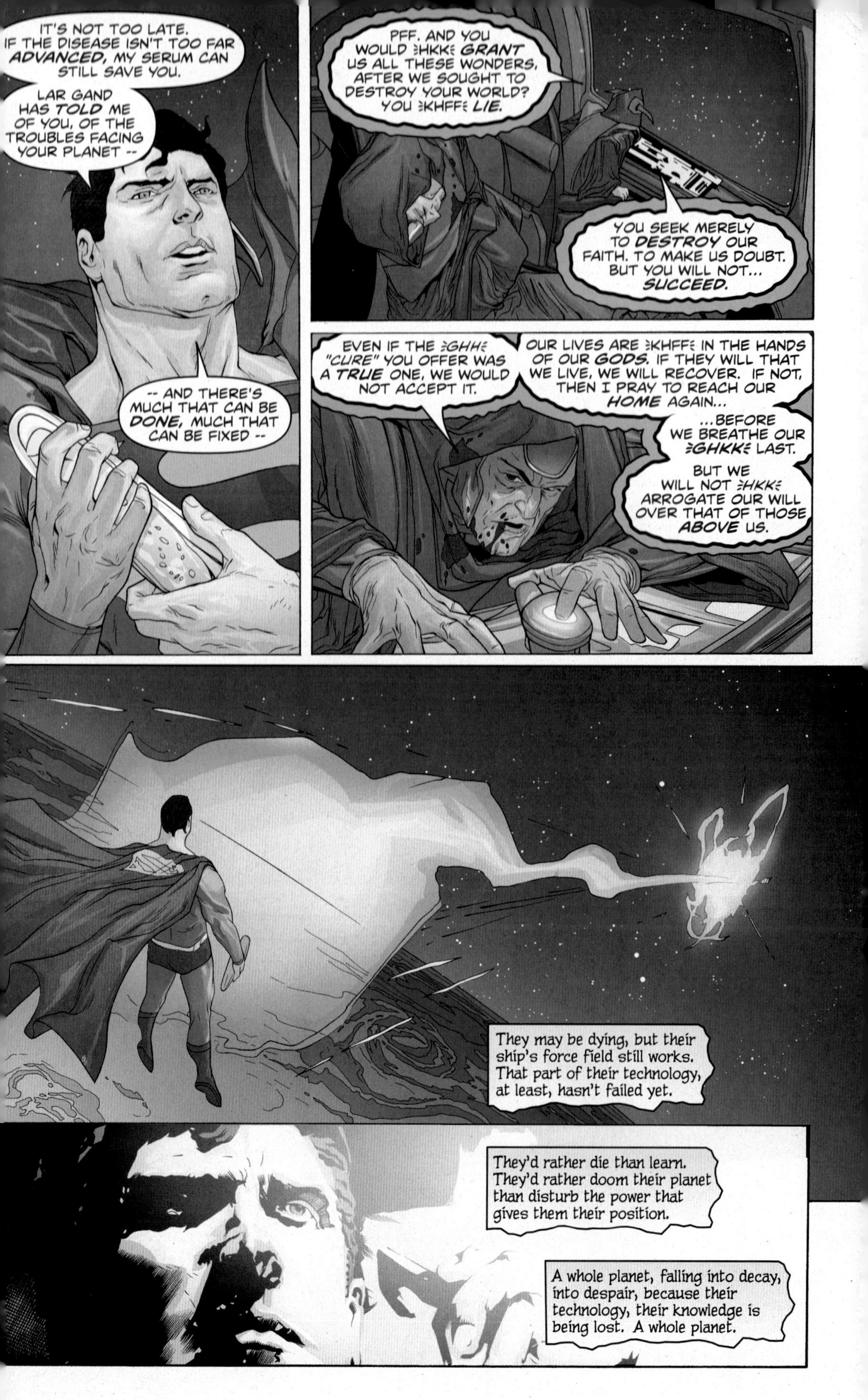
IT'S NOT TOO LATE. IF THE DISEASE ISN'T TOO FAR ADVANCED, MY SERUM CAN STILL SAVE YOU.
LAR GAND HAS TOLD ME OF YOU, OF THE TROUBLES FACING YOUR PLANET --
-- AND THERE'S MUCH THAT CAN BE DONE, MUCH THAT CAN BE FIXED --
PFF. AND YOU WOULD ⋮HKK⋮ GRANT US ALL THESE WONDERS, AFTER WE SOUGHT TO DESTROY YOUR WORLD? YOU ⋮KHFF⋮ LIE.
YOU SEEK MERELY TO DESTROY OUR FAITH. TO MAKE US DOUBT. BUT YOU WILL NOT... SUCCEED.
EVEN IF THE ⋮GHH⋮ "CURE" YOU OFFER WAS A TRUE ONE, WE WOULD NOT ACCEPT IT.
OUR LIVES ARE ⋮KHFF⋮ IN THE HANDS OF OUR GODS. IF THEY WILL THAT WE LIVE, WE WILL RECOVER. IF NOT, THEN I PRAY TO REACH OUR HOME AGAIN...
...BEFORE WE BREATHE OUR ⋮GHKK⋮ LAST.
BUT WE WILL NOT ⋮HKK⋮ ARROGATE OUR WILL OVER THAT OF THOSE ABOVE US.
They may be dying, but their ship's force field still works. That part of their technology, at least, hasn't failed yet.
They'd rather die than learn. They'd rather doom their planet than disturb the power that gives them their position.
A whole planet, falling into decay, into despair, because their technology, their knowledge is being lost. A whole planet.

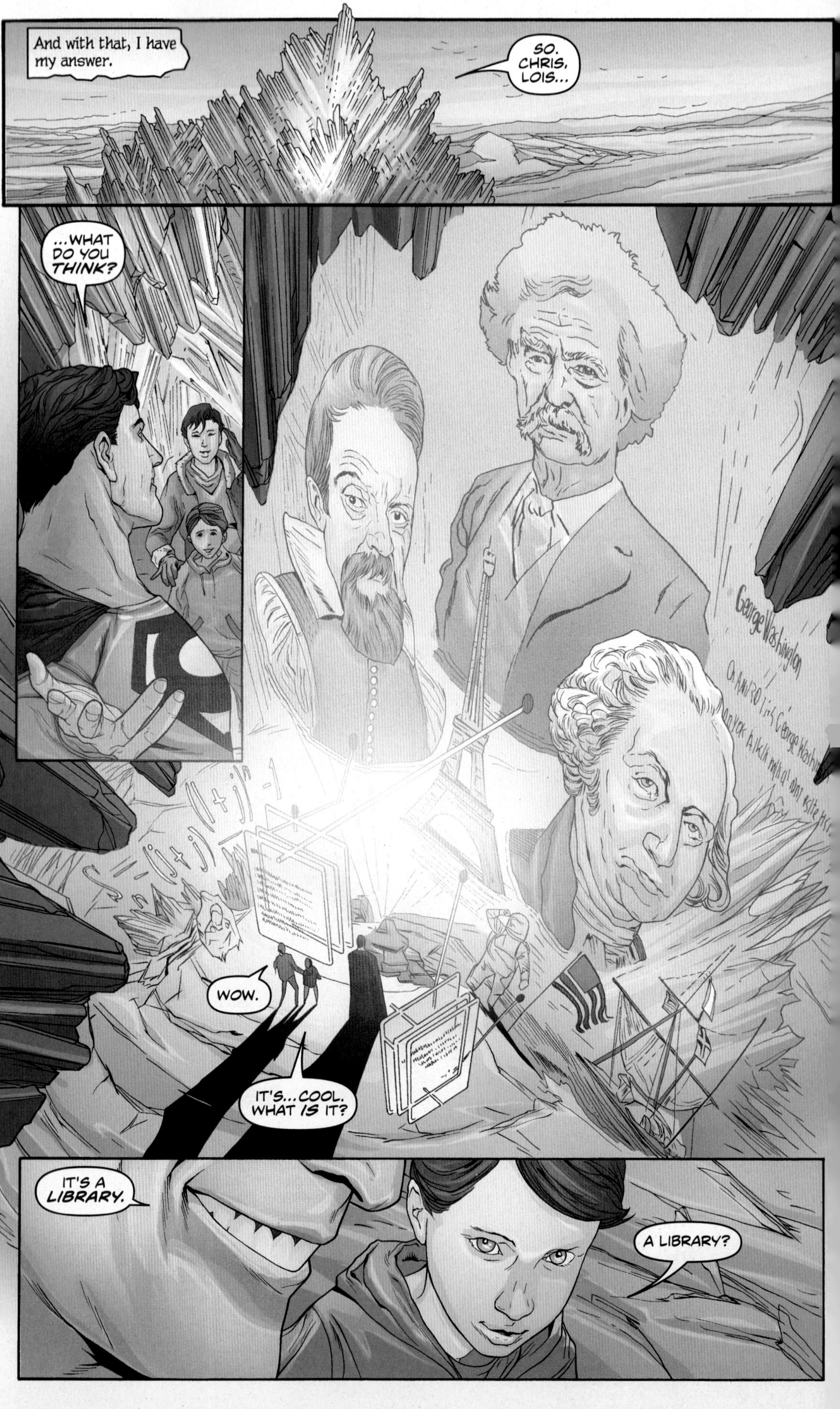
And with that, I have my answer.
SO. CHRIS, LOIS...
...WHAT DO YOU THINK?
George Washington
WOW.
IT'S...COOL. WHAT IS IT?
IT'S A LIBRARY.
A LIBRARY?

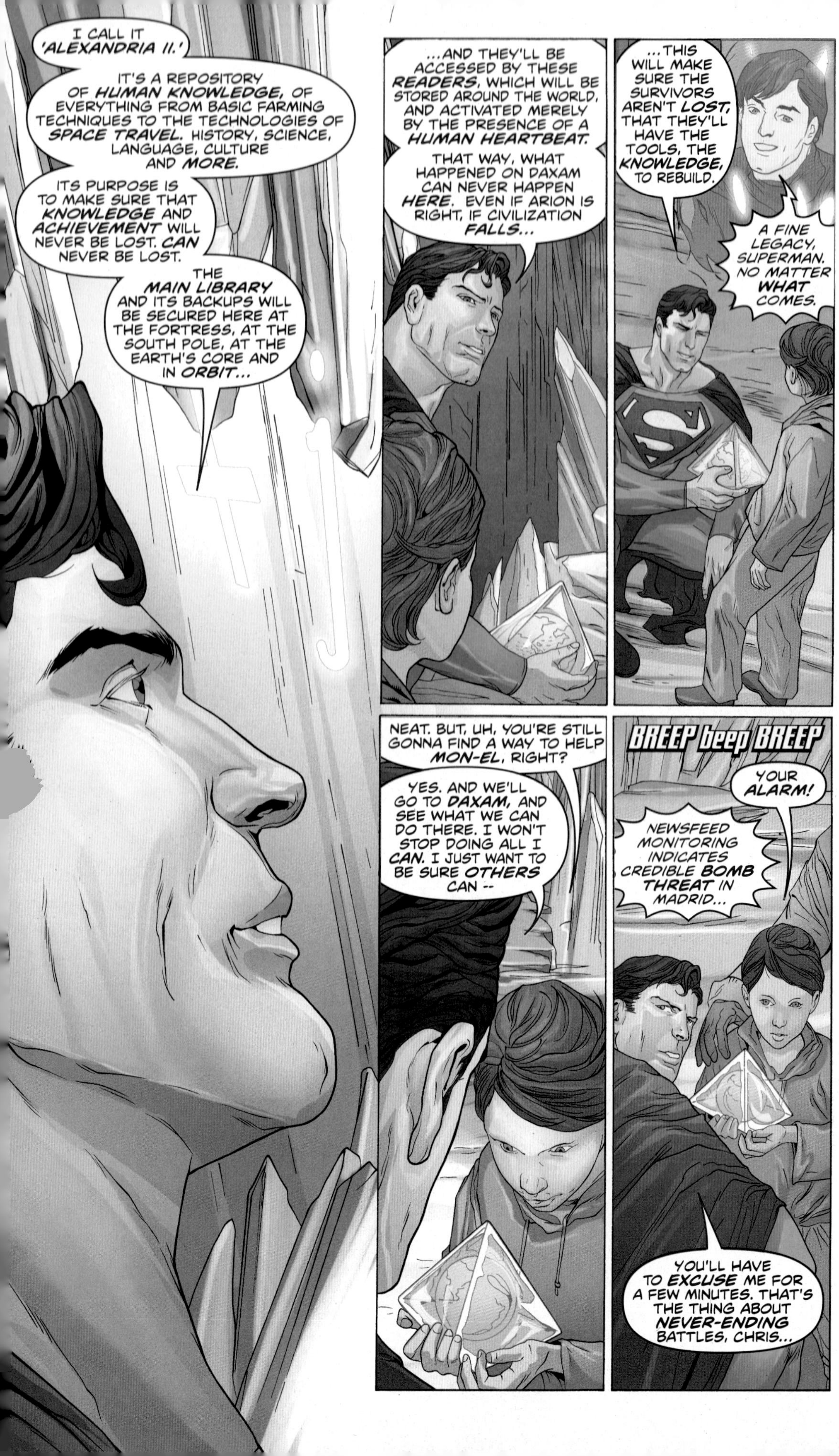
I CALL IT 'ALEXANDRIA II.'
IT'S A REPOSITORY OF HUMAN KNOWLEDGE, OF EVERYTHING FROM BASIC FARMING TECHNIQUES TO THE TECHNOLOGIES OF SPACE TRAVEL. HISTORY, SCIENCE, LANGUAGE, CULTURE AND MORE.
ITS PURPOSE IS TO MAKE SURE THAT KNOWLEDGE AND ACHIEVEMENT WILL NEVER BE LOST. CAN NEVER BE LOST.
THE MAIN LIBRARY AND ITS BACKUPS WILL BE SECURED HERE AT THE FORTRESS, AT THE SOUTH POLE, AT THE EARTH'S CORE AND IN ORBIT...
...AND THEY'LL BE ACCESSED BY THESE READERS, WHICH WILL BE STORED AROUND THE WORLD, AND ACTIVATED MERELY BY THE PRESENCE OF A HUMAN HEARTBEAT.
THAT WAY, WHAT HAPPENED ON DAXAM CAN NEVER HAPPEN HERE. EVEN IF ARION IS RIGHT, IF CIVILIZATION FALLS...
...THIS WILL MAKE SURE THE SURVIVORS AREN'T LOST, THAT THEY'LL HAVE THE TOOLS, THE KNOWLEDGE, TO REBUILD.
A FINE LEGACY, SUPERMAN. NO MATTER WHAT COMES.
NEAT. BUT, UH, YOU'RE STILL GONNA FIND A WAY TO HELP MON-EL, RIGHT?
YES. AND WE'LL GO TO DAXAM, AND SEE WHAT WE CAN DO THERE. I WON'T STOP DOING ALL I CAN. I JUST WANT TO BE SURE OTHERS CAN --
BREEP beep BREEP
YOUR ALARM!
NEWSFEED MONITORING INDICATES CREDIBLE BOMB THREAT IN MADRID...
YOU'LL HAVE TO EXCUSE ME FOR A FEW MINUTES. THAT'S THE THING ABOUT NEVER-ENDING BATTLES, CHRIS...

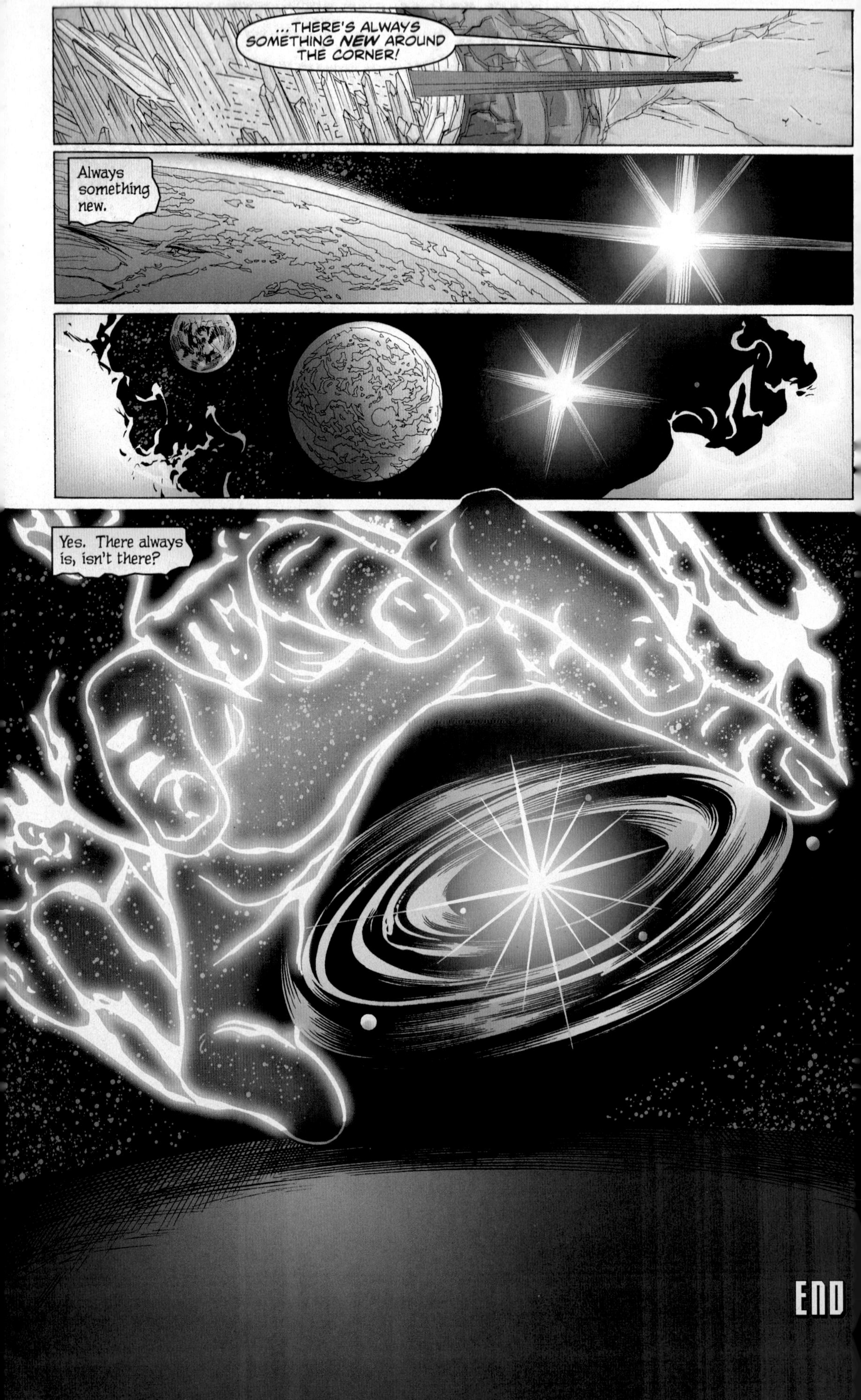
...THERE'S ALWAYS SOMETHING NEW AROUND THE CORNER!
Always something new.
Yes. There always is, isn't there?
END

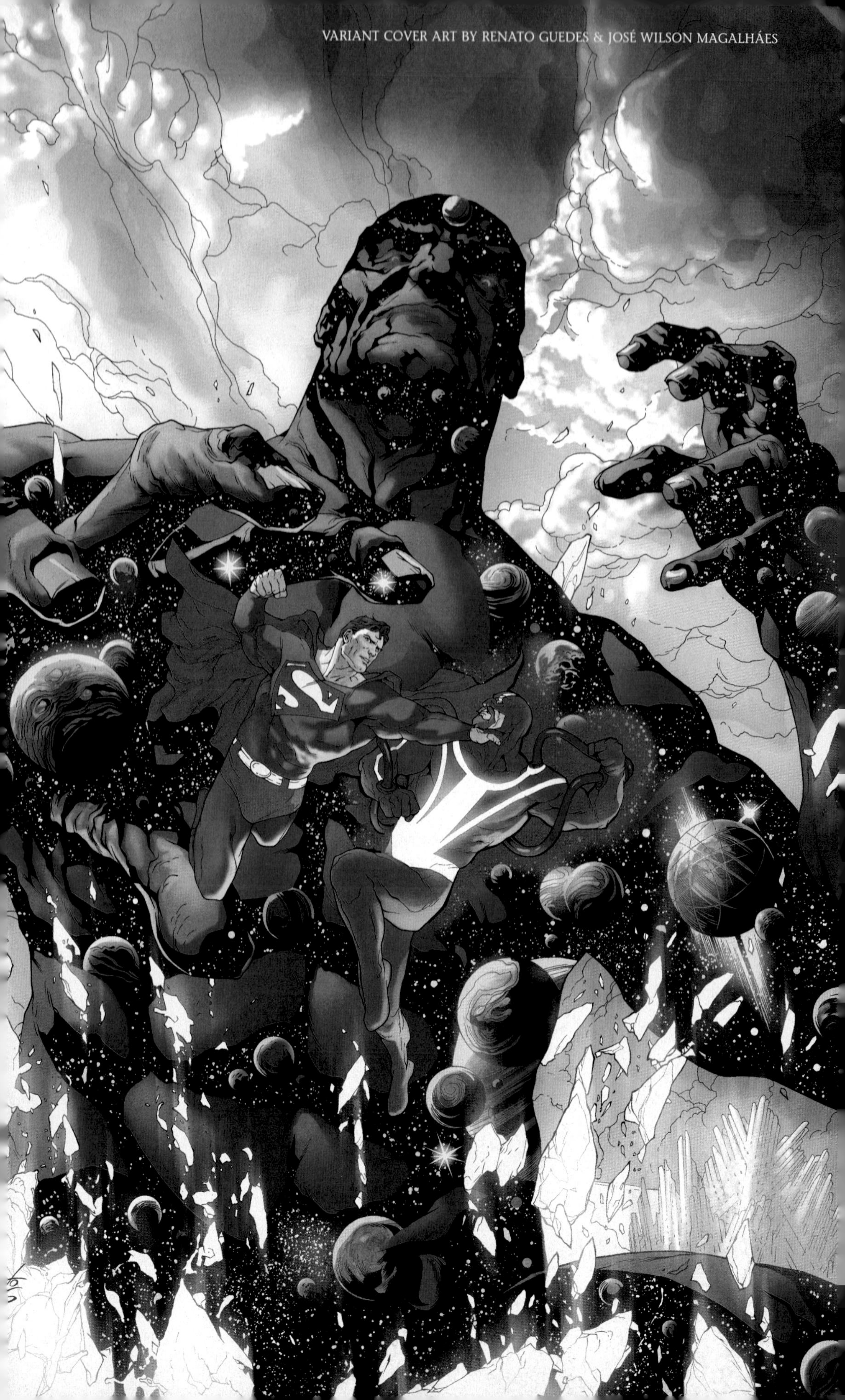

VARIANT COVER ART BY RENATO GUEDES & JOSÉ WILSON MAGALHÃES

ORE CLASSIC TALES OF THE MAN OF STEEL

SUPERMAN:
THE MAN OF STEEL
VOLS. 1 - 6

JOHN BYRNE
DICK GIORDANO
SUPERMAN
THE MAN OF STEEL

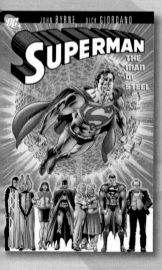

JOHN BYRNE

SUPERMAN:
BIRTHRIGHT

SUPERMAN
BIRTHRIGHT
THE ORIGIN OF THE MAN OF STEEL
MARK WAID LEINIL FRANCIS YU GERRY ALANGUILAN

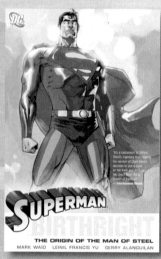

MARK WAID
LEINIL YU

SUPERMAN:
CAMELOT FALLS
VOLS. 1 - 2

SUPERMAN
CAMELOT FALLS
KURT BUSIEK · CARLOS PACHECO · JESUS MERINO

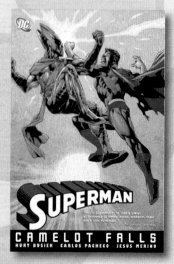

KURT BUSIEK
CARLOS PACHECO

SUPERMAN:
OUR WORLDS AT WAR

SUPERMAN
THE EARTH-SHATTERING SAGA OF THE MAN OF STEEL'S GREATEST BATTLE!
UR WORLDS AT WAR

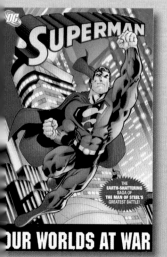

VARIOUS
WRITERS & ARTISTS

SUPERMAN:
RED SON

THE GREAT AMERICAN ICON... REIMAGINED AS A SOVIET HERO!
MARK MILLAR
DAVE JOHNSON
KILIAN PLUNKETT
ANDREW ROBINSON
WALDEN WONG
SUPERMAN
RED SON

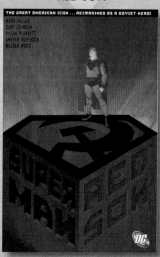

MARK MILLAR
DAVE JOHNSON
KILLIAN PLUNKETT

SUPERMAN:
SECRET IDENTITY

kurt busiek stuart immonen
secret identity

KURT BUSIEK
STUART IMMONEN

SEARCH THE GRAPHIC NOVELS SECTION OF
DCCOMICS.COM
FOR ART AND INFORMATION ON ALL OF OUR BOOKS!

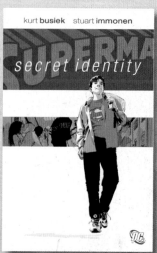